Inspired Thoughts
Can Reveal a Vista of Hidden Truths

from

The Little Scribe

Volume I

en Press

Copyright © Ron Bateman 2011

All rights reserved

No part of this publication may be reproduced, stored in a retrieval system, or transmitted in any form or by any means, without the prior permission in writing of the publisher or copyright holder, nor be otherwise circulated in any form of binding or cover other than that in which it is published and without a similar condition including this condition being imposed on the subsequent purchaser.

All paper used in the printing of this book has been made from wood grown in managed, sustainable forests.

ISBN13: 978-1-78003-198-9

Printed and bound in the UK

Pen Press is an imprint of Indepenpress Publishing Limited
25 Eastern Place
Brighton
BN2 1GJ

A catalogue record of this book is available from the British Library

Cover photo by Joan Christopher 2011

I dedicate this book to Brian who is the inspiration for it. And to Irene, without whose help and encouragement this book could not have been written.

Thank You.

Ron Bateman
'The Little Scribe'

Other titles by the author:

More Thoughts from the Little Scribe
Further Thoughts from the Little Scribe
An Anthology of Thoughts from the Little Scribe
Inspirational Thoughts From Afar from the Little Scribe
The Pathway to Inner Thoughts from the Little Scribe
Precious Thoughts from The Little Scribe
Thoughts of Comfort and Guidance from the Little Scribe
Know Thyself and Know Thy God,
  Final Thoughts from the Little Scribe

A few words of explanation regarding the writings in this volume. In March 2000, my lifelong friend and companion died, and soon afterwards I was 'prompted' to sit down and write, and what I wrote surprised me. I was 'told' via these writings that they would come from Brothers, who belong to what is know as 'The White Brotherhood', and that they would work through Brian, (my companion), and that I was to be the last link in the chains as it were, for their Teachings.

I am often awakened in the early hours and I go to my study, and write quickly for about an hour or so, then I go back to bed and sleep. When I get up in the morning, I read what has been written and then record it on a cassette, then I listen to, and hopefully learn from what has been written. I am just the scribe and can take no credit for what is written, but I feel very privileged to be part of this on-going teaching, and am very grateful to my Brothers and Brian.

To those of you who have read this volume I hope the words of comfort have helped you, and to those who are searching I trust you have found what you were looking for.

May the Blessings of the One on High be with you now and always.

A few more words of explanation regarding these two books that comprise Volume One and Volume Two under the title of – *Inspired Thoughts can Reveal a Vista of Hidden Truths*.

In my previous series of books under the heading of *The Little Scribe* I thought I had come to the end of my writing with number 9, and so I said in that book that this one would be the last one!!

Well it seems I was wrong, because I have continued with my **inspirational writing, much to my surprise!! And so I don't think**

I had better call these last two as the final ones, even if they do turn out to be so!!!

May I wish you, the reader, an interesting journey of the mind as you wander, metaphorically speaking, through the pages of these books!! Read with an open mind and rely upon your own intuition and you won't go far wrong I'm sure. Farewell.

'The Little Scribe'

Chapter 1

February 9th 2008

LIFE'S ADVENTURE!! on all LEVELS

Wake up to the reason and the rhythm of Life, for life is far more than what you may think it is!!! To live life as it should be lived is more than a day to day acceptance of what is normally thought of as living. To many people this form of day to day living is a 'job', of whatever description you care to mention, but that is just one aspect of your life, there are many aspects that go to make up a life.

And here we should mention the one that is known as the 'inner life', and that does not necessarily mean one of, shall we say, a monastic or highly spiritual nature!!! The inner life is composed of many layers, and substitute the word 'layers' for perceptions, and here we are wandering into the realms of the imagination, dreams and their waking variety that we call 'day-dreaming'. A very pleasant pastime that sometimes reveals knowledge that we were not aware of.

The imagination is a tool of extraordinary value, for out of the imagination very often comes positive creations of lasting usefulness to not only the one who is doing the imagining but also to others!! And that is just one aspect, one of many that go to make up this art of living and more importantly understanding of what this life of ours means.

But do we really give it serious, positive thought of where this day to day existence is leading us to?

You may well say that just getting through this day to day living leaves precious little time for trying to fathom out the reason for us living here upon this plane of Earth, let alone **delving into the unknown hidden depths of 'Why' we are here in the first place!!!** And if you were to tell the majority of persons, and here we are thinking of those in the Western Civilization, that this life they are living is but one of many that we travel **through either upon the physical plane or the 'ones' of the Spirit,** they would either think you were mad or certifiable to say the least!!!

Yet to many in the other hemispheres of this world the idea of many lives, or as some say re-incarnations, is a perfectly logical and acceptable explanation of the mystery of Life, and what it holds for us!!! Some are rather fatalistic about it all, but Fate is not necessarily the wicked spectre that sets out to entrap the unwary!!!

We can actually be the Masters of our fate and not the victims of it! It is all in the perception of what may seem to constitute Fate. Take a step back metaphorically speaking, and view this so-called Area of Fate dispassionately, and you may well find that you have an answer that will, to a certain extent neutralize its effect upon you. Positive thought can work wonders <u>when</u> you put your mind to it!!!

Take charge of your life, do not be afraid to accept the challenge of it, even if you cannot alter situations completely.

At least you've made a start, you are showing that within you, you have the makings of a 'Master', one who can with willpower, **make a positive difference to yours and other's lives!!!** We are not just puppets, waiting for someone to jerk the strings to animate our movements!

This earth life is just one of many training grounds that **constitute what truly is 'Our Life'**, and that life does not just end when the transition of the mortal body takes place. And once again the Spirit regains the freedom that it willingly gave up when it started out once again on its passage through its life upon the Earth plane. That period, now over at least for the time being, shall we say?

Perhaps a further incarnation may be considered necessary and **if not, well then a period of, shall we say, 'Heavenly bliss' awaits** the Spirit traveller upon this new round of life experiences!!!

And this form of second life living is really to stretch your Spiritual qualities, not exactly to their limit, but getting on for it! For the life upon the Spirit planes of existence is a never-ending realization of what your potentialities are. Things that upon the Earth plane would perhaps be beyond your reach are now seen in a fresh perspective, where thoughts that flow out of your imaginative process can become realities in their own right.

We could say these realities are limitless, and are only limited in their execution by your own standards of limitation!!! When working within the Universal law of 'cause and effect', miracles really do happen.

But miracles are not miracles, just reactions that are permitted by using the, law of the Universe, in other words by its boundaries of licence!!!

Once upon the Worlds of the Spirit and once you have learnt what it means to work within those boundaries, you will find that the vista of life as it is meant to be lived, stretches far, far into the distance, beyond the province of possibility to the one of positive reality. **Life then, is what 'you' make of it!!** There is no such thing as **'failure', for that word had another connotation, and that is, 'a pause for reflection'**, before the next steps forward.

If that formula was carried out while still upon the earth plane, how much easier and simpler life would become, do you not agree?

Once your Spiritual eyes are opened then everything becomes clear, and here we are not speaking of sight but of inner perception, the perception of the Mind!! For the Mind or Spirit awareness is ever present. Thoughts are not just confined to the human existence upon the earth plane, for Thought is the very essence of the 'life force' that permeates All Spheres of existence whether Physical, Spiritual or the ones yet to be made available to those who are searching. And yes, seeking the inner knowledge of that mysterious force we call 'Life', and its true meaning!!

The primitive energy that governs all forms of creative endeavour, that storehouse of Auric vitality, that Primordial chaos, spoken of in those ancient manuscripts as the 'Breath of The Almighty made manifest'. That then is just one of the mysteries that lie hidden from Man.

And here we speak in terms that reflect the word 'Adam', and all that, that word implies, which does not mean one man, but the nucleus of ALL FORMS OF MANKIND from the very Root source of all Divinely inspired Creation. The thought before it became a reality!! of Imperfect structure, seeking the perfection that would enable it to take its rightful place in the Halls of Eternity!!!

And here we feel is a good place to cease our excursion into the realms of the Eternal and leave you to ponder upon what has been written by that little person who calls himself a 'little scribe'.

We think differently and he knows that and so we will bid you, the reader, Farewell. And to you Brother we bid you a very fond Farewell and the love that surrounds you we also give to you from many who wish us to do so.

Farewell, Farewell dear friend, Farewell.

May Allah smile upon thee little person of the Earth!!!

Chapter 2

February 16th 2008

THOUGHTS TO TAKE YOU FAR!!!

Dear Brother in Christ we begin.

Had you ever thought that as the next realm that you venture to at the demise of your bodily structure, is it anything like the one you have just left behind? And if not, what are the differences? Or could it be that quite a lot of them are not so different after all!!! We know that those of the so-called Spirit very often continue to remain as far as looks go, very much as they did when dwelling in their earthly body, but does it stop there? Well, **the answer is No it doesn't, for when the Spirit is released from its** earthly companion, it carries with it not only memories, but of the most importance, its traits of Character that it has acquired during its sojourn upon the Earth plane!!

We never lose that, we build upon it yes, for that character was with us, though perhaps lying dormant when we began this incarnation!! But during our lifetime our character becomes even stronger. For life as it is being lived, brings us many conditions good or bad that affects our character in no uncertain way, even if it is only when we are in a retrospective mood that we can see how life has shaped us. Our thoughts, our actions, even our day to day working life, they all play a part in shaping our very own character that is like no other one, we are unique in that respect!!

Now what is all of this surmising leading up to? Well it's to prepare you for what we are going to elaborate on, and that is, we do not suddenly become different overnight so to speak, just because we have shed our mortal body and taken upon ourselves the garb of the Spirit!!! We begin to alter, but with some, the progress may be slow, it's getting to accept this new life and how we 'fit into it'!!!

The worry of the day to day living upon the Earth plane is no longer with us, but that doesn't mean that, shall we say, everything is 'plain sailing'! In other words expect the unexpected!! That really is what life, upon whatever sphere you happen to be, is all about. You wouldn't want it otherwise would you? Life is meant to be lived and live how you want it to be.

You'll have decisions to make whether right or wrong, but here upon the Spirit realm you learn how to 'cope', coping and learning how to compromise, in a way just like your former life. But here your efforts are rewarded straight away, because results are almost instantaneous. Not by some magic formula, but through your own commonsense and acceptance of the realities of how the Universal law works when you understand, that it is for the benefit of ALL, and not just for a favoured few.

You will meet, or shall we say 'come across' all kinds of people, and that means you may not even like them but that is no barrier here, because you accept them as they are. And in that acceptance you perhaps look for a reason for your first impression and quite often you'll see that your judgement was perhaps a little too hasty.

A valuable lesson learnt without you even realizing it!!

Life, when lived properly and that means harmoniously, is a wonderful experience and you are a part of it, it is your life and it is up to you what you make of it. There's so much more freedom here, not only of personal adventure but also of Thought! For thought is of paramount importance, especially when you have been taught just how to think in a positive manner, which results in positive 'realities'.

And that word can mean so many different things in the Spirit World, as you will discover for yourself!! Be positive and never negative, for negative is a backward step when travelling upon the upward spiral of evolution of the senses of perception!!!

As you have always been aware, the saying that 'Travel broadens the mind' is a very apt one, and is just as important here. By which, you will understand that travel upon the Realms of the Spirit far outweighs anything you may have done when living upon Earth. Upon Earth you have facilities for exploring other countries, other continents, other cultures!

Well here we are no different, for there are countries, continents, cultures, all waiting to be discovered and understood by anyone who wishes to do so. But here you do not need visas or passports. It is your 'Thoughts' that are your gateways to new destinations and those people who inhabit them! For Thought is the Universal language of the Spirit World and is understood by All Cultures and Religions.

Yes, we did say Religions, for though the idea of Religion is a Universal one, there are no restrictions or barriers as to how a person practices what they believe in!! Does that surprise you? I expect it does, because to most people upon the Earth plane they seem to think that the form of Religious Culture would be the same for everyone. But that would be denying the person's Free Will to pursue what perhaps they have always believed in when upon Earth!! Religion here is, shall we say, 'Open to All forms of Thought'.

You are not expected to suddenly change a lifetime's acceptance of a particular Religious Culture, just because you are now back in your garb of the Spirit! You can now see the merit, or otherwise, of the various cultures that are still practised. Gradually we begin to see what Religion and God are all about, what they mean to each other, and you may even find your own thoughts changing quite radically upon those subjects as your perceptions grow and alter in your upward progress!!

Just remember your life now is one of Freedom, freedom to think perhaps that to some, may almost seem the unthinkable! **The territory that you are now upon is God's vast vista of the Eternal!! The Eternal Now!**

Your perceptions of the Past the Present, and the Future, are **amalgamated all in the 'NOW'!! – 'GOD'S NOW'**, and not yours! Just remember that the word Eternity is just another word **for the Unknown, and as such is 'flexible' not for you, but for The Creator!!!**

We feel that this is where we will depart from this discourse, **for there are so many 'areas' of the Spirit World that need** explaining.

And this little treatise would need many volumes to do it justice. And so we will bid you scholars of the Earth plane and yes, also those who are with you though as yet unseen, but who can still be counted as scholars of Life upon all of its Planes of Existence. **We say to you all Farewell and we leave you in God's** care.

And to you dear scribe we leave you with all of our love and thanks for this period of joint thought participation. Farewell dear friend Farewell, ALL is WELL believe that and go forth in peace:

May the Blessings of Allah Our God of Mercy be with you now and in the coming days of endeavour. Farewell.

Chapter 3

February 17th 2008

THINK AND THEN THINK AGAIN!

We ask you to sit quietly and think, and think seriously we might add, regarding the life that follows on from this Earth. One, when the period of what sometimes seems to the Spirit as a period of semi, not imprisonment but of restriction, comes to an abrupt cessation, with the transition of the mortal body that is called death!! A word that to many people causes them to shudder. But it shouldn't really be so; it's mainly the thought of how this transition is to take place that is the cause of this disquiet!!

If it were just a case of going to sleep and then the Spirit waking up upon its former plane of habitation and leaving its recent shell of protection i.e. the earth body to be decently disposed of. Then all the apprehension regarding the death of the mortal body would be seen in a very different light.

Sadly though the denseness of this lower planet rather precludes this wishful thinking, even though in certain areas of this globe there are inhabitants who really can do just that. It becomes a natural act on their part, for that is what nature originally intended this parting of the mortal and immortal bodies to be, a natural cessation of one, and the release to a future life of the other!!!

The Earth life is but a prelude to the everlasting one of the Spirit.

It is needed by the Spirit to awaken within it, the realization of its true potentialities that it is heir to, regarding its relationship to its Creator the one many call upon as GOD!!! It takes many, many lifetimes upon many, many varying spheres of existence before we can even catch a glimmer of the truth that binds us with the golden strand of Divine Love to the Creator of all Creation. For are we not the offspring of the One we call upon as Father?

So much to conjecture with, when it comes to trying to come to terms with this speculative relationship of the Divine and the Secular and how the union of both can be accomplished!! Many great minds have sought an answer to this age-old problem of how can Man find the answer that will satisfy his longing. And yet still he is floundering, yea and stumbling around in the darkness of his muddled thinking looking for an alternative that does not require too much effort on his part, in changing his way of life and his pattern of thought behaviour!!!

Woe unto Man who is born of Woman and denies the very existence of the Divine Principle of the Life Force of the Immutable, and yea Unknowable Creator of All seen and unseen aspects of that created life force. That permeates <u>all</u> of existence, whether in this, our so-called Universe or those others that can only be hinted at because of their unseen existence beyond the perimeter of our known one!!

We see with our eyes of sight and not with the inner sight of our sense perception. So much to learn and yea so much to un-learn if we did but know it!!!

And yet we are upon this plane of Earth to learn about ourselves, and in the doing of it we can perhaps learn just a little bit more about our Creator or even Creators if we begin to think in the broadest of terms and with an open mind. The unthinkable need not remain so, to one who is prepared to ask questions, even of himself, for many lifetimes can bring forth much wisdom and knowledge when properly thought about in a serious fashion. Remember <u>you</u> are the Master of your Thoughts. We all are, and **perhaps we should say 'should be'!!**

Be a pupil and also a Teacher, the two are interchangeable if you can accept that premise. Share your knowledge with those like-minded acquaintances and you may be surprised at what you may learn from the exchange of spiritual values!!! We keep going back to the word Spirit do we not? And the reason is because we are basically Spirit Essence, part of the Essence that is the very lifeblood of the Unknowable Creative Force that we call Life.

For that word 'Life' is the unbroken cord that binds us all together all through those various lives that we live, no matter what plane of existence that we find ourselves dwelling upon. And this Planet called Earth is just one of the many that we reside upon on our inevitable journey back to the source of our creation, where we started out upon this journey of life as just a thought form. That became a manifested identifiable being endowed with God like qualities because we ARE part of that Creator GOD, yet we know it NOT!!

Hence this never-ending search that we embark upon to try **and find our very beginnings of this force we call 'Life'.** This Gift of the Almighty that in time should see our return to that Creative source of Divine Love. Destiny fulfilled as it was planned from the very beginning of Time itself!!!

So as Spirit we should endeavour to try and find out more about our Roots that stem from the Tree of life we call our Creator!!! This call of the Spirit that is ever with us while tarrying in the Mortal body of flesh that is only on loan to us for the brief period of one lifetime. Then back once more upon familiar territory namely this first sphere that is supplementary to the physical World, where we can assess what that brief lifetime upon Earth has taught us!

Gradually we become less and less dependent upon this physical existence, for the knowledge we have acquired over the centuries of incarnations have become the ground work for us to build upon on our inevitable spiral of Cosmic Evolution. This Earth is but a training ground where the Spirit learns about its temporary incarnation in a gross body of material matter, of its restrictions of movement while dwelling upon, what to some Spirits, is an Alien environment!! Becoming 'human' as it were, is the only way that the Spirit within can learn about itself and its possibilities, it experiences what it did not understand as pure Spirit Essence. That perfection has its counter balance called imperfection, and to become aware of what that implies, when studying the reasons for this seemingly never ending back and forth between the Realms of the Earth and the Spirit!!

When thinking in terms of the word 'Eternity', these lifetimes that we encounter from time to time, are, when properly understood, just passing phases of that strange commodity we call 'Time', which to the author of it are as Nothing!!! But as humans it is very relevant to our living within 'its' boundaries. As Spirit though, we can, shall we say 'live without it', for time upon the Spirit Realms is flexible! In other words we use it as we wish and are not bound by its rules as you are upon the earth plane!

You are probably thinking, 'Well, if we are predominately made up of Spirit essence, we should be aware of all of what you are saying.' Quite true, that is if your memories were in an active state, which they are not, when you are contemplating a return to Earth for a re-incarnation period. To remember past lives would be too much of a burden for not only the Spirit, but also the Thought pattern of the mortal body of residence to cope with!

Sometimes though a brief memory may surface, only to be thought of as perhaps part of a dream and dismissed as such!! 'Nature' comes to the rescue every time, we are but fickle yet complex creatures are we not? All part of what you like to call the 'learning curve'. Now you can perhaps see the logic behind all of these seemingly endless re-incarnations upon the Earth plane! They are necessary, a very necessary aspect of the overall pattern **of 'Life' and all that that word implies!!**

Accept your limitations, for they are for a purpose, but as you grow Spiritually, these limitations become less and less.

You learn how to become the 'Master' and less of the pupil when dealing with your life wherever it is taking place!!! For the present we feel that you have had enough information to be going on with, more will be vouchsafed to you in due course. **Isn't there a saying, 'Sufficient unto the day thereof…'?!!!** And we leave you there.

Farewell friends and scholars of Life and its hidden mysteries, Farewell!

And to our Scribe Brother, thank you friend, thank you. We bid you also a Farewell a fond Farewell from all of your Brothers in White.

Peace be with you Brother, <u>Your</u> world is intact have no fear. We are guiding you all of the way!!

Chapter 4

April 23rd–24th 2008

WHAT CAN I SAY?

Thoughts that have just come to me, first I must explain. Some while ago when it was my time to retire to my bed, I was aware of a figure to the left of me not very far from me. But I was not able to be aware of this (for the figure was Male!) entirety, by which I mean he dwarfed the area I was in and his head and shoulders were not in my sight. Though sight is the wrong word, I was only aware in thought of this presence.

He was to my way of thinking somewhat like the Ancient Samurai Warriors. Though his armour, if that is what it was that **covered him from head to toe, was of 'Leather' and not metal!** And there were degrees of, how can I put it? Colour variation of the leather, some parts dark while other parts were somewhat lighter, they were the parts I think, that overlapped each other!

Now though I was aware of this figure I felt no apprehension, for I felt he was watching over me in a protective sense and not one of antagonism!!

Since that first awareness I am conscious that the figure is there when I retire to my bed. But it is only a vague awareness, almost as if the feeling I have is that the figure is now, shall I say, a replica of the original and not the original himself! If that makes sense!!!

Well, now that I have explained that, I will now proceed with my thoughts on the subject! And that is, that there are unknown Masters of the Universe, the keepers of the Flame of Life that allows this Universe of ours to continue upon its allotted span of 'Life'! For I do believe that Universes 'come and go', in other words, are Born, have an expectancy of Life and then Die!! But not die in the sense as we know it!! They 'change' Shape, Density, and even Substance!! Though what that substance consists of I have no idea!!

These Masters, or Keepers of this Life Force are a race of Beings of immense proportions, and they come from areas of Space that do not belong to what we think we see as Space. For there Space is beyond the area of Time and location. They belong, and yet they are not a part of what it is that they Monitor and keep in check!!

For they are Not of the Human Variety and yet they could pass as such, but on a scale so vast as to be incomprehensible to Mankind's thinking capacity!!! And here I am being told to go no further in THE explanation of Who they are. For it is forbidden for me to dwell upon that subject any further, other, than I am allowed to say, if you can picture in your 'minds eye' what the word 'Giants' conjures up, you may have a very, very vague idea of what these Beings are like!!! And why they are like they are.

And now I am told to cease writing and put my pen down until another time. So this I must do right away!!!

I resume my thoughts!!

I wonder just how long they will remain mine? Not for long little one! not for long!

Well, that answered my question! So I'll proceed.

The Masters of the Universe that does the monitoring of 'its' progress are not creators per se, and yet Creation does come within their remit when considered as necessary. When, in certain circumstances an alteration is required, if the Universal structure needs either a permanent or temporary alteration! The Higher Beings that are part of the ongoing Creative process are 'Legion' in other words, there are numerous categories to which these Creators belong!!

The word Creation sounds so simple, and yet the outcome that stems from a creative thought is beyond human comprehension!! The onlooker so to speak, only sees the resulting creation whatever that happens to be. But behind the scenes so to speak there is much trial and error, before any form of PERMANENT creation can be considered as a viable creation.

For what has been intended by the Divine Thought Essence that stretches right from the Top to all of the subsidiary **manipulators that come under the heading of Creators, God's Beings of Light** – Masters, and Monitors of the very essence of the Life Force that is used for the many creative sources of shall we say, 'Human – kind'? And that word encompasses many, **many, many variations of Man's perception of what he calls the Human Race!!!**

'Human' is just one word that covers just a small part of the Creative process of 'Life Forms'. In all of their wonderful variations from the original conception of identifiable original identities, of the Unfathomable, Unknowable, Essence of Thought Creativity, of the One who remains Nameless!!

Universes, and there are many, believe that. And they are still being brought into existence in the areas of Space that exist beyond the Space that your Universe has dominion over while it holds it captive!!! For Space is forever attempting to regain its lost freedom when it was, as it were made a prisoner within the outer **confines of the inner perimeter skin of the Universe's structure!!!**

Space cannot be identified as a quantifiable amount, for it is boundless and is forever replicating itself, beyond the beyond of the so-called knowable beyond!!! Do not try to fathom that out little scholar of life, accept and know your limitation is for Your benefit. Believe that, while you dwell upon your Earthplane, we hasten to add. And we leave you to think beyond that if you wish!!

Such is the vastness of 'All Creation', and shall we say, 'Those who Create'?!! You, that is Mankind has no yardstick with which to conjure up in his imagination what, and who, these Creators actually are!! Do not think of flesh and blood, or Spirit Essence. There are, shall we loosely call them, 'substances' that defy any kind of Earthly description.

They go beyond any human conjecture that could accurately pinpoint a definite objective as to what it is!!!

For it 'IS' and yet it 'IS NOT'!! and we do not propose to go any further than that at this stage, in Man's evolutionary progress!!!

The little Scribe scholar would love to delve further, but this is not the time for him to divulge any of his own hidden knowledge on that particular subject!!! And here we feel is where we will depart from this discourse of joint minds, Ours from Afar, his from within Earth's confines, a meeting that has given us much pleasure, which we hope to be able to repeat in the near future.

We thank our fellow Brothers of Light for allowing us this privilege of Thought manipulation and know our work is on a Universal scale. And not confined to even one Universe and its many inhabitants, which in this case, we refer to the diverse planet's constellations and Worlds without number!!!

We leave you in Peace and true Brotherly Love. Farewell little friend we shall meet again, have no fear!! We part!!

Well Brother, quite a journey of the minds was it not? Farewell and God bless thee little scholar friend.

Allah be Praised!!!

Chapter 5

April 26th 2008

THE AVENUE OF THOUGHT!!!

Dare I venture down the avenue of Thought and see where it leads me? Am I thinking that I already know what it is that I am anticipating, thinking upon? Or, am I expecting thoughts to come to me from an outside/inside influence? Perhaps I had better wait and see what avenue opens up a vista of knowledge not yet quite realized by me!!!

My 'own' thoughts favour the pursuance of the previous discourse from those Higher Beings from Afar, I will pen what those thoughts of mine are and see if I receive any enlightenment either from myself or Others!!! So please accept that what I write is all hypothetical conjecture on my part as it usually is, isn't it? For whatever I write, or say or think cannot be verifiable from a human standpoint can it? Especially when dealing with, shall I call it, Psychic phenomena from a vibrationary force that is beyond my own human comprehension!!! In the previous discourse there was mentioned Masters, Keepers of the Flame of Life Force, Creators, Monitors, Gods, Beings of Light, and no doubt there are many more descriptive adjectives to describe those Creative Beings that permeate Space and what it holds!!

I believe there are 'degrees' in the Hierarchy of Creation and all that it entails. 'Degrees' yes, but not in the sense of competitive achievement!!

For Creation is for the Benefit of all 'Creation', yes, and even for those Creations yet to be created by the outstanding Thought process of those designated to begin that process!! And you notice I have said, 'Begin that process'. Think upon that, and know that an original thought creation need not remain within the boundaries of the Creator whose thought produced the original conception!! That created subject is passed along the line of those Emissaries of 'Higher Beings' whose 'job' shall we say, is to evaluate the Creation mentioned!!! Trial and Error are the joint pathways to ultimate perfection!! Does that surprise you? For you have probably always thought that a creation when Created by those in Higher Authority, would of necessity be perfect from the word Go! so to speak!!!

Not so! And if you care to think about it, most 'things' that are thought created, reach the end stage of perfection through what has been said, trial and error!!! And even the thought that perfection has been achieved need not be quite accurate, for quite often another 'pair of eyes' metaphorically speaking, can perhaps discover not exactly a flaw, but a room for adjustment if considered it warrants it!!!

Such is the eccentricity of 'Life' wherever that form of Life exists!!! 'Perfection' begins as 'Imperfection' and then in stages the imperfection is eliminated, and once again the original conception of what was envisaged as perfect, has now been achieved!!! So it would seem that Imperfection in so many ways has its place in the scheme of Creation in general!!!

You may not agree with my thoughts upon this subject but it may give you food for thought on your part, and that is a worthwhile thought, is it not? I will now pause and continue this treatise at a future date!!!

'Angelic Hosts! What part do they play in the Celestial Hierarchy of the Divine Force that we Mortals call Our God? I believe they move on a completely different vibrational wavelength to those other vast Beings of Creative Energy!! They are perhaps a liaison that can be tapped into when studying those

Beings aforementioned!! But I feel that one would need to be on a very high Spiritual level to have acquaintanceship with those Angelic Beings, who, because of their Spiritual qualities and Higher Psychic awareness, we poor mortals would hardly ever be able to contact those vibrationary areas where they dwell.

And yet I feel that they are very aware of Man's need for further Spiritual growth, hence the Masters, the Saints, and the Savants who in their wisdom, can enlighten those who aspire to acquire the knowledge of those hidden mysteries that await the **dawning of Man's higher Spiritual qualities. This will allow him** to be party to those forces that are to be present upon this lower plane of Earth in the far off distant future!!!

As with all organizations there are stratas of different aspects that go to make up a coherent whole and so it is upon the realms of the Spirit worlds, everything in its place and a place for everything!! Well organized, but in such a fashion as not to be, shall we say, intrusive upon the freedom of will.

That all life forms in the creative genre known as 'Man' and his Spirit counterpart enjoy!!!

The complexity of the Creative Principle and its effect upon the whole of the Creative element is, in itself, so simple as to often be misunderstood, it is complex, but only to those of us who are part of creation and Not to the Creators of it!!! Man and his offshoots have such a long way to go before they can come to terms with what the Essence of Creation can be understood and accepted as a mystery that must remain as such.

And is therefore one of the many mysteries that Human Mortal Man cannot be expected, or even allowed to unravel. Only the Gods can do that and though Man can aspire to emulate his Creator, as a creature of dubious mortality he will never achieve that distinction while he dwells upon the plane of Earth!!!

So let some mysteries remain a mystery and accept that a little knowledge is a dangerous thing. **And that statement is for Man's own benefit**, believe that for it is a fundamental truth, in fact, a fundamental Universal Truth!!!

Man at present is confined to this his known (rather a misnomer of a statement 'his known') Universe and that is where he belongs, he will not be allowed to pierce the perimeter of the said Universe and venture outside of it. For chaos would reign should he be able to accomplish that feat, which, to put it bluntly, there are means of stopping him before he even thinks of such a venture into the unknown!!!

'**Sufficient** unto the day is the evil thereof'! to quote an age-old saying!! A very apt one to be sure!!!

Though we can hint that more is known about this, your Universe, by those Outside of it than you can imagine!!! Shall we say that the transparency of the fabric of your Universe has been noted by others, even though to you its appearance is one of '**Volatile Solidity**', which is actually an understatement of the fact. And here we do not intend to enumerate any further regarding the merits or otherwise of this Universe. But we can say they (the other Universes in existence) vary greatly in structure and substance and let that be an end of that form of conjecture!!!

The scribe brother has nearly come to the end of his 'supposed thoughts', and he understands our meaning, and so we will bid him our customary Farewell for the present! Keep on with your thoughts and your writing Brother, your work is not over yet!! You will know when it is, and then you will understand the joy that will bring us all together in continued friendship and Love.

Farewell little Friend. Farewell. God bless You.

Chapter 6

May 2nd 2008

JOURNEYS OF THE MIND!!!

I seem to always be talking about journeys, and yet quite honestly I haven't made any, that is, of any importance. But here I hesitate, for I have made many journeys not of the physical body, but of the mind. And when I say, 'of the mind', I am not referring to the imagination! I know when I'm going to embark on one of those, because the final destination has already been mapped out in the imaginative process!! No!! I'm talking about those journeys that I sometimes take, shall I say, in the Spirit?

Those journeys I have no idea about, where they will begin, where I am going, and where will the minds destination finally take me to? And when I say, 'Minds destination', it's not 'my mind' I'm talking about, but those other minds that impinge their thoughts upon mine so that I go willingly wherever I'm being taken!! And so everything is new to me and comes as a surprise!!! Are they lessons I'm being given? And then seen how I respond to them there and then!!

Though sometimes it's only when I look back in retrospect after the journey's end that I can see what it is that I've been shown!! Though here I pause and say not all of those journeys I feel are for 'lesson learning'.

Some are for real pleasure of the senses, where I can enjoy my new surroundings and experiences. I've never felt apprehensive as to the outcome, because I seem to know that I am accompanied, and by whom? Now that is a question, for I know 'they'? or 'he' is behind me usually to my left, and I can feel the presence and yet I do not 'see', 'them', or 'him'!! Strange!

Some of my 'journeys' seem to be as I am writing, as I am now, almost as if I am remembering and I have no real 'control' as to what is being written. It's only afterwards when I read back what has been written that I can appreciate the experience I've been through!! Sometimes the memory is so vivid that I never forget it, even after years have passed and I can recall where I had been and what had happened that had so impressed me!!!

Are they journeys of the Spirit? Or should I say, 'an aspect' of the spirit, where the mind in 'thought' has imprinted upon my conscious awareness of psychic phenomena. That the parts of me that can 'travel' without any conscious form of a 'body of reference', but of a 'mind substance' that can transmute Time, Space, and the Now, into the Whole!! And the 'Whole' being what? The Universal Mind? Or should that be 'The Mind of the Universe'? Is there such a thing? Wake up little Brother! You know the answer to that one!! Think!! There!! Now proceed with 'your' narrative!!!

Sometimes I have felt, how can I put it? I have felt part of the Whole, as if I am no longer the Me who I think of as 'Me', but I am an infinitesimal part that 'belongs', but 'belongs' to 'Whom'? or to 'What'? Yes, I know the answer but it cannot be put into 'words'.

It is beyond the language of the tongue or even of the pen I am using! It is a 'feeling', that even goes beyond that word, it is a knowing, and yet even that word is still inadequate, so perhaps I should leave that all unsaid, and try another avenue of thought, that my physical and mental awareness can cope with!!! Tall order Brother, but carry on!!!

Well, this all started out as journeys!! And where has it got me? If I say I feel 'contented' that doesn't explain anything, other than, I feel that my morning's 'dip' into the waters of the mind has given me some positive elements to mull over. I haven't sunk without a trace, but I'm floating upon the surface and I feel quite buoyant and I think I'll finish right there, before I get carried away with fancy metaphors that probably would mean absolutely nothing!!! Well said little Brother!! Write the word Finish and we will depart from your morning's travel of the mind, of which we have been a part of!!

Farewell little friend.

God be with you and remember all is well!

May Allah guide you upon your chosen path of esoteric wisdom and knowledge.

Praise be to Allah, Praise be to the God of your choice! Little Chela!!!

Chapter 7

March 5th 2008

SPECULATIONS!!!

These are going to be my thoughts, at least that's how they are going to start out but who knows how they will end up? Most probably not mine!!!

Well to begin, just **recently I've seen two television programs** one dealing with the Big Bang theory, the other one discussing the finding of a Planet that appears to have a similar structure to our Earth One. But is umpteen millions of miles away out there in Space!!! Well, **I don't think I qualify as a person who can give** any constructive comments upon either. Only to say that in both cases they have left out, to my way of thinking, the most important element when dealing with what I shall loosely term 'Life' and all that that word encompasses!!!

The reason I say that is because the word **'Spirit' is always left** out. Or shall I say completely ignored, when dealing with so-called **'facts and theories'** regarding this Universe of ours, let alone any other Universes that may be lurking outside the perimeter of Ours!!!

They (that is the Scientific fraternity!) put forward calculations and diagrams, which are all very plausible and no doubt perfectly **accurate by today's standards.** And I hope you notice that last sentence 'by today's standards'.

For that implies that by tomorrows and here I speak theoretically regarding the scale of time! 'By tomorrows standards' they the former may be considered either obsolete or perhaps lacking in verifiable substance!!! And here I come back to that 'verifiable substance', for what I write about cannot possibly be verifiable by mortal man upon this Planet you chose to call Earth! If you only knew what that word 'Earth' really means you would not consider that it applies entirely to this Planet!!!

There are other so-called Planets that structurally are nothing like this planet that we dwell upon, and yet they have the substance if you like to call it that for Life to exist!! Maybe not, as you upon Earth visualize 'life' but never the less it is a form of Life that can be recognised as such, by which I'm referring to our form of Life upon this lower sphere, which is but a 'form' of many such, so-called, 'Life Forms'. Some that resemble Man, and some that can be, shall we say, recognized as an, not exactly an offshoot of mankind, but of another form of 'Root' creativity.

Some might even say they are an improvement upon the so-called original, which we tell you, Man, as you have come to know him, is 'not' the original conception of an idealized version of the Creative Genius that many label as GOD!!!

All of Creation, whether seen or unseen, known or unknown are all forms of 'Experimentation', whether you like or dislike that word is of no consequence for to us it is a 'fact' and to us a very verifiable one in every respect!!

And here we are told to say, 'You must make up your own minds' as to what has been said, and you are under no obligation to accept our word on any subject we care to impart to you. You have a mind of your own and the freedom of the Will to use it. So please do so. The scribe writes what he is impressed to do; we know his thoughts on these matters for he is a willing participant, for which we are eternally grateful.

We now proceed.

There are things that are to do with the Creative side of Life that Mortal Man in his present frame of mind can just not comprehend. And we say to him, accept your limitations for they are for your own good. And if you are wise and of the thinking class you will understand that Man is still in his Infant stage regarding his relationship to his Spirit counterpart, and the Creators of that counterpart! And read that word again 'Creators'!! And just remember what we have said regarding your free will!!!

Worlds, planets, in fact everything are all in the experimental stage! There have been many such forms of civilizations that peopled those unknown Worlds and Planets and other 'structures' that could be loosely called 'places of habitation'. You must learn 'NOT to LIMIT' your Creators and Gods in their form of 'Creativity'! For Creation is forever ongoing and does not cease, that is to say it may slumber prior to being re-awakened in a different form, but Creation is as it has been said 'Creation'!! and will ever be so.

Creation could be likened to an empty void awaiting gestation.

Yet within that so-called empty void there is life in abundance! For even Space is full of life substance even if it cannot be observed as such, and remember you, that is Mankind, has no real knowledge of what constitutes the 'Art of Creation'!!!

Even when there is a period of so-called 'in-activity' it is merely the cessation of 'action', but action is forever present in one form or another. Quite an anomaly for you to consider, is it not? Think about it and you may comprehend that statement!! So to bring this treatise to a culmination, we return to the word 'SPIRIT' and all that it implies. And so we say to you, when Scientists put forth theories that may sound feasible to the man in the street, remember they are dealing in facts as 'they' see them.

On a blackboard they can prove or disprove whatever they wish, but they dare not bring the word 'Spirit' into their equations, even if some of the more broadminded have leanings in that direction!! So it's up to you, the seekers and searchers of this world to come to your own conclusions and we sincerely hope and pray that you may find what you are looking for, even if you at present cannot verify it on a personal basis!

We bid you Farewell and leave you with the blessings of those on High.

Scribe!! Brother of Light! Your work has not yet finished dear friend, but remember we are ever at your side. Farewell! Farewell! Farewell!!

Chapter 8

March 6th 2008

JUST THOUGHTS! JUST THOUGHTS!

I woke up last night thinking about the previous discourse, and a lot of thoughts came crowding into my mind. I should have got up and put pen to paper but I fell asleep again! So what I shall be writing are only vague remembrances of those thoughts, so I trust you will bear with me if they are a little erratic and probably not in proper sequence!!!

The one I remember most clearly was about the Universe! and how it changes its shape from a form of round to one that almost resembles a rugby football. And then one that seemed to be **'elongated'**, as if all of the pathways that intersect the Universe were stretched lengthwise, say from left to right or right to left **and not 'up and down' to put it loosely!!!**

And these pathways or corridors as I have written in some of my books, together with their various appendages i.e. Worlds, Planets, Galaxies and what have you, would in a way be displaced, and so may present a completely different picture than was previously thought of!! In fact now that I think about it perhaps some of those planets etc. might even find that they were now in a completely different corridor of existence, having been **'squeezed' out of their previous orbital belt and now find** themselves in a foreign dimension!! Now how would that affect their equilibrium?

Some perhaps might amalgamate with others and so forming gigantic Balls of Nucleus Energy and becoming Planets or Worlds that would be almost unrecognisable!! **That's just one of my** thoughts, but I suppose you could say that the same procedure could be attributed to when the Universe opts for another excursion in one of its many phases of Evolution!!!

Another thought was one of Space, and by Space I mean the **'area' beyond the perimeter of our Universe where dwell** I presume many families of Universes, Big and Small, empty, or full of Heaven knows what!!!

Universes may even have within them another Universe, and that brings me to the thought I had about a Biblical text, which I **think said, 'As Above, So Below'!** Now just supposing that could **be altered to 'As Within, So Without'!!** Meaning that the Spirit Matrix would be the one that, as it were, gave birth to the other one that should resemble the Original. But would be of a denser form of matter that would then depend upon its ability for furthering its Evolutionary standing by acknowledging its dependence upon its Spiritual Progenitor. Who like our Spiritual side of our Earth life, would to all intents and purposes, be **'Invisible' and yet perhaps not to all of its inhabitants!!!!** Do you follow my line of thought?

Back to the Outer Space once more!! I say Mankind! but that word cannot do justice to all of the Created forms of Life of which Man as we know him is but a small fraction of Creation. **Well then, I say that 'Mankind' will Never know the extent of that outer vista of unlimited 'Space Matter'.**

I call it Space Matter for I believe that Space is a living 'organism' if that is the right expression, which I feel it is not!! And so to try and confine it to shall I say a specific area of identification is absolutely impossible, and we should leave that thought in abeyance!!!

What other thought is now surfacing in my mind? Shall I say GOD? GODS? DEITIES? or The UNKNOWABLE ESSENCE OF THE FORCE we call 'Life'? That essence that defies description and yet is ever there, hovering in the background to any thinking person who will try and think about that subject with an open mind!! Thinking is one thing! Knowing is another!! And I feel the latter is the one we should accept as the one that we shall 'Never' be able to come to terms with, either in this life or the many others that in our evolutionary scale we may traverse!

I personally have no problem regarding GOD! GODS! or however many you may conjure up in your mind. I firmly believe in the One we upon this Earth call, Our GOD! I will not dwell upon how or why I feel that I fully accept the way I feel, and that suits me fine. And I'm not likely to change my attitude regarding 'Him' and I know that that phrase 'Him' does not really apply to our Creator. But with our God given free will, we are allowed to see that Creator in any way that, shall I say, brings us closer to our vision of what a God figure, a Heavenly Father means to each one of us.

It's not GOD who changes, it's in our perception of what that word really means. And as we grow older and perhaps a little wiser our vision alters and perhaps we see GOD more in an abstract way.

Not perhaps so personal as Universal, universal as in all of the Creations that we attribute to Him, the ones we see around us all the time and take for granted!!! And what is so wonderful is that We are part of this Creation, that never ceases but goes on and on just as we do when the transition of the mortal body takes place. Nothing created ever dies it just alters, that is the natural course of events. And has been ordained by that Unknown Deity!!! I was going to say I will leave you there, but I feel it would be more appropriate if I said, 'We will leave you there and you know just what I am implying!'

And so it is, We who say to you and the Brother Scribe, Farewell and may the blessings of Those above be with you now and in the days to come, and we also add:

May Allah be Praised.
May Allah be Praised.
May 'your God' be ever with you, 'you students of Life'!
Farewell.

Chapter 9

March 11th 2008

MINDS IN UNISON!!

I awoke last night, thinking about a television programme I had watched earlier, which had left me thinking 'Well I haven't learnt much from that, if anything!!!' What has made me put pen to paper is the fact that so many scientific persons accept Creation and yet ignore the Prime Creator!! In fact many seem to think creation just 'happened' and leave it at that!

To my way of thinking I find that very arrogant on their part, they obviously accept 'their' powers of creativity whether of the mind, the body or, I was going to say, the 'Spirit'. But I don't think any of them even credit the fact that they have one!!! And I make no apologies for using the word 'fact', for to me the Spirit is the dominating force in our whole period of existence,

whether upon this evolutionary plane we call Earth, or upon the other planes that the Scientific fraternity would probably deny existed!

Just because they have yet to discover their own Spirit counterpart that is the immortal part of this liaison between Physical matter i.e. Body, and the governing principal Mind, or Spirit, if you wish to call that elusive invisible substance that is at the very core of all creative matter. Seen or unseen, visible or invisible all words that signify 'nothing'.

For to explain the <u>true</u> origin of the force of Life, can never be explained in terms of physical reality. For to my way of thinking the Force of Life is 'Spirit', and physical matter or substance is a form of a 'Bi-Product' that stems from the experimentation of those Creators that are not even recognised as existing, either in the mind or in reality. 'NOT OUR REALITY', but theirs!!! For Creators whoever they may be, are all aspects of the Divine Author of Life Itself!!

Just as 'we' are, in a humble way. Though the word 'humble' I feel does not sit comfortably upon the being called Man!! That is 'Mortal Man' and not his Immortal Spirit of amalgamation!!

Why is it that the Spirit side of Man, and yes even of our World, and go one step further and say 'Our Universe', has never been explored in the way the Physical side of Life force has? Is it because it is what we 'see' with our physical sight, but ignore the inner 'sight of feeling'!!! There's so much more to 'Life' than just this lifetimes sojourn upon this tiny orb floating in a sea of unexplored and unexplained so-called Space!!!!

To study earth, the planets, the stars, the galaxies, in fact the whole Universe, look first to its 'Spirit Origins'. And when I say Spirit, do not think I am bringing Religion into this equation. The true force of 'Life' does not need a religious form of interpretation to unravel its mysteries and its Truths!!!

Religion as such, I feel has been, and yea still is a stumbling block to rationalized thought upon any subject that is to do with Man's place in this vast unknowable landscape.

The thought process of the Author of All that there is, or ever was, or ever will be!!!

Man is but a fraction of that Thought process, even if he deludes himself to the contrary!!! There are Many, Many, Many, 'Manlike' experimental structures created, and yea even being created in the Vast Cosmic Mind Conclave or Unknown Creators, that are 'Your' Creators, call them what you will. Words and language are but outward expressions of inward thoughts!! Be they of the physical body or of the Spirit!!!

Learn to communicate by Thought, words only confuse and even deceive, but a thought is from the Soul and is True!! Believe that, for in time (your time!) communication between races will be in Thought Form. And any form of written treatise will be first in Thought participation and acceptance of all parties, and so War will cease to have any significance in the unification of this World and yea, Universal integration!!!

But your Religious convictions will have to be put aside before Mankind can enter into that phase of evolutionary progress. And here we are talking about the Universe in general and not just a handful of like-minded planets orbiting in their allotted space!!

Universal Unification is far more than personal ambition, it supersedes the personal and becomes **the 'Universal Whole' That** is the Future that has been planned and Ordained and <u>Will</u> take place. Accept that, for it is the <u>Truth</u>! Remember, You do have your place in the scheme of the Author of your future existence.

But you must play your part and know not only your limitations, but also your responsibilities towards All other forms of Creation!! Learn from the mistakes of the past and yea, even of the present and dare we say it, even those to come!!!

Be warned, for enemies often start from within and by that we mean from the one who takes it upon himself to try and alter **what he has not fully understood, regarding another's way of life.** We speak not only of persons but also of Nations!!! Pocket your National Pride and replace it by being Proud of being a member **of the 'Human Race'.** Think about that and act upon it!! For your **future and your very lives depend upon your attitude to 'right thinking'**, and that means for All people, and not just the so-called chosen few!!

We withdraw from this excursion into the passive mind of the person with the writing implement, it has been an experience for us and we hope to encounter it again in future times. We bid that one a Farewell and extend out hands in perpetual friendship.

It is now time for our departure to take place. We leave you in Peace.

Well Brother! It was not we who took over your thoughts this morning, you have been blessed, believe that. Farewell little Scribe, Farewell.

And to those of you who may read what has been written we bid you Farewell and God bless you, in your seeking and searching for the meaning of Life and its mysteries!

Farewell.

Chapter 10

May 6th 2008

THOUGHTS!!

Have you noticed that when people give their explanations regarding the realms of the Spirit, they usually speak or write on terms of what they know of the Earthplane! What I'm trying to say is that all of their descriptions are, shall I say, 'biased' towards what they are familiar with! Quite understandable really, in fact I'm just as guilty as they are, because I too describe things and places with a slant towards the Earthplane. Yet I am sure that 'areas' and even 'things' is difficult to describe adequately, what is unfamiliar to human senses!

I seem to remember, I think it was the prophet 'Nostradamus' in his descriptions of what he 'saw' mentally that he had to use the language of the day in his descriptive verses. And it's only in modern times when the actuality of those descriptions are viewed in reality, that his flowery descriptions can be seen to be true and pretty accurate when the, shall I say 'objects'? have actually been invented, and in many cases now taken for granted.

So what I am getting at is, are we, that is human beings, limited regarding our mental images of those 'unknown things' that we 'see' in our mental imagining? And so we call them by a name that is familiar to us and yet does not perhaps do justice to what we are trying to come to terms with, regarding our limited form of reference.

When we are describing what we are trying so hard to convey to others, who are just as limited in their viewing capacity and understanding!!!!

I'm also thinking regarding one of those 'Sci-Fi' books or articles that were fiction that has now been found to be a reality, and the word was, I think, 'Kryptonite' or something similar. And it was purely a figment of the author's imagination, but now the scientific fraternity have 'discovered' that there really is a substance from Space I think, and it has been called Kryptonite!!! So much for 'Fact and Fiction'! Are they interchangeable? And are we living in a Factual World or one of Fiction??? Somewhat mind boggling is it not?

So if I were to say, that on one of my Spiritual Mental journeys that my Brothers / Guides had taken me on, that I walked down a wide boulevard and lined with trees that shimmered in the breeze. Giving off the most alluring scent and their leaves were like living jewels, not of green but of iridescent hues that changed, and then changed again. And the little birds that played at hide and seek amongst the branches were themselves like sparkling jewels, weaving a spell of enchantment and sheer magic to me, the wanderer, along this avenue of bewilderment.

And sheer ecstasy that was taking me to a building of extraordinary beauty that scintillated in the mornings dew, that was like liquid diamonds of many hues creating a path that caressed my bare feet. So that walking became almost non-existent, I was floating so gently that I hardly noticed the movement!!

The building! Well that word does it no credit.

It was like a Heavenly mirage that came and went, only to reappear entirely different, it almost floated above the ground, for it seemed supported upon gossamer like clouds, that were forever moving in a languid fashion? This building, this edifice of

The Little Scribe

perpetual motion, was inviting me to enter, but where was the entrance? I saw none and yet I felt I must now be a part of this fabric of eccentricity, for suddenly I was aware of Jewel-like windows gazing down at me. And as they opened wider there floated back and forth silken-like curtains, that were there one minute and then were gone. And in their place was left a bejewelled bird crowned with soft white plumage, and as the head was moved, came forth a sound of distant harps and the scent of Jasmine!

I must have found an entrance for I found myself within the building, in a courtyard octagonal in shape. The floor, I thought **at first was of water, but it wasn't yet it bore the reflection of the** sky above it, and as I gazed, the stars from the canopy sky gently dropped down to the liquid below. And as each one reached its destination there arose vapours of colours I have no knowledge of, and yet they seemed familiar in a strange way.

I felt that I had strayed into the area where souls were to be born stars that had descended to become the Saints of the future. The eyes of God, manifested as saviours of the lost races of humanity, that were to be returned once more to the Gardens of Allah to await the verdict of the Eternal One who must remain nameless!!!

I looked around me, for I could hear voices, but they came from within and I knew that my time had come for me to return, but return to Where?

And here is where this strange narrative ends!! Even though I have tried to describe the journey I was taken on, I know that my feeble attempts at description have fallen far short from the '**reality**', if that is the correct word, which I feel it is not! So I will conclude this form of narrated experience and say, Thank you, to those who have made my journey possible!!

We bid you a fond Farewell Brother, a very fond Farewell to be sure!!

Chapter 11

May 21st 2008

A JOURNEY!!!

Let us take a journey, shall we say, a Hypothetical one for your benefit dear students of the occult. And by 'Hypothetical' it is for you to think about, for we cannot in all honesty prove to you as human entities that what we are about to vouchsafe to you, is an accurate description of the plane and the events that follow those 'entities' that inhabit it. So now let us begin this journey into the Hypothetical planes of the Souls experience, and life upon what is loosely termed 'The Soul Plane'!!

In previous dialogues on the subject of the Soul, that is 'your soul' that we are talking about. We have told you where the 'soul' in its plasticized embryonic thought substance dwelt, before it was deemed appropriate for 'it' to descend as it were, to the planes of matter. We hesitate to call them lower planes, because your understanding of the word 'lower' is quite, quite, different to our interpretation of it!! Just accept that 'lower' just means another direction from the original plane of conception. Where thought, that is 'Divine Thought', is the guiding principle of the life force that animates that wonderful but virtually unknown aspect of the Divinity!!! Namely, the Soul!!!

We continue. The embryonic substance that is called a Soul is now upon the Soul Plane, where it will remain during its 'whole' life form.

It never leaves this plane until the time comes for it to return to the Higher plane that adjoins the one of its inception! But that will be a very, very, long way off in your human understanding of Time! Which to us, that is 'All' of the so-called Spirit entities, has very little actual meaning, and so for augments sake a thousand years is but a fraction of a second, if you can follow our train of thought!

So ignore the use of the word Time, for Time is Timeless and is virtually flexible it can be manipulated by Those in authority who have jurisdiction over it!! Time can be stilled so as to be non existent, or can be speeded up to virtually confuse those who are unacquainted with Times eccentricities!

The Soul, when it is ensconced upon the Soul plane becomes part of a 'group', those who are considered to be, shall we say, compatible to each other in their ever-ongoing evolutionary progress. Each soul, shall we say, remains in this 'group class', but also has a 'One to One relationship' with its mentor and Spiritual guide, and so each soul also inherits some of the values that that mentor has over the centuries acquired. And so the Soul benefits from this liaison, and because of it no two souls are actually alike in their outlook of what is being shown to them.

Though here we pause, to say that some souls are almost 'twin souls' because of their attachment to each other during this period of learning and so this bond remains forever.

During all of the centuries that the Spirit, which the soul has been allowed to create, reincarnates upon the various lower spheres of spiritual attainment. More of this later!

Now how can we describe to you in layman's terms, what soul looks like and what it is 'made of'. Well we will try. Soul in its first embryonic stage now is ensconced in a protective vapour-like envelope that is constantly changing and full of movement and colour. This protective covering is only a form of outer 'garment' that stimulates the latent mental substance that the soul has been endowed with, but as yet has no knowledge of how to use this wonderful organ of thought mechanism!

Soul is in a way cocooned in this vapour-like essence it is not restricted, for the cocoon or garment is a form of liquid, where the embryonic form can move, or remain inert as the case may be. Do not think that at this stage the soul resembles a human being, for it does not, and yet it has all the latent capabilities of actually creating a likeness of one at a later stage in its learning!

It is actually a very beautiful almost transparent substance that reflects all of those thought patterns of colours that defy description. For colour here upon the soul plane is in the form of a musical note that as it vibrates, gives off this sound of colour. Each note or chord responds to another and so the Soul is like one harmonious vibration of exquisite notation that actually promotes its inner spiritual growth!!

The Souls guide and Mentor who is now a life long friend and companion monitors all of this activity, and so as the soul progresses the guide gradually encourages the mind substance to expand, by imprinting upon it, various picture images, and the soul then responds in various directions. The guide can now evaluate the progress and at a certain stage the outer covering is replaced with a lighter variation, that allows the Soul within to venture outside of this vapour covering. And yet it has what might be termed an umbilical cord that joins the outside soul to its 'spirit core' that remains within the confines of the vapour shield!!

Gradually and with much patience the 'guide' encourages the Soul's aspect to become more adventurous. It is then that the Soul has the ability to clothe itself in an egg shaped oval skin of vapour substance, that can move with ease in the, shall we call it, the 'outside world'? of its existence!! Along with all of the other Souls they now form a 'community' of basic understanding of what awaits them as they learn the rudiments of creativity.

This is a very carefully monitored stage in the Soul's development. And gradually their picture forms of thought are shown, and how they can project them to the outside of their Mind substance. And then the guide and mentor shows them how thought then needs a 'physical' tool for the construction of their thought form, so that it can be animated by the thought process! By 'tool' we are not suggesting arms, hands, and legs etc. The 'tools' used in the world of the Spirit are, shall we say, 'electrical currents'.

These become 'positive constructions' that carry out the orders of the blue printed thought patterns. All thought form patterns vary according to the sphere where a Spirit form happens to be. Upon the 'first sphere', shall we say 'up' from the material world, your world in fact, Spirit entities often use, shall we say, their spirit replicas of their previous human bodies, i.e. Hands, arms, feet etc. Because that is considered the 'Norm' upon this first sphere!

Whereas upon the 'Higher' ones the thought blue print of electrically charged animation is all that is needed, even when the 'thought tool' is on an invisible wavelength! Do you follow?

And now back to the realm of the Soul!!! The soul now has the ability to create for itself Spirit forms or essences of its soul creator, to perform the various functions that are needed to give to the Soul the information it needs in its Spiritual Growth upon its evolutionary path back to its original source of Creation! For Soul in its original state is Perfect! But without any knowledge or what Perfection is all about!

And so it creates for itself Spirit essences that can become entities in their own right and in that way they can experience what the Soul upon its plane of habitation never can. But there is a line of communication that stretches right down and up from the very earth plane itself, and all of this information is sifted and analyzed not only by the Soul, but also its friend and mentor. And so the Soul is gradually coming to understand the true meaning of 'Life' and what part He or She as Soul plays in this evolutionary path of everlasting growth.

This takes in so many various life styles and forms that the Spirit has to take on, to fulfil its destiny towards its surrogate creator, The Soul!!

And now we come to an anomaly! Not all Souls are fully aware of their potential, and so what we have written cannot be taken as a generalization. This is all taken into account by the Masters of Creativity and we feel we must not venture down that path in this narrative of the Soul and its creative process!!

The actual Soul Plane is one of extreme beauty it has a translucent aspect about it, almost one of magical quality. The Light is constantly changing, as are the clouds that encircle this Plane of existence. There is foliage everywhere, trees and shrubs the like of which is beyond Earthly description. There are areas where many souls congregate and this is where many life long friendships are made, and they really are lifelong.

Here too, the souls sometimes bring with them some of their identifiable Spirit creations, which though not exactly human like they do have a verifiable identity somewhat ethereal and dreamlike. And of an extremely Spiritual quality of expression, and by that word we are not signifying human facial expression, but an Aura of tranquil beauty and sound so soft as to be almost inaudible but not to those who are associating with each other.

It is the blending of these colours and sounds that contribute to lasting friendships and bonding. And this can surface when the **Spirits are upon different planes, and when two 'souls' meet and** the vibrationary tones connect, and then recognition takes place and memories are awakened.

This then is the meeting of a true 'Soulmate'. And this then is transferred to the Spirit Human Companion of their present incarnation!! We can leave you to dwell upon that statement and judge for yourself if perhaps you too, have experienced such a meeting.

Remember what we said about time and its non-relevance to those upon the Soul plane? And remember also that not all Souls mature at the same time, it really is an ongoing process, some slumber, while others are very active. The actual plane is divided into many areas or continents and so life is very rewarding in so many ways. For not all areas are the same in either structure or **'life style'**!!! The soul is constantly learning and being shown how other Planets and their inhabitants live, as well as there own. **Creativity is the main, shall we say, 'lesson' that the Soul is** learning about, and also bringing forth their latent capabilities that they can, if they wish, pass on to their various Spirit creations!!

If we say to you, think of the child prodigies, the geniuses, and the often misunderstood gifted ones, and you can then speculate as to where sometimes these qualities originated!!! As we have said many times before, Thought is Paramount upon all spheres of existence whether in the realms of the Spirit, or upon the planets that whirl about in so-called space. In fact, Thought is Universal, and we do mean Universal, in its multitude sense of Universes other than your own!!

Thought is Life Force before it is manifested as such.

So think then of those who are the Creators of it and their responsibility to that Unknowable Substance, that Essence that defies description and always will!!!

And believe us when we say that Creation in its many forms and construction can never truly be understood by the lay person, whether of the Planet Earth or one of the many millions more that you know nothing of!!! There are such varying stratas that go to make up what you loosely call a human being. And that being **is 'Not' necessarily the 'end product'** of Thought, that is manifested everywhere but is not confined to any one place or **plane of existence and that need not mean 'human existence'**!!!

So marvel at what you, that is you, you speculators of human existence are created of, the many layers that go to make of you, who you think you are, and know that who you think you are is not who you really are!!! And also remember that whether humans or Spirit, or Soul essence, we all owe our life force to the Creator of it!! We are but clay in the Divine hands and Mind, of that Omnipotent Omnipresence all Embracing substance that cannot be identified as like anything else in existence. For it is the very existence itself and therefore has no parallel with which to judge it by!!!

Your very Soul is that part of the Creator that **through 'His'** Love is endowed with the freedom of Will, to choose whether you believe or not. You belong to your Creator as your creations **belong to you! You are indestructible you are 'Immortal'**. And this is a Universal trait, believe that for it is a truth.

Never think that the vehicle you use, (the human body) is the only one you are heir to.

For you are many, and they all emanate from that original Soul concept that seeks to return to its very source, knowing now why it was allowed in the first place to descend only to re-ascend. **With the acquired knowledge of 'Why' this many**-bodied journey of many life times was the only way to self-awareness of the spark of the Divinity that dwells within all of us. **And by the word 'Us'** we include all created life forms, known and perhaps still unknown, awaiting their turn to appear upon the stage of Life to fulfil their destiny!!

Remember that the Soul essence is not a replica of the human shell that the Spirit inhabits from time to time. It is beyond the likeness of a **human identity and we stress the word 'human'**, for **an 'identifiable entity' can be recognised as part of the Divinity** itself. And that means the Soul has that God given aspect, which transcends all human like aspects and becomes that ethereal quality that we as humans call Angelic, and Saintly.

The glory of the Almighty manifested in all of those who have surrendered self, to become selfless and in unison with all of creation!!! Your discourse on Soul and its many aspects must now come to a close. We have only been allowed just a glimpse of Souls purpose to pass on to those who are searching and seeking answers to questions that no doubt will still be asked a hundred years hence!!!

Such is life, Question and Answer! Question and Answer! That is Life is it not? We leave you little travellers of the mind and bid you Farewell.

And to you Brother we say to you, Fare – Thee – Well, little scribe of the written page!!

Your journey is not over yet and we know you understand our meaning!! Farewell little brother Farewell. We are always near you believe that for it is a truth!!

GOD'S BLESSINGS BE UPON YOU!!

Allah be Praised!!!!

Chapter 12

May 23rd 2008

OUTER! OUTER SPACE! AND WHAT DOES IT HOLD??

Let us take you on another journey, a journey of the mind, where all things are possible but difficult to prove. So it is left up to you, you searchers after the truth, to accept or reject what is presented to your inner screen that registers what some people like to call the imagination!!! Which, of course is a product of your own inner thoughts, that can be influenced by thoughts from other directions, by which we mean from other people, either deliberately or by accidentally tapping into the thought streams or wavebands that circumnavigate your Earth Plane!!

And now let us begin our mutual journey of the mind and see to where it will lead us!!! First we say to you relax, not only your body but also that receptive area of the mind that will allow us to influence you on our joint venture. We take a step as it were, off this little whirling globe you call your Earth, and looking back and down upon it, it almost looks like a toy version of your world suspended in an ocean of blue. And is gradually taking on a mantle of sombre darkness as we approach the outer limits of your known perimeter.

Where the darkness is pierced by the ever-changing vista of stars and galaxies, planets that seem to be wandering as if searching for a haven of refuge, they do not know that their allotted area of Space is carefully monitored. And their wandering is in fact, already programmed and so they are really behaving in a normal fashion according to the immutable laws of Universal habitation!!!

We are rapidly approaching what appears to be a gigantic ball of Fire, that is not a ball at all but a series of many, many smaller nuclei like stars that are bonding together. And then breaking away leaving streams of coloured translucent vapour trails, that have the appearance of clouds that obscure the originators of this fierce energy that goes to make up this seen Ball of Fire. Every so often fingers of what looks like molten lava shoot out from this **fireball and 'pieces' break off and are actually planets in the** making.

These lava fingers are not hot, but cold, though some seem to have a certain quality of Heat and the pieces that fly off them gravitate to the colder ones, forming somewhat larger areas of planet substance. And these are the ones that will eventually become life-forming areas of habitation, not necessarily of the Human species of life force, but of experimentation of other areas of Life forms. As yet not identified as any particular species that can be classed as an evolved previously known life form!!!

This area of Space is one of 'perpetual activity' and though of interest, is not one that we wish to stay too long observing!! So we move on once more. Space, no longer dark and gloomy but radiating light that is beyond any earthly description.

It is Life Force energy that seems almost like a sea, where the waves and currents jostle each other for supremacy. Strangely though, there is very little sound attached to all of this activity. **It's almost as if this area is waiting for a catalyst to give it the** spark that will generate the life force. And will enable all of this silent activity to become a volatile force of untamed electrified energy that can be harnessed for certain uses in the coming eons of time.

When electrical generated energy will become the normal food of all living creatures in fact, of all created creations. This energy will be **the major part of the 'make-up'**, and food as it is known now will become a thing of the past!! It will, we are told, be just a pleasant pastime, but of no particular value to the promotion of the growth of any particular species, human or otherwise!!! The idea of killing any living organism will be unheard of. All life force will have in its possession the ability to withdraw that force whenever it wishes, or shall we say, certain intelligent species will be able to change their actual form and become a higher version of their particular genre!

And all of this is just a minute part of the overall plan for the promotion, or shall we call it the Evolution of the various areas of Space that warrant this introduction of Cosmic Experimentation. For not all Areas of Space are deemed suitable, they may well become acceptable sometime in the future but for now some Areas of Space are just slumbering their time away. And these at present are of no interest to us and so we will hastily leave them far behind and turn our attention to what lies beyond this frozen perimeter of time!!!

We approach a junction of corridors and wonder which one to choose to explore in this venture of ours to limits far, far beyond the vision of Mankind upon that awesome little World that you know of as Earth!!! We decide to turn to the East and so we are propelled along that corridor at break neck speed, passing whole avenues of little planets that bob about in what seems to be an ocean of liquid that never seems to be still. And so these little planets have a hard time avoiding each other.

They are not inhabited by any form of life energizing matter, **they are in fact sterile, until they are required, and that's all we** know about them!! Our corridor twists and turns, and is not what we expected of it. But it does make for variety, for we do not know what awaits us round the corner so to speak!

Suddenly our corridor stops and ahead of us is an empty nothingness that is paradoxically teeming with life! Yet we cannot perceive it, we only sense that it is there, for there is a sound, a murmuring, not of voices but of movement. But what is causing this movement eludes our senses, until all of a sudden it stops, and this emptiness comes to life, it is as if clouds have parted and we see what is going on beyond them!

It is like an ocean of light, a light of such subtlety that we are unaware of its source. And then the surface of the ocean is disturbed in many, many places, islands appear from out of nowhere, actually they have come up from the ocean's floor. And as they float gently back and forth and some seem to propel themselves in a different direction, we hear the sound of laughter.

And gradually our eyes become accustomed to seeing what was invisible to us before. People, lots and lots of happy carefree people of all ages, it would seem that this coming up from the Ocean's floor is an event that the inhabitants look forward to at each turn of a season. It's a holiday that turns out to be a working holiday, but one that they all enjoy, for now comes the time when all their efforts while upon the ocean's floor can come to fruition, almost overnight so to speak.

Trees and shrubs grow at a terrific pace, as does everything, their crops are harvested and then another lot grows in its place. It is an abundance that never seems to stop. We are told that this goes on for quite a long time, that if you could measure it, it would amount to several Earth years!! But to the inhabitants it seems but a few months, and then the islands and their people return once more to the ocean's floor, and store all of their produce, which will last them until the next surface time arrives! They seem able to live either under water or upon dry land, and yet to our eyes they appeared, shall we say, 'quite normal', even if at times they seemed to almost disappear in certain lights!!!

All of this we viewed as if we were watching a film, they were not aware of us and we did not infiltrate upon their life style. But all extremely interesting and somewhat uplifting in a peculiar

Spiritual way. We were sorry to leave them, but all of this experience seemed to take no time at all. That is if you are conscious of the passing of it!!! Which we are NOT!!!

We now pass over this vast expanse of Light and ever changing cloud formations, and can see that our designated corridor continues in what now appears to be a straight line!! Once more upon it we feel an upsurge of energy that carries us along with absolutely no effort on our part. We pass scenery of spectacular beauty, sometimes rugged, sometimes lush and meadow like, and then again we see endless vistas of sand dunes. But these sands vary in colour, which includes the foliage that seems to spring up in the oddest of places.

They sparkle like jewels and actually radiate some form of light so that these pockets of coloured foliage act as beacons to any traveller upon those vast sand areas, and point the way to what look like settlements, but settlements of rare beauty. The houses and gardens appear to be of a permanent nature, but we understand that they actually move, shall we say, lock, stock and barrel!!! **To other areas, it's as if they float as it were a few metres** above the ground and to view the procession of multi coloured houses gently floating along, which also include their gardens, is a view not to be missed!!!

These houses we are told are made of a synthetic material, very strong, but extremely light and when they wish to, shall we say, **put down 'roots'**, that is exactly what they do! They project a series of spike-like arms, which anchor them into the ground and these can be withdrawn when they decide to move again!! Each **house has a 'plot'**, which includes the garden area, all very ingenious and very effective!!! We seem to be encountering quite exotic landscapes and their inhabitants on our journey Eastward.

Cities that we pass over all seem very well ordered, well planned in a grid-like fashion, but, how can we put it? in a flexible fashion that allows for variation and personalization of group areas? And so whole areas of a city can resemble complete contrasts to each other and yet nothing seems to jar, and yes, the variety makes for an extremely interesting melange of architecture where each area is almost like a complete city in microcosm. And these cities are constantly expanding as new groups of people join the thriving community where harmony is the main ingredient for a happy and contented lifestyle! We can envy this form of Utopia and wish that the same system could be applied upon our Earth, or rather your Earth!!!

As we travel Eastward we keep encountering various Suns, some are white hot, while others seem to be of a more moderate temperature and yet again they vary in colour taking in a whole spectrum of, shall we say, Rainbow colours? These colours are reflected light from within the core of each sun and so landscapes etc. take on a surreal appearance, which is most intriguing, especially when the light is reflected in the seascape.

And you cannot be sure which sun is casting which light, for sometimes it seems there are more than just one sun, we have counted as many as four separate ones in just one area of a world we are passing!!! We feel that when there is more than one sun involved then the volume of heat from each sun seems to be regulated in some way, otherwise the heat radiated would become too intense if there were inhabitants involved!!

We now seem to be in more than one area, it's as if there is a junction here it's almost as if it's a 'melting pot' of many different kinds of, what is the word we are looking for, of some form of **'matter' gaseous matter of an unstable nature, where 'things'** become different from what they were. They are being amalgamated with other matter, which we think is the prelude to a new Star being formed. This area is all very turbulent though wonderful to observe, but from a safe distance we hasten to add!!!

We have been informed that it would not be in our interests to venture any further along this corridor of uncertain space, and so we prepare to return to where we started out upon this Eastern corridor of unexpected, but nevertheless most interesting of areas, hitherto unexplored by Mortal man!! Perhaps next time, that is if there is a next time, we may venture down one of the many other corridors that intersect what we know of as Space. Which seems that the more that we know, the more we realize how little that is, when visiting Space and beholding its wonders!!!

And so dear companions of our minds we bring you back safely to the starting point of this journey into some of the depths of Space, that seem to have no end!!!

We bid you Farewell and may God's blessings remain with you now and forever. Farewell.

And to you our dear Brother in Christ consciousness, we thank you for your co-operation and the joining of minds, yours and ours. We also bid you Farewell, but only in thought and not in Spirit!! Be patient just a little while longer and all of your desires are to be fulfilled. This we have been told to tell you little one. Farewell, but NOT Goodbye!!!

Chapter 13

May 26th 2008

VISITORS FROM AFAR!!!

Imagine, dear friends of the Earth, a large tree whose branches are laden, no! not with fruit, but leaves, so many leaves that the branches curve over to form a shady umbrella from the heat of the noon day Sun. And seated round a central figure are many, many people of all nationalities and colour. They are in little groups and their seats are the warm grassy soil, soft and enticing, for other people are wandering past and some stop to listen to what the central figure is saying. Some remain and join a group while others stand in the background for a while and then continue their interrupted journey.

Has your imagination captured the picture that has been painted for you? If it has, then you can join those groups of interested seekers of the knowledge of Why!! Why this World? Why this Life? And what it is that awaits those whose transition from one sphere to the next is all about?? You dear earth friends can join us in your minds, while those that have been described to you are here with us upon that next sphere. For the message that is being imparted to them is also meant for you as well!

Our teachers of the mysteries of the occult, the continued life cycle that is forever expanding with what is known as evolution, the evolution of each and every individual that is created.

The human body is just another aspect of the evolutionary process that began when a Soul was brought into existence by Divine Thought. And that Divine Thought Creator has many,

many diverse forms of intelligent Beings, whose sole aim is to be of service to that nameless Essence of Divinity that is everywhere, and yet is Nowhere!! An anomaly perhaps because what cannot be seen does not mean that it does Not exist!! For there are dimensions that are not known about in their entirety and, in fact, they never can be explained and never will be to mortal man, or even to his immortal Spirit counterpart!!

That knowledge would be so staggering that no form of known intellect could understand its abstract complexity, and in trying to do so would result, No! Not in madness, but in absolute annihilation of the created essence and so, we, that is all of the **'programmed' entities that cover the whole spectrum from Soul birth to Spirit awakening, will never reach that stage in thought activity.** And the reason is obvious is it not, little searchers after the truth!!

For once you enter the path of the searcher and become a devoted disciple of the art of seeking; you can never turn back. And yet here we pause and say to you, sometimes a searcher has to retrace their steps in order to proceed further along that path of esoteric knowledge! Confusing? No, not really, it is a form of re-evaluation of learned aspects that can sometimes only be properly understood when put in there right and proper context! And that **can only come about in, shall we call it, 'hindsight', a much used expression in today's colloquial language from all corners of the globe!!!**

We have said 'Globe' and you can if you wish alter that word to 'Universal acceptance'. For knowledge and teaching, learning and accepting, searching and seeking, is a 'Universal' trait and is not confined to just one small part of what you humans call 'The Universe'!!!!

We, that is 'We' who are, shall we say, the 'Outsiders' who monitor the various planes of existence, the Planets and Worlds if you wish to call your places of habitation, 'We' then, are beyond what you would call 'Intelligence life Forms. We cannot in our capacity of 'Observers' comply with your wishes of further knowledge of just Who and What we are. Sufficient to say we are, shall we say, 'Another Branch' of the Evolutionary Tree of expansion of Eternal knowledge of Creation!! And here we must leave that as has been said!!! Accept, and question no further on that particular aspect of creativity.

Let it be known that we have your interests at heart and comply entirely with the Laws of the Universe. That is, 'Your Universe'. And make of that what you will!!!

And by that statement you may infer that Universes in general can and do converse with each other in ways completely unknown to you upon this Planet that you have named Earth!! A word that denotes many things in many places that cannot be covered by your interpretation of what that word signifies!! To You!!!

'Creation' covers a multitude of different interpretations, of which your Scientific fraternity with its very limited knowledge of Creation has absolutely no real idea of what it involves.

When we say to you, if you could 'step outside' of the confines not only of your minds but also literally of your very Universe, you would get just a glimmer of what Creation can actually accomplish, when Thought is brought to bear upon what is loosely termed as SPACE!!! You! We! All dwell in Space. Whether it be confined within the perimeters of your Universe, we hesitate to call it your 'known Universe' for to us we feel you know very little of this confined Space that revolves in the outer limitless areas of many layered stratas of Unseen matter that you call 'Space'.

For Space is not what you think it is!! It is 'NOT EMPTY'!! It is teeming with life forms before they are 'forms'. A conundrum for you to think about! If they are formless then who or what makes them seem forms of active life? And is that life invisible?

And if so, why? And to whom? And **if not 'who or what' is it that can observe what is being created??** And think not just in terms of **The Humanities'** for **that word covers many different forms of** living species if you did but know it!!!

We know!! For <u>We</u> come into that category!!!! Speculate on that, little person who is doing all of this form of communication between Minds from different vibrationary spheres of Thought participation!!!

We feel that we are nearing the completion of this form of communication, between the various forms of Created entities of identifiable aspects of what is termed Creation!! As you are aware this form of creativity encompasses much, much more than any of us can be aware of, we speak of you dear Brethren of the Earth.

You do have much to learn and, shall we say, un-learn about the reasons for the existence of forms of life (Man included!) upon the various Worlds and Planets that exist within the **Universe's grasp!**

You are creating forms of communication between the various groups of Nations that was not known about such a short time ago. And yet we can tell you that communication between nations has been in existence before this modern era of it that has thought to be of such high technology, is NOT as modern as you may think!! There have been civilizations upon your planet that have long since disappeared leaving no trace. And yet they emerged upon another Planet as forerunners of our advanced **civilization that 'one day' you upon Earth will come across in** your Space wanderings, that seem so primitive to us, who really **'do know' how to use and 'tame'**, space and time, which are the **two sides of your 'proverbial coin'**!!

It is there to be used and not abused, as you will in due course find out. Beware of transferring back and forth units of unknown viruses that could cause serious disruption of populations that may become contaminated by them! Be warned and be prepared!

Not all areas of Space can be trusted, so watch out for your immune systems you travellers of Space, there will have to be a great deal of thought taken regarding the health of those who choose to dwell upon your man-made satellite imitation planets of habitation!!!

We have moved quite a long way away from the shady tree of **the imagination haven't we?**

But our non-verbal form of communication has been not only for you dear children of the Earth, but also for those who we spoke of in the beginning of this narrative. Those of the Spirit World who also search and seek wisdom wherever it can be found, as you are, and no doubt will continue to do so when your transition takes place in due course.

So until we meet again in Thought manipulation between Us and that little person who writes so laboriously with that peculiar implement he calls a pen! When thought, when used properly could do the same work in a fraction of the time it has taken him to do it!!! We nevertheless do Thank him for his efforts, which has been a no mean feat on his behalf. Take great care of yourself little person, you do matter, you really do. We are told to bid you a Farewell and so we do. Farewell! And we also are told to say to **you, 'May God bless You!!'** This also we do.

Farewell Earth, Farewell!!

Well Brother, Yes! We are here and have been all of the time! For it is through our Thought Channel that is connected to you that makes this work possible. And, has already been said dear **Brother, 'You do matter.'** Both of You! Believe that for it is a Truth.

Farewell, Farewell, Farewell!!

Chapter 14

May 29th 2008

A DISCOURSE TO THINK ABOUT!!!

Do you sometimes wonder just how you upon this little World, fit into the overall scheme of this Universe? For you are such a very small particle in this vast, vast cosmic ocean of Space. You view what you think of as the permissible vision that your probes and telescopic instruments allow you to do and yet they fall far, far, short of showing you what is actually Out There!!

For what is 'out there' is constantly changing, it fluctuates with the seasons of birth through to the end, called death, and here we are speaking of Planets, Worlds, Galaxies etc. and not of your species called Humanity!!! Which in some cases is merely a bi-product of the Created essence you call 'Life'. For 'Life' can have many interpretations if you were able to judge the formula that constitutes what is known as 'Creation'.

Creation is NOT just a passing fancy of those who, we shall call, The designated Creators of the matter that you choose to call the 'life force'. For life force in its embryonic stage that begins its journey in the Thought substance of those aforementioned Creators. For contrary to many speculative questions about 'The Creator' of known Antiquity that you call 'God', there are many, many, creators who are allowed that privilege of creativity.

That, shall we say, owe their allegiance, nay their very existence to that Higher Unknown Essence of, shall we still call it, 'Life Force'. For that force is but an abstract dimension of an unknown quantity of 'unexplainable matter', and even that feeble explanation falls far short of the actuality of something that defies explanation and description!

So how on Earth can Man ever come to terms with what Creation is actually a part of! For believe us Creation is not the 'be all' and 'end all' of what that unfathomable Mind substance is capable of!!! It is 'Limitless' in its capacity of, shall we call it, 'Illusion' and we have to leave you to interpret that as you wish!!!!

We have to use the word 'Creation' for that is what this form of mental discourse is all about. We are told that we may not go beyond that word at this present stage in Man's mental capacity for understanding, what cannot be understood by language of the Earthplane, but only by an advanced inner feeling of acceptance of unverifiable esoteric abstractions. If you can follow our line of thought!! Which could come under the heading of 'doubtful', and we mean you no disrespect we are just stating an observation!!!

Abstract usually denotes a certain form of explanation about something that perhaps defies a 'logical' interpretation, and here we use the word 'logical' in your language for we have no example that corresponds to it!! So what do we know about Abstract possibilities? Shall we be honest with you and say that even We, with our advanced knowledge of the Cosmic Enterprise have not been able to penetrate those hidden mysteries.

That follow on from where Creation does not actually 'leave off' but rather takes on a more, yes we will say it, 'abstract form' of activity that we find difficulty in defining as a verifiable certainty!!! In other words in Our present stage of Evolution we have not reached that position of being presented with a solution that we can actually comprehend!!

Such is the Mystery of, shall we call it, 'Cosmic Illusion' that were we to be shown what we would consider a verifiable solution we would most likely, be in a grave error. For what is verifiable 'today', (and read that word as 'Thousands of days or years' take your choice!!) could well be just an illusion that takes on the mantle of reality, but is in effect just an 'illusion' of it!!!

Quite a lot for you to conjure with is it not dear scribe? Do not stop now to try and work things out, they will come to you when you are ready to receive them! You are as it were like a 'sponge' you absorb much, but until you are metaphorically squeezed, then, you are in a position of passing on your gleaned knowledge however you have come by it, and shall we add, and by 'Whom'??

When one, and here we are speaking in general terms regarding those whose minds are open to explanations and interpretations that are at variance with the prevailing thoughts of the day!

You have minds and free wills, use them wisely; and if you cannot 'go along' with what is being written, do not worry, just file it in your memory storehouse.

And let it surface when you are ready to reassess the knowledge you have been vouchsafed not only by Us, but by others who also are on the path of esoteric evolution. Even if some of them are unaware of their position as Teachers, to teach is to learn and to learn is to listen, and by listen we speak of the inner senses of 'feeling'. When instinctively you know when something being said or shown to you is the truth and we should add 'a truth at present'! And you must use your own judgement regarding that remark of ours!!!

Nothing pertaining to 'Life' stands still; the movement is one of continuity both of Mind and Body. Do you not agree? If we stand still then paradoxically we begin to stagnate, though sometimes a period of cessation of deep thinking can in a way be a forward step and not a backward one as can be thought!! To reassess ones values both of the past and the present, can result as a leap into the future!!! And the future of the 'thinking' person can be very, very, bright and rewarding in the most unusual of ways!!

Remember always, 'Look before you leap' and learn to 'Walk before you attempt to Run!' When you have left the Wheel of Life upon your Planet Earth then your Real life will begin in earnest, that is if you wish it to, your free will is your inheritance and is with you forever. Not every Spirit wishes to pursue a life of, shall we say, 'expectation', and that is their choice and is respected as such.

We return to the beginning of this discourse regarding this your Planet of Habitation and its place in the Cosmic Subtlety of this your present Universe!!

You may wonder what we are going to say next about your precious little World. Well as far as we can tell, the changes that are affecting it at this present time are, how shall we put it? Perfectly Normal in their witnessed Abnormality that your Planet is going through! We stressed before about the constant movement in connection with All life forms, and that does include your Planet, which is a living, vibrating, structure of intense activity within the bowels of its outer coverings. These coverings and what goes on beneath them are all part of the growth of this Planet, and growth usually means upheaval of some sort somewhere. Like the snakes of the forest they shed their dead skin to release the growth of the new one underneath, awaiting its turn to become a creature of light once more!

So your Planet in its own fashion is shedding what it no longer needs to allow the growth awaiting its turn beneath the surface, and yea even deeper than that!!! You witness what you see, but you do not see what is causing all of this chaos, and we say to you, be thankful for that. For to be a party to that great disturbance that rocks the very foundations of your Planet would literally be the end of your mortal body and would leave a scar even upon your Spirit that would take many, many lifetimes to erase!!

You will have to learn how to adapt to this epoch of change that you, at present have to endure. There have been countless civilizations that have gone before you leaving no trace whatsoever! They too passed through changes that stunned them and left them bewildered and thinking that the end of the World was in sight!

Well it was for them!! But NOT for the planet upon which they dwelt!! Cause and effect, Life and Death, all part of the same Cosmic illusion of reality that really is no more than the 'growing up' of a Stella particle of Thought matter. That one day we do not say, (will cease to be) but will change and perhaps become amalgamated with another particle (Planet) that is also part of this unknown growth that is forever changing the Space. Wherein it has its programmed allotted time scale of Birth, Death and RESURRECTION!!!

These then are just some of the mysteries that pervade all known Universes and their inhabitants and we do not mean the Humanities, though of course these events do effect them and we suppose always will. That is as long as there is a need for the growth of mortal man in his search for his true identity and when that search is over, then Earth Planets will no longer be needed for that purpose and we leave that there. For we are informed that that does NOT concern present day Man or the foreseeable future of that species!!!

So you can see, little people of the Earth planet, there is much **that has to be withheld from Man's enquiring mind.** For the whole of Creation is far more complex and is indeed far outweighed by probabilities as to its eventual outcome and we dare not hazard a guess as to when that Omega aspect will come about!!!

This lesson (for that is what it is!) has been to try and give you a glimpse of what lies beyond Man's perception of why He and His kind have been chosen to be, NO! Not 'Guinea pigs' but forerunners of a species yet to be thought of as viable examples of a perfection.

That far exceeds any known form of that word, which seems to be reserved for those Higher entities that you call Gods!!!

Does that make you think of those words from Ancient Scripture when Your God Creator announced to those celestial beings around Him, 'Let Us Make Man in our Own IMAGE!!!' That day has yet to dawn, for the species known as Mortal Man it seems is a far cry from those uttered sentiments from on High!! Perhaps if we attune our thoughts to the entities you know of as 'Spirit' we may come nearer to what was envisaged by those lofty thoughts in those far off legendary days before Creation was even Created!!!!

And here we feel is where we must end this discussion that flows from the pen hand of that earnest little person who is called a scribe!! A word that in olden times denoted one who was far wiser than he was ever given credit for, and we leave that just there. For it is making the scribe anxious as to what we may say next!! Fear not little one, we have said all we were going to say on that topic!!!

And now it is time for us to abandon our brief sojourn upon this lower plane of learning and return from whence we came from!! We bid you Farewell, for we do understand the meaning, And to the scribe. Brother! We greet you as one who once we knew, in times long past!!!

FAREWELL. May your God be with you now and for always. Farewell.

The Little Scribe

Yes Brother we are here with you, guiding your hand and your thoughts. It is now our turn to say Farewell and this we do with all of our Love.

Farewell from all who hold you dear!!

Chapter 15

June 4th 2008

ALL PRAISE BE TO ALLAH

May the Peace of Allah be upon you little friend of ours and in His Name we will proceed if you are ready?

Along the pathway that we call Life it is far from straight, for it twists and turns, and yes even doubles back upon itself when you perhaps least expect it! But then that is the variety that keeps mortal man upon his toes! For if all of Life was, shall we say, straightforward, there would be no incentive to change and progress either physically, mentally or Spiritually!! And that dear friend is what we are programmed to do! Change and move forward. Yes we like all of the animal kingdom and others are programmed, however irksome you may think that is, but as you know we, that is the Human species, have been given the gift of Free Will!!

A priceless gift, but also one that carries with it a great burden of responsibility. For when it is used properly as it was intended to be, it becomes a wonderful tool of near perfection. But when used for selfish ends and reasons that harbour deceit then it is a Knife of Razor sharp intention and can only result in what is known as 'Bad Karma', that in one way or another must be erased whether in this Lifetime or in one to come.

And here we are speaking of the reincarnation period where it is left for the Spirit companion to judge how it's now physical 'mortal being liaison', can make amends for its previous incarnated protégé's bad Karma that 'it', the physical side of this partnership failed to amend. Justice has to be done and yes seen to be done. You may think that that strikes you as unfair, so it may seem, but then the present mortal partnership should be aware of what Karma is all about. And Bad or Good Karma that the mortal man generates has its profound effect upon its Spirit companion of this present life span!

So you can see that this partnership must be understood in its proper context by the physical partner, each one helping the other in the evolutionary cycle. **That really is the Spirit's main concern,** for as you are aware, Spirit is the Real one that never dies it is immortal, whereas the physical body that is the temporary dwelling place of the Spirit, is mortal. And has an allotted life span that ceases upon the bed of Death, and then the released Spirit can now return to its true home that mortal man calls Heaven, which it is, but only one aspect of what should be called **'The Heavens' that are without number.**

'Life' is one long continuous journey of discovery, it really is never ending, call it Eternal if you wish, for the wor**d 'Eternity'** has many meanings and translations and Man's idea of Eternity is 'His idea' and may very well bear no resemblance to the reality of it!!! Life, Death, Resurrection, all words to try and explain something that in a way is unexplainable and that is What Life is! We can only see it as it affects ourselves, which is only natural.

But 'Life' encompasses all living aspects of Creation, and what 'we' do as a person has an effect not only on our immediate circle of family and friends, but like the ripples on a pond when a stone is thrown into it, they radiate in all directions until they reach the surrounding banks where they come to rest!! That is just what your 'actions' do, cause reactions, even when they may not be noticed or anticipated! You see that word Karma creeps in again! There is no way of escaping it!! Its other name is 'Cause and effect' and you upon this War-torn Planet are well aware of those results!!!

To be a human being is only one facet of the whole created principle that we think of as representing the identity of the person that we call 'Me'!! When 'Me' is just a covering, a garment of flesh that the 'Real Me' needs for reference purposes, while once more reincarnating upon the lower sphere called Earth!! Spirit as Spirit is a 'product' of the world of the Spirit and as such does not belong to the material world of the flesh. It needs its outer garment partly as protection and partly for recognition purposes!!

The material world of matter gives to the Spirit a fuller understanding of the complex workings of what is commonly called 'Life'. This lower plane of dense matter is the ideal training ground to bring out the latent possibilities that the Spirit Essence has, but is not always aware of!! It may take many incarnations in a physical body to become a fully rounded being that is ready to progress upon other spheres of learning and understanding!! And there are many of them, and not necessarily called by the name of Heaven!!! Which in many cases can be a state of awareness and not a plane of existence!!

Such is the progress of the 'Human Spirit'. We use the word 'Human' advisedly for even as Spirit we still retain many of our Human qualities even if after a long time we lose some of them, to be replaced by more Spiritual ones!!!

Remember that 'time' as such is held in a very different way upon the realms of the Spirit. And so you cannot begin to judge the passage of it from a human standpoint. A day, a month, a year! Just words that do not convey the reality of it, and yet even that word is an anomaly for 'reality' is non existent in human terms, for today can be tomorrow, or even the tomorrow can remain the today!!!

It is all in the 'mind's perception' and that means the individuals perception, which may well differ from another persons even when they, shall we say, are engaged in conversation or any other form of contact. Do you follow? It just means that if you were to ask each person 'what day it is', you would probably get two different answers and yet each person would be stating what that period means to them!! That is why time as we have said is irrelevant in everyday thinking!!! Now you can begin to see why the whole concept of Creation in its broadest sense is such a complex state that almost defies a logical explanation!! And the Human and Spirit variety are just two aspects of the multi faceted jewel called Created Creativity!! Much to learn and much to be left, shall we say, 'Unlearned' and just accept that Not to know is in itself, a form of Knowing! A paradox, but then that is what we are trying to say All of Life or Lives can be termed a paradox.

And yet it all makes sense when you think about it!! But don't try too hard just yet dear friends upon the Earth. For change is ever present when dealing with the many aspects of the World of the Spirit, nothing remains the same, and yet it has its roots in the past, so in a way nothing has changed, just another form of paradox for you to conjure with. But do not think that the mortal being known as Man doesn't have his place in the scheme of the Creator's plan. For he does, His place is to shape this Planet Earth with his accumulated knowledge and in doing this he is preparing his own evolutionary progress that with each passing generation enriches, not just the few, but the many.

And this can only be accomplished by a physical Mortal being that is Guided by his own 'Spirit companion'. The two become one, and one without the other is not complete. The gross matter of the Earthplane has to be tempered by the Spirit, for eventually the Mortal Man must one day take on the mantle of Immortality. In other words he will have reached the goal that has been set him, 'Physicality' will have been surpassed by 'Spirituality', as it has been ordained from the very beginning of time itself! Spirit we are, and to return to that state will show that the lessons of the plane of Earth have been well and truly learned. And so the

Planet Earth will be transformed from its gross heavy matter to one akin to that of the Spirit World from which in very truth it was originally spawned!!! And when that cycle has been completed, then another one will take its place. The cycle or circle can never be broken that is the immutable law of the Universe.

And that word hides the very identity of the Supreme Creator of all that 'IS' and ever was and ever will be!!! And here is where we are bidden to cease our thought participation with the Scribe of the implement of the written word. This we will do and we leave you in the care of your Maker and Creator. Peace be with you all.

May Allah be Praised! May Allah be Praised!

All Praise be given to Allah!

Farewell!!

We also bid you Farewell Brother and those who search and seek the truth wherever they can find it!!

Chapter 16

June 6th 2008

THE DARK GLASS

If we say to you look into the glass darkly, you may wonder what else we are going to ask you to do! Well looking into the glass darkly is really just a hypothetical way of saying to you Look into the Mirror of your life and you may well be surprised at what the imaginary reflection will show to you!!! There are many areas in ones life that, shall we say have been obscured with the passage of time! Perhaps now is a good time to look more closely at those half forgotten areas that were pushed into the depths of that metaphorical dark glass!!!

It takes a lot of patient endeavour to bring those areas back into the light of day. And then even more endeavour to analyze what you are witnessing with your inner thoughts upon that hidden screen that has been lurking in the darkness awaiting the spotlight of retrospection to illuminate it. And hopefully bring forth results that may amaze you, for not all hidden dark areas of the memory are ones best forgotten.

Everything that one does during ones lifetime upon earth results in actions of some sort, good, bad, or indifferent! Now you will have the opportunity for yourself to piece together the results of those past actions, and see how they have shaped the person who you are today.

In other words what effect have they had upon your Character, the one that your companion Spirit of this lifespan will take with it on its return journey back to where it calls home.

Though that first sphere is one of the many 'homes' that Spirit will inhabit during its various manifestations that will eventually result in reunion with the Creator of its Destiny!!!

Now back to your looking glass once more and see if some of those dimly remembered areas of, perhaps not complete darkness, are showing you anything that can be of use to you in this form of soul searching that is probably giving you quite a jolt.

For sometimes events that have occurred in one's life have been well and truly forgotten, perhaps deliberately if they have resulted in what is now talked openly about as Karma! Cause and Effect, Good and Bad, **and shall we add also 'in-between'**!

You know it's not such a bad thing this looking back at some of the mistakes or errors of judgement that have cropped up during ones sojourn upon the Plane of Earth! In some cases you may even be able to reverse some of the consequences that resulted from those errors of judgement!! Had you thought of that? No!! **Well now is the time to rectify those 'errors' before it is too late!** And you know to what we refer regarding, 'who' will eventually take upon themselves the burden of putting right, what you the present companion of your Spirit has neglected to rectify, when you had the chance!!

No! It is not all Doom and Gloom by any means, for you do have in your memory bank plenty of good Karma that can be called upon to offset some of the Bad Karma, that you can now see in retrospect that you perhaps unwittingly allowed to accumulate!! We all have gone through these periods of retrospection yes! Even now while we dwell upon the Higher spheres of the Spirit Worlds. **We aren't perfect by any means!** After all, our many previous incarnations in human bodies have left an indelible impression upon our Spirit Psyche, in other words We are only Human!!

Does that make you feel better; knowing that Life and its ups and downs really does go on?? So many people have the idea that being Spirit suddenly makes you perfect in every way!! Not so, dear friends. Not so!! **Perfection doesn't come easily, it has to be worked at and worked for!! Believe that for it is a 'Truth'.** We, and that includes you all, we are learning all of the time, that is what life is all about, we progress, and sometimes that means we have to retrace our steps metaphorically speaking!!

A time to pause and evaluate what we have learnt, or as the case may be not learnt!! This is just what we are saying to you via the penmanship of the little scribe!! We are in no way criticizing you, just stating facts as we see them!! So this journey that you have mentally embarked upon, is very worthwhile if it has alerted your senses regarding what has affected your life. And also how You have affected the lives of others! There is a saying is there not that **'No Man is an Island'** meaning that we all have influences upon others, whether we realise it or not!

Has your experience of looking in 'the glass darkly' been of any help to you? We sincerely hope so. We were going to say that **you needn't make a habit of it! But on second thoughts we say, 'every so often when you are perhaps alone and wondering just what this life is all about, a look in the Mirror of Life can be rewarding after all.'** That is if it teaches you something, and here is where we are going to pull the veil over the mirror and return you to your everyday activities! We bid you an earnest Farewell and say, May God bless You and keep you safe, Farewell!

Brother, Farewell once again but only in words and not in deeds!! Farewell.

Chapter 17

June 7th 2008

THE PLANET, BOTH HUMAN AND OTHERWISE!!!!

We wish to speak to you about your Planet and the reasons for what you are experiencing, due to what you term 'Global Warming'. Well, to quote one of your observations that is only the 'tip of the iceberg', so to speak! For the origins of all of this disruptive activity has its 'roots' deep, deep within the bowels of this volatile little Planet!! The core of this planet is almost like an active volcano only in reverse, instead of pushing lava out, it draws it in upon itself! It is in effect its 'fuel', which it needs to keep this world upon its equilibrium to keep it stable within the orbit that had been set it, since its very inception as a Planet that could be used for a number of different forms of experimentation!!

The whole of your Universe is a form of a vast ongoing experiment!! Your world is by no means the only one experiencing these changes both in climate and in its very destiny!! All over, or should we say, 'in' this Universe there is violent activity. For it is this activity that keeps this Universe a viable Area of habitable units and the word 'units' denotes, Worlds, Planets, Stars, Galaxies, to name just a few of the 'Visible' forms of creation, and by visible we mean to you the Humanity that occupies this World that you consider is 'Yours'!!

Error number one! 'It' does not belong to you, you are its custodians and are allowed the privilege of dwelling upon what is still a very beautiful 'Cosmic appendage' that contribute to your very life force, your destiny in the overall plan of those who you can, if you wish, call 'Creator Gods'. And please do not take offence at those words 'Creator Gods'. For we do know what we are talking about, contrary to what may be the accepted ancient doctrine that you pay so much attention to without always giving it the serious thought that it warrants! Just an observation and not an idle criticism on our part!!!

Planets, Worlds, what have you, come and go, sometimes leaving no trace at all, for what you call 'Debris' is merely the building blocks in disguise!! Activity, is the very lifeblood of 'ALL' Creation, even when the activity seems to be lying dormant, it never really ceases in one way or another. And that is exactly what is happening to your Planet at this time in its Evolutionary Cycle of cause and effect.

What you are witnessing and being a part of, has not just suddenly erupted, it has been slowly building up over the centuries. And we use the word 'centuries' for your human's benefit, for in the 'life' of a Planet, time is Unimportant!! Especially to 'those' who Monitor its life force and how it affects the created 'elements' that occupy it!! Such is the Complex Nature of Creation itself!! It cannot be fully comprehended by Mortal Man! Maybe one day he may be allowed to become party to this Creativity, No!! Not as a Creator but as a bystander, an onlooker as it were!!

And that is all we can say regarding His part in that future evolutionary period in His, and His Worlds!!!

Mankind at present is unaware of the great privilege he has **been given to play an active part in his World's destiny!!** He may think that with all of this turmoil going on around him, and the disasters that culminate in the life span of many being cut short, that if that is a privilege then he would rather go without it!! We understand those sentiments, for have we not in the past also been affected by climate change? But we are still Alive to tell the tale so to speak! That is a Truth, even if some of you in the Western Hemisphere do not go along with the belief in the 'After Life' upon the inner Worlds of the Spirit!!!

We have said that Creation as such is Complex and if you really think about it deeply you will perhaps get an inkling of what we are trying to convey to you. You as Human beings are part of this complexity, even as we ourselves are!!! And that is just two of the many, many, variations of Created Creation!! Which encompasses so much more, that these pages would have to be many volumes to truthfully explain all of the variations, offshoots, whatever you wish to call them, that make up the agenda called Creation!!!

So now you can perhaps understand why all of this shall we call 'Unseasonal Disturbance' is in effect perfectly 'normal'. It is Natures way of ensuring that the life of this Planet will continue upon its allotted course.

It will no doubt change in its appearance, some areas will disappear altogether but the loss will be compensated by the re-appearance of areas that have been forgotten ever existed!! A hundred years from now and you will hardly recognise what you now observe as your 'homeland' and even the populations will have changed, we can tell you that life then will be far more superior to what it is today. Of course you of today will not be around to see all of this, but who knows, some of you will observe this change from our side of Life, while others will have perhaps re-incarnated once again on their path of learning and understanding!! We have said Life is continuous and it really is wherever in this Universe you happen to be, and that includes Our version of the Universe and we leave you to speculate upon that Statement!!!

We have said 'Our Universe' as if it is different from yours! Well in a way it is, perhaps we should elucidate and say our

Universe is Yours but in Reverse!! No! Not literally but in 'perception' and yes we will say it, in its illusionary qualities!! For illusion plays a very big part in the ongoing saga of 'Evolution'!!! Though make no mistake about it, Illusion is a very potent force and can even be called at times a form of 'Reality'!!

Rather paradoxical you may think, and you would be right but then isn't the Whole of Life, and shall we say 'Lives', a Paradox. Just witness what we have said about Illusion versus Reality!! Interchangeable in every respect and here we have to bring in that word 'Complex' again. For the very nature of Creation involves so many variations that it is difficult to pick out one and say, 'This represents what Creation is about!!'

For Creation is a many faceted jewel the like of which cannot be imagined!

And believe Us, Creation is forever ongoing, somewhere in the Universe and perhaps that should read 'Universes' and we leave that left unsaid!!! For you have enough to consider when dealing with the eccentricities of it!! Do you not agree??

The Brain of Man, that too, is a complex piece of created activity, which present day Man is trying hard to understand. He will in due course, but he must not be too hasty or impatient to reach the goal of complete understanding, lest he comes to the wrong conclusion regarding its various functions and capabilities!!! We stress the words 'ongoing creation', nothing stands still; there usually is room for improvement of the original conception and that is fully taken into consideration when a new form of species is being considered! And we leave you to draw your own conclusions as to what we have hinted at!!!

Mankind is the Microcosm of the Macrocosm, he is in effect his own world his own Universe, if you like, study the body human, and identify its structure and conception in relation to the Universe in which you at present dwell! You will be amazed at the similarities but view it with an open mind, as should all things to do with learning and studying and yes, in Teaching as well!!! Be viewed and observed!!

When you have learned to accept that Knowledge, unless properly understood, it can be a very dangerous tool to wield before a public not yet ready for that information!!

Complete Knowledge is for the very few, see to it that if you seek to know it that you are worthy of its calling!! Just like the **saying of old, 'Many are called, but few are Chosen!!'** Accept your own limitations, and work within that perimeter until you are told otherwise, and that response will come either from within or from without, and do not discount the written word, for your **teachers' are legion!!!**

We began this joining of the minds with the words about your Planet and the consequences of its present form of activity, and **now we have ended with thoughts concerning you as 'Human Planets' of intricate design!!** And here is where we are to conclude this work. We trust that we have been able to open the windows of your minds to let in the light of understanding and whet the appetite to seek and search even further along the pathway of life. And so we say to you Farewell students of discovery, and may **'Your God' be the inspiration for it!!!**

Brother Scribe! You already know by thought what we wish to say to you and so we will leave you with our Fondest love for a fellow Brother in Christ Consciousness!! **We, of the 'White Brotherhood' salute you.**

Fare – Thee – Well!!

Chapter 18

June 10th 2008

THE KINGDOM OF HEAVEN!!

Seek ye first the Kingdom of Heaven, and all things shall be added unto you! What exactly do those words from Ancient Scripture mean to those who are living today? And indeed, what did they mean to those who listened to those uttered words so long ago?? 'Heaven' really meant something then, it was a place of Holy Sanctuary, where all was bliss, and God sat in Judgement surrounded by the Angelic Host, and Saints from a bygone era!! And it would seem that the majority of the population really did believe that if they lived a God fearing life then their reward would certainly be a place in one of God's many Mansions!!!

Now what about those of today, who view those ancient doctrines with perhaps a 'jaundiced eye'!!! Has the past nothing to offer to the Youth of Today? When they observe the antics of the so-called Adult population, there is no wonder that they feel bewildered, lost, and what on Earth does the future hold for them?? The role Models paraded before them seem to have feet of clay and very little substance to bolster up their shrinking egos!!! What then can be the cause and yea, what can be the answer for it? Money!! Yes, that is the seen and worshiped God of today!! If you have it then let everyone see that you have it, and if you haven't, well is there an answer to that?

There should be, and the answer should register 'Fairness for all of God's Children'. Prioritise your sought after ambitions, you may very well have got your Priorities mixed up and in the wrong place!! You are witnessing the results of the greed that many leaders of the various Nations pay homage to!!! And it doesn't end with the acquisition of wealth, for the lust for Power over other people's lives is a drug that seems insatiable!!

And if they can't be brought into a form of subjection by fair means, then use the foul ones and the results are quicker!!! But are they? We say to you Never!! For coerced subjection fosters a wound that one day will bring forth sores that go on multiplying and multiplying!! Past History tells you that, time and time again, but do the Powers that be take any notice of what History shows them? Sadly Not!!

It would seem that it will be left to Nature at her rawest to bring you to your knees, and it will be the innocent who will suffer! They always have and it is then that the Name of God is uppermost in their thoughts either of pleading or supplication. If, and it is a very big 'IF' God was a real part of their everyday living, and we mean by their actions as well as their words, then your War torn world could be turned around. And then become once again the Garden of Eden that was what it was intended to be. 'A Heaven upon Earth.' A mirror of the ones above that we are promised one day to inhabit!!

But the price of entry into those Heavenly Spheres is the demise of the physical body and its release of the Spirit inhabitant that has been its erstwhile companion for the life span of the mortal being.

We as human beings, the Highest form of Animal Creation at present!! upon this Earth, should be able to have our 'Heaven' here and now and not have to wait for some promise to be fulfilled at the parting of the ways from mortality to Immortality! We've been given the tools with which to bring this about and these tools are A Mind of intricate design and a Brain to do its bidding!!! You have all of the ingredients for this, and the ingredients lie beneath your very feet in so many various ways. Can you not see that?

Yes, you can, but you exploit those whose very home is the land that possesses all of this abundant wealth of natural resources!! They were meant to be SHARED, NOT HORDED in Underground vaults, GUARDED night and day!! Do you not remember the saying about storing up your wealth where rust and thieves will take their toll!! And the irony of it is YOU CAN'T TAKE IT WITH YOU!! You come into this world with 'NOTHING' and Nothing Material or Physical will you take out of it when Death comes knocking at your door and demands Entry!! Which, as a paradox should read EXIT!!!

But there is something that can show that at one time you did dwell upon this Plane of Earth. You have that God given power to Create, and that word encompasses far, far, more than you give it credit for. You! not only as individuals but whole Nations can be a force for Good.

Start with the individual and you'll be surprised that those individuals are the bedrock of a Nation. Goodness can prevail against the Evil of corruption, but it has to be worked upon, it doesn't just happen overnight. It may even take many, many, generations, but if each one can be a bench mark in the power of Evolution, evolution can one day be something to be proud of being a part of. It starts with the family unit and grows from then onwards; you leave behind a generation that YOU can say I am a part of that, I helped to make this world a better place to live in. And those that follow on from you can be grateful for what you the ancestors achieved, and now it will be their turn to carry on that Good Work, that God work, so that the idea of Heaven upon Earth can indeed become a reality in every way.

And here is where we will end this morning's chapter on Heaven and all of the possibilities that that word conjures up. We bid you Farewell.

The Little Scribe

And to the little Scribe, Farewell little patient Brother. Farewell and may your God shower you with the blessings of inner knowledge and understanding. Farewell. Farewell. Farewell, we now depart!!

Chapter 19

June 11th 2008

RELIGION!!!

Before I actually begin this writing I feel that I ought to give you a few words of explanation! All that I write I have to admit is in a Hypothetical vein! And the reason? Well, if it was about this world of ours it should be able to be verified in some way by somebody, somewhere!! At least I hope that it can!! Now we come to where my Hypothetically conjecture comes in!!

If what I write is to do with the Spirit and Spiritual side of Life, then I as a humble (I hope!!) scribe have no physical way of verifying what is written!! I may well be informed via my thought process that it can be verified by **those that I'm allowed to call my Guides and my fellow Brothers. They are known by many as 'The White Brotherhood' and the word 'White' refers to the garments** that are worn and NOT to the pigmentation of the SKIN!

Well, now that that is over I can proceed with this narrative!

Brother! We speak to you about that very emotive word **'Religion'**. Probably most people who are open minded on the subject of what, to a lot of people is called the After Life, tend to think that Religion is only an Earth planet form of communication with their chosen version of GOD! And here we stress that the word GOD covers a multitude of various appendages to that name!!

Well, to return to that word Religion, though it is a Man made appellation of their particular Faith, and shall we add calling, it is known and practised All Over the Universe under various disguises!! Also we in the World of the Spirit are well aware of what that word Religion means to ALL peoples who **'wake' up after the transition of the Mortal body and find that** their life has in fact continued! Albeit upon a different vibrationary sphere, which nevertheless has to all sense of appearances a definite likeness to the World that they have just vacated!!

To some this seems unbelievable, while to others it is just an **accepted fact, even a pleasant reminder of the World they've left** behind!! Now, to say to you the reader of this form of tuition, upon this first plane of the Spirit World, which in fact is just one **of many, many different shall we say 'Perceptions'.** And what awaits the traveller now that the ordeal of the transition is well and truly put behind them, and they are ready to explore this new and vibrant world of the Spirit!

For it is vibrant, vibrant with life expectancy, and yes sheer wonderment at what they see around them. Though much of **what they become aware of is new to the 'senses',** they still retain (that is The Spirit) they still retain very strong memories of their 'physical past'!! What the mortal body learned and observed had an indelible effect upon its Spirit companion of that life span and is in the form of Character. The Character that is one of **continuity upon 'All Spheres' whether of perception or Spirit Reality!!!** Food for thought little pilgrims upon life's path!

What we are coming to is the 'Religious factor', which is carried over, in your new extended life!! You do NOT, suddenly become aware of ALL of the Mysteries associated with the practice of any particular branch of Religion per-se!!! Contrary to perhaps what people imagine, All Religions don't become as One!!! Upon the Spirit Plane there is plenty of room for All forms of Religious Culture, or even None at all!!

We are, shall we say, very, very, tolerant of peoples persuasions!! And strange as this may seem, You will find that you now acquire the same form of toleration!! You see things for what they are and you are content to leave the Judgement to those who understand the true meaning of that word!!!

There are areas set aside in various parts of this first sphere, which are entirely devoted to the study of ALL KNOWN and yes, UNKNOWN forms of Religion. Where Temples, and Churches rub shoulders with Mosques and Buildings that almost defy description in the Complexity of their chosen path that will lead them to the Godhead of their choice and Faith!!

What is more All Faiths are OPEN to anyone who is an earnest seeker and searcher after the truth! For as we have stated quite often Faith, and Religion in general is a multi faceted jewel of Enlightenment. Turn the jewel around and in the Sunlight of the rays of intuition you will glimpse another aspect of what is being shown to you. Remember that what we said in the **beginning, Religion is 'Man Made'**. GOD, maybe the focus of it, and as an anomaly All Religions, All Faiths lead ultimately to the ONE who is Nameless.

But who is known to all, through the Wonders of Creation in all of its aspects!!!

You perhaps wonder what about those people of no faith, even those who believe that there is NO GOD!! Shall we say that if they can remain open minded about all things, then that is NO stumbling block, here upon the Spirit World. Belief in something requires thought and a case of trial and error, and disbelief usually has its roots in past misunderstanding. Misunderstandings can be ironed out, when toleration is brought to bear regarding them!!

Time is Nothing to those who are the Creators of it!! So cease your wondering about how long enlightenment will take to become Universal!! It already is Somewhere and we leave that just there!! You will know when you are ready and not before and it doesn't have to be at your transition period!! Do you follow what we are implying? Good!!

Remember that Religion or Faith is entirely personal to each and every one, and you cannot coerce another person to accept what you believe or even what you do not believe! Toleration, **that is the answer to all of Life's misunderstandings, practice it** and you will be amazed at the positive results you achieve. For that is what we teach and practice in the World of the Spirit, which is 'your' world as well as ours. We have only dealt with one aspect that affects our Spirit world, but we think that that one word Toleration could well apply to all other aspects not mentioned!! And so we have come to the end of our treatise on Religion and Faith. As your scribe has pointed out, He cannot verify what has been written on our behalf.

We can and Do, but that really is cold comfort for you is it not? You will just have to wait and see what the future life holds for you and then you can verify everything for yourselves!!!

We know that the Brother Scribe accepts what we have impressed him to write, so at least we have one convert have we not?? We take leave of you all and bid you a fond Farewell.

Farewell Brother, Farewell, and shall we add

May Allah look kindly upon you, little scribe of the earth! Be at Peace for all is well!!

Chapter 20

June 12th 2008

WHAT"S IN A WORD??

Reincarnation! Another word for Resurrection!

We bring to you a thought and the thought is: 'REINCARNATION'!!

Now why is it that Peoples of the Eastern Hemisphere of your Globe have absolutely no problem with that belief! Yet those in the Western Hemisphere have difficulty in trying to come to terms with that idea? Why should that be? Mainly we suspect is that they are looking at it from a Human standpoint and NOT from one of the 'Spirit'! For it is the Spirit that is the reincarnating entity and NOT the Mortal physical being, that thinks of itself as ME! For 'ME' is just a cloak of protection and identification that the Spirit has to use, when reincarnating upon the lower plane of Earth!!

Not everyone who believes in reincarnation, gives any thought or credit to the other part of them that is an Identity in their own right!! They may speak of their Spirit almost in an abstract way and not, shall we say on a 'personal basis', which it most certainly is!! People sometimes equate thoughts about memories of the past as actually belonging to their now Human body of existence, when if it is thought of very carefully they would realize that the Human vehicle is only Mortal for one lifetime!! And any previous memories of a past incarnation come from the 'Spirit' who is now part of this their present lifespan!!

When the Mortal human being dies, the shell of that body remains and the Spirit companion vacates that protective covering of Human flesh and returns to its proper Home in the World of the Spirit. There too, shall we say evaluate its recent past incarnation, with its accumulated knowledge shared with its earth companion during their sojourn together upon the Earth plane!!!

Now sometimes a Spirit, who is intending to reincarnate once more upon the World of dense matter, may well favour the idea of again becoming a member of a particular family, where they were happy and perhaps were not able to accomplish all that they had wished to do. Hence when they, the Spirit is once more part of that family via the birth of a new infant, it brings back to that new companion memories of the past. And those memories awaken in other members of the family, ties that unite and bond with the new arrival when it has grown in mental awareness of who they are!!

Such is the complexity of Created life. For Immortal Spirit and Mortal Man, complete the circle or cycle of Birth, Death, and Resurrection of the Spirit!!! **Now, doesn't that make sense?** Past, Present and Future!!! All One, as it has been ordained!! Always remember, a body a Human body, needs a Spirit for its growth not only for its physical side but more importantly for its **'inner Spiritual growth'**, that will complete the cycle of the predestined map of Divine Intention. That brings the Immortal Soul back to its Creator, through the many lives of birth, death, and re-birth!!! Life really is forever, death merely heralds the dawn of a new life.

A new round of learning and experiences that contribute to the ultimate design of Perfection!!! Those of you who adhere to the principle of KARMA are well aware of cause and effect, and it is up to every human being to try and make their life one of **'GOOD Karma'**. And not continue with the ever turning Wheel of Life that makes of Mortal Man a slave and forces the Spirit to continue this ever demanding round of incarnations to expiate the deeds of 'Bad Karma'. Which, perhaps it was unable to inspire its previous Mortal companion to take on the burden of **its predecessor's misdemeanours and irresponsible behaviour** patterns!

Justice must be done and Justice is done, believe that for it is a Truth!! Accept that, when perhaps you feel that life has dealt you a poor hand!!! There is a reason, and the reason is sound, even if you cannot see it. Fate! **Karma! Say what you will, 'The Lords of Karmic Ties' know their duty and always abide by the Universal** Law of Divine Judgementation!!!

We wonder what those beings in the Western Hemisphere will make of that lightly sketched explanation of incarnation, reincarnation birth, death, and Resurrection!! For that is a fact, and Resurrection of the Spirit is an every day occurrence, when you think of all the infants that are being born all over your globe! You do have a prime example of Resurrection that somehow the Church Authorities pay so much heed to.

When, if they 'truly believe' in those Ancient texts they would know that what the Master Jesus said about Resurrection was referring to the Spirit and NOT the mortal body of a human being. And when you look at it from that standpoint, then the idea of Resurrection makes far more sense than thinking that it is the physical body that goes through that phase of Immortality!

The human body is only programmed to last for a certain period, long or short, makes no difference, when you know that the physical body must at some time allow the Spirit to return from whence it came. And the transition as far as the mortal body is concerned, is the only way for that release to take place!! That may signal the End of the human side of this liaison of the two bodies of exploration and learning that has always been the Divine intention and always will be. Until the time comes when Man as Mortal Man, will have become more like his counterpart

Spirit, and when the two are now One and the same, then the Mortal side of this experimentation will have been completed.

And there will be no need for Mortal Man to remain Mortal for he will have put on the cloak of Immortality. And this cycle of Mortal Man and His Immortal Spirit will culminate in His (Mortal Man) his transference to another Dimension to make way for the next influx of a form of Humanity. That is more like what the Gods have envisaged, and worked to bring this about through what you like to term Evolution!!!

For as we have expressed in previous discourses, **'Evolution and Eternity' are the two sides of the same coin!!** And it is up to you, that is Man to comprehend the meaning of both of them!! And when and if you do, remember that neither can be called **'Immutable'**! For the whole concept of the meaning of Life is in the one word CHANGE! Nothing, but Nothing if it has any sense of value can remain as it is, to really be alive to the Art of Living one has to be conscious that change is inevitable, if life has to fulfil its Created Intention!! And that dear friends is where you can use without fear of being misunderstood, the word **'RESURRECTION' for that word heralds a change of direction** in more ways than one!!!

So when thinking about Life and its meaning, use that word in a different way to what you have always thought it was meant to represent. So instead of thinking that Death comes first and Resurrection comes after, think in terms of what we have said. It's a form of change, change of heart, change of direction, change of inner and outer perception, in fact, you can use that word to denote so many things, not just One!!!!

We wonder just how many people, East, West, North and South, will find comfort and understanding in this day's treatise on that very emotive word, RESURRECTION!!

And so it falls to us to say Farewell to all of you students of the Mysteries of Life and why, not all Mysteries need to remain as such! Farewell, Farewell.

And to you our dear Brother, we wish you well, and your endeavours do not go unnoticed. Believe that for it is a truth that has been expressed to US!!

Farewell dear, dear Friend. Your mission has nearly been accomplished so take heart and go forward in Peace!!

May the Smile of Allah wipe away all tears from your face and in your heart!!

Praise be to Allah!!

Praise be to GOD!!

Chapter 21

June 15th 2008

WHAT'S IT ALL ABOUT??

Wars! Wars! And Rumours of Wars!! Global Warming! Climate change! Volcanic eruptions! Turmoil! Turmoil! Turmoil! It must seem to the human population of this Planet that What more catastrophic occurrence is going to be the next one to devastate the very lifestyles of the peoples All over your World!!

We know that what we are going to say will bring very little comfort to those who are doing the suffering. But we have to say that 'It's all happened before' and most likely will go on happening time and time again! But the Human Race is a very resilient One, and after the 'Storm' comes a period of Peace and fragile security!!

You notice we have said 'Fragile Security', and that is all dependent upon 'Mankind' and his comprehension and understanding that much of the outcome of these 'Natural Forces' are just that!! It's Nature's way of trying to restore the balance that has somehow 'got out of hand'. And unfortunately Man has, in his way contributed to all of this upheaval by his thoughtlessness and yes, sheer arrogance when dealing with the very Fabric of this Planet. He wants to go his own way and hang the consequences. That is until they catch up with him and then he looks around for a scapegoat that he can blame but never himself!!

The Little Scribe

Nature comes in for severe criticism, and even God it seems doesn't escape Man's denunciation for all of the catastrophes that he cannot find a reason for!!! This in many cases puts a strain upon some people's faith, while to others it's just the opposite. 'Their Faith in the Almighty' is strengthened and it really does get them through all of the hardship that follows on from these disasters of Nature!!

But what about the Man made disasters? And 'WAR' is the prime example. Nations decry the wars and havoc they produce, but they still go on buying arms and weapons of Destruction from anyone willing to sell, doesn't matter to them 'which side' it is, as long as Money and lots of it are forthcoming. And so you get one Nations Youth being slaughtered by weapons of 'their own making'. After having done the rounds of those Markets of destruction and death!!!

Where, oh Where are your priorities in Life? You erect vast memorials to those who have lost their lives and more tragically, those who are wounded and maimed not only physically, but mentally as well, and often for the rest of there shattered lives! And the results do not end there, for the immediate family also suffers, and so it goes on! and on! and on! You say this or that War is to end all Wars, But has it? We see no sign of it either now or in the foreseeable future!

But there is a glimmer of Hope on the far Horizon and the spelling of that word is 'WOMANKIND'. Yes we are very serious about that.

For too long now your Planet has been governed by Male domination! And that was NOT the intention of the Creator Gods!!! Or if the plural offends your senses then we use the singular word God!! Whoever He may be in your Multi Religious World!! It will come about IF there is enough impetus by All of the Womenkind of your Globe.

Women are the Homemakers; they are the bedrock of the Family. This World should be one of 'Sharing and Caring'. And that means tolerance in all matters that affect Mankind and Womankind whatever the race or Colour or Creed!! Believe in the Sanctity of Human Life, for we are supposed to be made in the image of the God Creator and His Hierarchy of Celestial Beings are we not?

Has it not occurred to you that the 'Original Root Races' could have been Created by more than One God? And so the variety of the species could be accounted for in quite a different manner to what has always been thought of!!! **Don't close your** eyes and ears to unaccustomed Thoughts. View them with an Open Mind!! And then use your Free Will of thought expression, you may well be surprised at the thoughts that come out of that form of experimentation regarding Life Forms and their origins!!!

Nothing is impossible when dealing with Creation and those who do the Creating!!! And here we are going to leave you to your own thoughts and bring this treatise to a close, and do we say Farewell to you? Yes we do, so Farewell you searches after the **Truth, but don't be** surprised if the Truth you discover is not the Truth you thought it was!!!

Scribe, we also bid you Farewell. We feel we know you now, and look forward to renewing this friendship another time.

Farewell, may Your God of Your choice smile kindly upon you!!!

We depart!!!

Chapter 22

June 20th 2008

JESUS THE TEACHER!!

When you think or talk about the One called Jesus the Christos, what are your thoughts on that very emotive subject? That has been speculated upon for over two thousand years and if we are honest, do you know any more about that **Teacher and Master of Illusion? Now don't rush to the dictionary** and look up what it has to say about Illusion!! For that word can convey so many different meanings to so many different people!!!
Forget the accepted version of what a so-called Magician of today creates, to amuse, to tantalize and yes to actually deceive you into thinking that reality is just a myth!! Which of course it is when you are comparing it with what you yourself normally associate as reality!! Reality very often is a perception, a perception of the mind and we all know that perception can very easily be misplaced, if you are dealing with someone, who shall we say, perhaps appears to know far more than you do.

And so you may well accept their version of what is being perceived, and put yours to the back of your mind!!! Remember what we have stressed in previous discourses, Free Will and Intuition. **Both commodities that are exclusively 'Yours' and no one else's!!**

So what we are getting at is, Use your intuition when either **listening to another person's thoughts on a particular subject or** even if you are reading something that is unfamiliar to you and sets your thoughts racing with perhaps new ideas, test them for yourself! We know that that is not always an easy thing to do, and that is where Your Intuitive powers of deduction are your personal safeguard. Especially when dealing with anything to do with Occult teaching, and trying to unravel those mysteries from the past where no one of today can possibly accurately verify, either to your satisfaction or even to their own!!!

So read on, dear reader and come to 'your' own conclusions about what you are about to read!!! And where shall we begin? Jesus was born into a typical Jewish family, he was the first born, the family eventually became larger for Jesus had two more Brothers and two Sisters, Rachel and Ruth. We have never really been told very much about the rest of the siblings, but the family was a close-knit one and enjoyed a reasonable, shall we say, middle-class life style.

Joseph, Jesus' father was a Master Carpenter and was much in demand, and as the boys grew up they were all apprenticed to the firm of Master Carpenters Guild of which Joseph was high up in that Society!! The boys, and indeed the two girls were well educated but Jesus was in a way not content to become a Master Carpenter, he desired a more challenging form of existence but wasn't sure how to go about it!!!

This turned out to be quite an exacting period in Jesus' life, He knew of the Society that called themselves 'Zealots' they were in a way the equivalent of today's 'Freedom Fighters'. Their only aim was to rid themselves of the yoke of oppression that had been imposed upon them by the Roman Authorities! Though not all of the Jewish population saw the Romans in that light. Especially those of the Jewish Sanhedrin who found that as long as there was no trouble amongst the younger groups of the population life could be quite tolerable, at least for them it was!!

Jesus joined the band of Zealots, but was more of an onlooker and not a participant in their rather reckless behaviour, which seemed to be getting them nowhere at all! Jesus who was also a scholar of Jewish traditions and culture, felt that there must be a better way of getting along with their unwanted oppressors other than direct conflict!! And so he asked his father for leave of absence from the family business, knowing that his brothers were more than capable of helping Joseph to cope with any work that needed personal attention! Joseph, after much prayerful thought **agreed to Jesus' request, hoping that he would eventually return** to his rightful place as the first born.

And so began Jesus' wanderings about the countryside, getting to understand the feelings of others. Though he never intended to become a teacher, he nevertheless found he had an aptitude for speaking openly to those around him.

He also found he had a gift for creating not exactly illusions of reality, but by his words he was able to paint pictures that created in his audience a feeling of rapport and understanding. Jesus showed them the hidden side of the ancient scriptures and was able to answer their questions, sometimes before they even voiced them to themselves.

Gradually people began to talk about this young man who seemed to have the wisdom of the Ancient prophets, but with one great difference. He spoke to them in the language of their present day, so that they could fully understand the meanings of those ancient scriptures that had for so long been shrouded in mystery. To really question the words uttered by those in the Synagogues Hierarchy had long been taboo for the laymen. And so the words of Jesus came as not only a refreshing change, but he spoke with such sincerity and yes, quiet authority that to say His fame spread like wildfire would be an understatement!!

As he wandered about there were those among the population who wanted to know more about their heritage and gradually they formed a group, a dedicated band of followers, who in a way were a form of protection, keeping some of the crowds at a safe distance.

All this time those High and Mighty figures of the Sanhedrin were becoming worried for they found that those people who used to frequent the Synagogues were now gathering in open spaces to listen to the Words that came from Jesus' lips. Words that seemed at variance with their orthodox teaching and preaching!!

To avoid any unpleasantness regarding those in Authority, Jesus and his now strong band of followers retired to distant parts of the country where the people had only heard of this New Teacher, and wanted to know more about the things he was espousing in the name of Jehovah!!

This then was also a turning point in Jesus' life. At times he would retire to the Mountaintop and leave his followers behind. And here it was that he was 'touched' by the Hand of God, and given powers that would amaze some and to others would create animosity because of the Power that emanated from Jesus without him even noticing it. Some said they could see a figure of light that seemed to almost cloak him, it was in fact His own Spiritual Aura that was now a 'seen' part of Him. His calling had been given to Him in the Silence of the Mountaintop. He knew then that He was a chosen vehicle for God's work and that that path was to be His destiny upon Earth, and that whatever lay ahead, he would have no power to change it!!!

Such was the power now within Jesus that he was able to 'split' himself in two, quite literally in other words There were now Two Jesus'. One of physical and the other of Spirit, who nevertheless was of a solid appearance to others and yet at times could be shrouded in a mist of vapour-like substance from which the Spirit Jesus could now depart from physical sight and re-appear elsewhere. Hence Jesus could actually be seen in two different places at once!! One with the band of followers and the other with those chosen by him to be what we have come to call them, His Disciples!!

The 'Spirit' Jesus gave to them the hidden Esoteric mysteries, while the physical Jesus gave to the crowds that gathered around him those wonderful parables that still stand the test of time!!

At times the two became One, sometimes wholly Spirit and at other times purely physical. This then was for a purpose, which has remained a mystery to the layman but not to the adepts of Cosmic understanding!

The Disciples were unaware of the two 'forms' of Jesus and only thought that at times He was somewhat different! In actual fact there were far more than the twelve we have been told about, though it would seem that it was those twelve that have been singled out by Historians as the main ones. And the others have been somewhat neglected, but they were important in spreading the teachings of Jesus, both of Them!!!! And one day they will be recognised for there are manuscripts that do tell about those other friends of Jesus, which incidentally involve far more Women than has been officially documented.

Jesus treated both Male and Female as equal and in some of **the 'lost' documents it is shown** that he encouraged those Women to be partners with the Men in all that was being done to bring love and understanding to the populace. For He understood that Women are the Homemakers and they can influence society in ways that Men are not able to!! And that is the Spiritual side of **humanity, which is also the softer side of Man's intended Nature!!!**

There are two women Ruth and Naomie who one day you will hear more about when certain ancient parchments are brought out into the open!!!

The Spirit Jesus was well aware of what lay ahead, but the actual facts of what was to befall the physical Jesus were withheld from him, for obvious reasons. Such a lot of what really happened **regarding the life of that perfect Soul, that has been 'lost'**, has really been misplaced and not entirely lost as will be seen in the not too distant future, when more manuscripts will make an unexpected appearance!!!

Jesus' family was none to sure about their Brother's obvious calling to be the physical vessel for God's work, but they did not oppose his desire. Though Mary his mother, was sorely troubled by some of the talk about her Son, but refrained from any comment in case it upset Jesus. For she realised that not only was he different from his youthful days, but that he was genuinely sincere about the mission he had embarked upon.

The Spirit Jesus was able to give Mary deep Spiritual comfort that in a way helped her to see that her Son's destiny had been planned long, long, before he was even born, and this she did accept as God's will. Joseph on the other hand couldn't quite understand why his first born Son had chosen the path he had, and not been content to follow in his father's chosen profession of Master Craftsman!!! But he was proud of what his son was and gave him his blessing to continue as he saw fit.

Jesus loved his parents dearly and knew it was a heavy price to pay for them, as well as for himself!! As for Jesus' appearance he was above average height, muscular and well proportioned. He had a somewhat swarthy appearance, of one used to being in the open air.

His hair was luxuriant and of a reddish brown colour and at times he wore it long, at other periods it was much shorter. His eyes varied in colour according to his mood, neither brown nor blue but always kind and perhaps a little soulful. His gaze was straightforward and to many people somewhat disconcerting, for it was as if he knew their very thoughts even before they had thought them. He knew all about mind control, but only used it for certain occasions. He could, and did, mesmerize a whole crowd with his firm but gentle voice, and his Aura though not visible to everyone, was like a blanket of vapour and covered everyone in his vicinity, yea and even further. For others far, far, away told of a feeling of almost 'waking sleep' that left them refreshed and in a way enlightened spiritually. Quite beyond their usual comprehension!!!

Jesus the Man was ahead of His time, and yet He has, or rather his teachings are timeless and belong to All of God's humanity upon this plane of Earth! Whatever the language that interprets those precepts. For they are God given whichever way you look at it!!!

His life's work was catapulted into three short years as was intended! Believe that for it is the Truth!! His Spirit self had been the inspiration for many of the named and yes, unnamed Christs through 'All ages'!!! And yes, there are more to come before the Destiny of this Planet has been fulfilled!!! Christs are not born, they are chosen for their willingness through many lifetime incarnations that have fitted them for this sometimes harrowing period in their life's work!

But know that not all Christs are visible as such to ordinary man, and further, not all Christs are of the 'Male gender'. Accept that and know that God's work is done by many 'He Chooses', and then they are Chosen!! So look not for a second coming, for your Christs are always with you if you have the eyes to see them and the ears to listen to what they say. And yea, even the courage to follow what your heart and mind tell You is the Truth, but Not the empty rhetoric that cannot stand up to careful scrutiny. So beware of the ravenous wolves that parade themselves in Sheep's clothing and voice aloud that they are the Chosen ones! They are chosen, but by themselves and NOT by GOD!!!

The Words of the True Prophets of whatever creed or culture, will stand the 'test of Time' and you can witness this for yourselves time and time again. And remember not all Christs can be recognised as such, God chooses from the very humblest of those who dwell upon this planet to the very Highest!! A Christ can be your neighbour, had you thought of that? We are all endowed with the 'Christ Spirit'. It is God's gift to 'ALL of HIS CHILDREN', not just to a few!!!

And remember A Resurrection can be a physical awakening to a Spiritual truth, in fact an acknowledgment of your own Spirit Force. Your Immortal Self that is your guiding light in what to some, must seem like a sea of darkness called Life!!! Those hidden chapters of Jesus Christ's ministry will one day reveal the True meaning of that word 'Resurrection', and then All peoples upon this Earth will understand that Death is just another word that heralds the continuation of Life Immortal! Man and Spirit's true Destiny.

And here we leave you to ponder what has been written by the little scribe of today. We bid you fellow travellers Farewell, and to that little one we say 'MIZPAH' God be with you little friend. God be with you.

Farewell. Farewell!!

July 1st 2008
(APPENDAGE TO CHAPTER 22)

Regarding the Healing qualities of Jesus. He understood the laws of the Universe, which is Cause and Effect. Look for the cause and the correction can result in what has been termed 'a miracle'!! Jesus was a past master of the manipulation of another persons, shall we say, error to the life force that is within us all. So many illnesses have their roots in this form of misunderstanding of what this 'force of Life' really is!! It is the force that in its perfected state ('which means complete harmony') should govern all of our actions. Unfortunately we neglect the very basic rules of Harmonious living and that starts with the mind substance that invisible yet oh! So potent commodity that rules our very lives!!! If we only knew it we are our own healer.

Jesus knew this and was able to bring to the surface of an individual their own healing powers of Thought and Action! Miracles are part of Natures hidden assets, therefore you can call a Miracle a 'Natural phenomena'. One day Man will be able to Heal himself with his own natural healing power, that in a way will be almost like a separate part of the Brain's capacity for restoring equilibrium to the whole body. That part will 'Think for Itself'!! And will know how to put the healing procedure into action, regardless of what the individual concerned is thinking!!!

So you will have your own 'private doctor' taking care of you!!

And what a step forward that will be, and there will be more to come as Man begins to reach his true Spiritual peak of understanding of The Universal Law of God!!!

As has been stated in the Scriptures of old, 'Man was made in God's image.' Therefore that should mean that we have a replica of some of God's attributes, and looking at it like that We all have the potential to be 'Gods in the making'. So why not try and act like one instead of being this tiresome wayward creature that classes itself as part of Humanity!!! We say unto you, It's about time you 'Grew Up'!! Not a criticism just a statement of fact!!!

We bid you Farewell fellow travellers upon life's path. Farewell!!

Little Brother your morning's work is finished. Fare Thee – Well little scribe. Fare – Thee Well!!!

Chapter 23

July 3rd 2008

HEAVEN! HEAVENS AND ARE THERE MORE??

Welcome Brother, you have already thought that we wish to communicate with you and so without further ado we will commence our treatise on Heaven and its invisibility to be seen, or truly comprehended, by Man in his present stage of Evolution!!!

First let us say that not all that we will say actually refers to what you like to term Heaven, or should that read Heavens? For in truth there are indeed many of these so-called Heavenly abodes!!! Now that will make you wonder, if there are many, do we all go to the same ones or are there perhaps degrees of 'personality' that suit certain aspects of those created areas of expectation! We leave you to think that one out for yourselves at this stage!!!

Now to go back to the term 'Invisibility'. For that is a word or perception that is open to many contradictions that are nevertheless viable explanations when looked at in depth!!!

Your scientists have long known about certain Invisible 'substances', in fact even centuries ago some of the more enlightened ones were aware of these 'Invisible substances'. But how to prove that they existed was at that period of History beyond their comprehension, and for a very good reason we are told, 'too fast', 'too soon' is the recipe for chaos!!!

Witness the interest that has always existed regarding that mythical? Continent of 'Atlantis and its tragic populations'!! But we dare to say Not all of them were subject to that disaster, but that requires a subject on its own and here is not the place to pursue it!!!

Invisible only applies to those who are not physically aware of its existence! What is invisible upon one dimension is perfectly visible upon another one, or even more if those dimensions have similar vibrationary forces that allow for the participation of intimate contact!!! So you now can see that the term of something or yes, even 'someone' as being invisible does not obscure the 'reality' of what we are discussing!! You upon Earth consider yourselves as physical matter, for that is what you are because you inhabit a Planet that is made of grass and heavy matter and so you are able to survive upon it with comparative ease!!

Transfer you to another dimension and you would cease to exist!!! And yet as an anomaly those who you loosely term as Spirits can and do inhabit not only their own dimension, But can also inhabit (if that is the correct word?) your dimension, for as long or as short as they wish!! So what price 'matter' and what price 'Spirit'?? Quite a conundrum is it not??

Yet it is a 'Fact' and we not only witness it for we are Part of it!!! Even if to you we cannot be proved or verified to your complete satisfaction! One day perhaps, but not just yet we are informed!! Now back again to this invisible substance, that is in reality All Around and yes, within You!!

Even though your body is made of heavy matter it is 'governed' by invisible substances. Quite a paradox!! You are made up of 'electrical currents' that respond to the mechanism of Thought, that is then transferred to your very own conduit circle of the Brain, where much invisible activity takes place, All of the Time! Do not forget that, you are subject to the Universal law of 'cause and effect', work within it and you have equilibrium, violate it and you have chaos and illness, you call it disease, which it is 'dis – ease'!! The antithesis of Harmony and wellbeing!

So invisibility is actually a part of the human psyche, that is why so many people are physically affected by adverse conditions that have their roots in the electrical currents that are part and **parcel of your World's make**-up!! It all depends upon the individual, some are not affected at all by strange phenomena, and others seem to thrive upon it!! Such is the make-up of each **individual upon this Planet! Notice we have said 'This Planet'** upon others, yea even in your own vicinity their whole life force is of a different nature, it is one that is compatible with their surroundings, as yours is with your own environment!!!

Yes you have assumed rightly they are Invisible to you upon **Earth, but nevertheless they 'Do Exist'! And are as real as you are!!** Believe that for it is a fact, and one day will be verifiable to **Earth's Mankind sometime in the not too distant future!!!** We pause here for a little while and return to the subject of Heaven and Heavens and how their invisibility affects you mortals upon Earth when your transition takes place!!!

Heaven is 'NOT' a figment of someone's imagination. It is a 'REAL LIVE PLANE of EXISTENCE'! We should know for we frequent the many planes of that name!!! Yes we are travellers upon the Cosmic Space held within the confines of the Universe! To us, distance, or should we say the perception of distance and time is no obstacle to our travelling. Whether in the Realms of the Spirit Worlds or those other Unknown Worlds to you, that have their orbital belt planned out for them before they were even created out of the Cosmic chaos of Primordial Matter. That is still a part of this ongoing Universal structure!!!

Creation as such never ceases, it may alter, it may even seem to slumber, but there is always a form of activity present, even so-called inactivity!! Man has not been programmed to search the hidden depths of what Creation really means, and Who it is that does this Creating!! And perhaps we should have added 'Who They Are!!' For Creation has many Creators, and we will leave the rest unsaid so as not to offend others sensibility on the subject!!!

The Worlds of the Spirit vary greatly, both in character and in structure! For example some appear to be quite dense, almost like the World that you now abide in! But there the similarity ends, for the one we have in mind has all of the good points of your Planet but none of its, shall we be generous and just say, unpleasant atmospheric aberrations!! In other words, no erupting volcanoes, no earthquakes or violent disturbances. These events are part and parcel of your Planets make-up, they are in fact just **natural geological phenomena that try to keep the Earth's balance** in perspective!

We, that is the Spirit Worlds have no need of this 'outside influence' to keep our Worlds intact and free from those calamities we have mentioned.

As we have said some of our planes of existence have **similarities that mirror the Earth's, but ours are so much more** beautiful and harmonious in every aspect of their creativity! We, that is the resident populations are in complete harmony with our **surroundings, for we are actually 'part' of them!! What affects one affects All!! And that includes 'ALL' forms of Creation, Light and** Shade in everything, for we, as it were emanate the light around us we are part of what we see. And so when, shall we say there is a crowd of people, the Light from within creates a spectacle of such beauty without, that it is absolutely magical!!

Difficult for us to truly express what it is we feel and extend to each other, but it is such a wonderful bond of Love for just about everything and everyone that we are in contact with! You feel this love emanation everywhere, because you are that Love and it is tangible and vibrant, it is our Life Force in action!! There are no other words for it, and we have only touched quite briefly the meaning of being in Heaven!! And there are so many of them, that await the traveller who is earnestly seeking the true meaning of the continuity of the life force that is from the fount of the Eternal and we may not add what comes after that word the 'Eternal'…!?

So you see Heaven is what you make for yourselves and others, it is a perception and not always a place of existence!!

If you can follow our line of thought.

The perception of Heaven can change in the twinkling of an eye, it all depends on who you encounter in your travels through the other Cosmic Universe, that one that 'IS' but also 'IS NOT'!!! And That one is the one that the human Spirit is heir to and the one that is invisible and yet is a true reality, a paradox that is worth exploring in your inner mind, for you do have an 'inner mind' you know. You are Not confined to one mind in spite of what others may say to you is an impossibility!! Nothing either in this World or any other is impossible! When you understand the mystery of Creative Illusion!!! Of which without you knowing it we are 'all' a part of!!!! Yes, both Mortal and Immortal Man. Use your intuitive powers when reading that. For Illusion and Reality are all part of Life or Lives!!! Regarding life upon, shall we say the 'first Heaven' that you find yourself upon when your transition has been accomplished!

Your first impression is one of absolute joy! And the reason? It's all so familiar, and why is that? It is because you, that is the physical you, are back in your own territory! And here we are speaking of You as Spirit and not Mortal Man whose BODY HAS BEEN left behind. And yet looking at yourself, you will be amazed that you look just like you used to look when upon Earth! It is, and we are stating a fact, it is a form of illusion!!! Your Spirit has for a lifetime been associated with your mortal body and consequently has absorbed much of what that body went through during its three score years and ten, metaphorically speaking!!

And so the facade that you see is still, shall we say, a form of replica of the original earth life form! You will also see that all your loved ones and friends look just as you remember them!! All part of Spirit's illusion qualities, and intended to make everything and everybody familiar to your senses, that is until you have become completely adjusted to your new, though in actual fact, 'old surroundings' You soon accept that from now on you too are complete Spirit again, which also means you can use your mental powers of 'adaptation and creation', do you follow? You now see all things in a different light. Your mental adjustment will show to which 'area' of, shall we say, 'habitation' is open to you!!! Remember you are still 'living and yes, learning'. But now as Complete Spirit with memories of the physical world that will gradually begin to fade, as your progress resumes in your now permanent or maybe 'semi permanent' mode of existence!!!

You now view everything from a 'Spirit's' point of view and NOT as a physical one, and so things are not going to be quite as you expected them to be if when upon Earth you thought of Heaven and all that it holds for you!!! You had to make your own way when living your earthly life and yes, your DECISIONS whether right or wrong!! Well things haven't changed that much for you now that you are once again on familiar ground!!

Your life will take on quite a different colour! You can now see 'things' and events as they really are and how they affect you now!! Life goes on, different Yes! But it still needs thought and subsequent action on your part to, shall we put it, 'to make it work!!'

It's not a bed of proverbial 'Roses' as some people think Heaven is! This first plane of Heavenly abode is a working plane!! No! Not in the earthly sense!! But neither is it one of doing nothing in particular! That might suit you for awhile but you'll soon tire of that mode of existence and crave for something positive to do!! And believe us there are plenty of Positive actions that require positive thought to bring those actions to a satisfactory conclusion!!!

There will be unexpected twists and turns in this new life of yours that will keep you in a positive creative frame of mind!! Yes!! Life really does continue, believe that for it is the Truth, as one day you will find out for yourself! And if you truly think about it you will know that, that is what you really want to happen! Forget the little cherubs' forever chasing each other across the clouds of damask hue! That's all a myth propelled into existence by Artists of the past and bear no resemblance to the reality of Children of the Worlds of Spirit!! For like all of life, children grow up, and it's no different here. We leave you for awhile and resume later!!! Yes, that is the little scribe making that DECISION for us!!!

Once again pen to paper dear friend and we will continue our discourse. You will naturally become part of a like-minded community of souls (No! not the soul.) And so you will have ample opportunity to explore all the avenues of creative activity and as we have already stated, there are plenty to test your perhaps, latent abilities or even new ones that you have never experienced before on the physical plane.

But do not run away with the idea that these capabilities will just fall into your lap! They won't! They need effort and PERSEVERANCE, just has always been the case. Just because you are now of the Spirit fraternity you do not suddenly acquire magical powers! Those powers are there for you to grasp, when you learn how to use them, for all powers of creativity Universal law of cause and effect. You are now aware of what that law entails and how you can take advantage of it by learning how to work within its boundaries!! You can see now can't you? how life matures into a comprehensive pattern of pre-ordained conception!!

You now are freer than you have ever been, no 9–5 working days to keep the wolf from the door!!! That's a thing of the past. Your true Spirituality has been awakened, as we have said, it is all up to you, what you now make of your continued life force!! We do not exaggerate when we say to you, 'Now all things are possible to those whose eyes are open to what the Spirit life has to offer.' And here we have to add; not all people wish to change their ideas and are quite content with the way things are, regarding their life style!

You grow at your 'own pace' and no one else's!! So accept that this Spirit World is one of understanding of the principle of Live and let Live! You are not expected to agree to everything that you see or what is put before you. You still have your Free Will, so use it and use it wisely that is why it was given to you in the first place. When used properly and with discretion then harmony for all concerned is the result!

So we will end here and say that when your time comes for you to return to your true homeland we wish you all the best for the new life you are embarking upon. Make the most of it for it is your destiny and the pathway to Eternity and Eternal Bliss!! We bid you travellers of the mind Farewell.

And to you Brother we have no need to preach to you for you are an 'Old Hand' at this ongoing form of life, and lives lived and yet to be lived!!! We will remain with you dear friend both in Spirit and in Thought!!! Farewell dear Soul, Farewell!! And we have chosen our words wisely and sincerely!!

Chapter 24

July 22nd 2008

THOUGHTS on my part!!
THAT NEED EXPLAINING!!

Liquid Electricity!! – Life Force or Light force. Same thing!!! This form of Electricity is not as we know it! In its raw and natural state it is absolutely phenomenal! It is volatile, unstable and yet it has the power to bring forth 'life' but not as we upon Earth understand 'life'.

There are, shall I call them, Extra Terrestrial life forms that have the ability to change their outer shape into anything that the 'Thought Molecule' desires. And yet the matrix or blue-print of their original identifiable exterior is never lost, for they can in a trice resume their 'originality' and it is perfect again. Their whole 'make-up' stems from this liquid electrical substance that when it is understood can be, as it were, 'tamed' – diluted if you like so that it resembles a form of 'claylike' molecular structure that can be directed into any shape or form that is desired!!!

In other words it is the nucleus or nuclei of, shall we say, A human-like identifiable creation that can if desired, pass off as a being known as the human being termed as Man!! But the resemblance is purely superficial for their form of 'interior workings' shall we call them, are completely unlike the human variety.

Man needs a dense form of matter to sustain his life force, whereas these unknown aspects of that can be classified as coming under the heading of Human beings of Identifiable image, have a completely different life force that animates their being!! It is all generated and governed by THOUGHT! The biological aspect of creation has no parallel with which to compare it to!!

In other words To create a Birth is brought about entirely by the Thought process, therefore the Creator of this 'born' image is both 'Father and Mother' if the desire is to create a family Unit starting as it were with a new born babe!! Otherwise the Creation could well be another adult with all of the capabilities and shall we say characteristics of the Creator! Yet the 'created One' if an adult is his own 'Man' so to speak and so is not beholden to his Creator in any shape or form!! His life and all of His potentials are His own, He is in fact another being and is therefore in complete control of his own life and the ones to follow!! If you can accept that premise of Creation and the Created!!!

If Earth Man and Woman really understood the intended principle of the art of Creation, and here we are talking in terms of the human family, They would know that any child that had been conceived by those parents is not just an extension of its progenitors. Even though it may inherit certain genes as characteristics it is in fact, an entirely separate human being, with a life expectancy in all things of its 'Own'! Parents cannot expect to live 'through' their offspring.

Give them Love and guidance by all means, but do not expect that they will abide by everything that is suggested to them. Parents should learn to accept the unexpected, however much it may hurt them, a child that will eventually mature into adulthood is 'their own person' and that is what some parents feel they cannot understand or even come to terms with! But once they accept the principle that it is the Spirit that has been allowed to use the human vehicle for its own Spiritual expansion, and therefore that child of the womb is the vehicle of choice of the Spirit Entity for its sojourn upon the lower plane of Earth!!

It does NOT tamper with the Free Will of the individual of its choice, likewise that individual has no power of its own to influence the Free Will of its Spirit companion during the life span of the human vehicle!

The intention of allowing this union of the two separate identities was always assumed that the two would work together in harmony for their mutual benefit! In some cases this has happened and people call them Saints or Masters, Teachers of the Esoteric mysteries of the known, and yes unknown aspects of the Universe, that houses so many Planets, Worlds, and such diversities of those two words as to be unimaginable!!

That is the Blue Print for Mans ultimate destiny upon this Planet, and then when Spirit and Humanity become as One then **the 'real' journey of those two aspects of the Divinity will herald a** new chapter in their everlasting search for what some like to call **the 'Quest for the Holy Grail'!!** We will not enlighten you any further on that particular subject, for though vast, is actually very simple!!!!

We proceed upon another subject!! UPON AN UNKNOWN PLANET! We are going back to the fascinating subject of Liquid electricity that is the main stay of the very life force of that particular planet in question, where those unknown (as yet) inhabitants dwell! Electricity is far from being just one thing, it has many aspects and not all of them resemble what you may think!! The main and dominant aspect of the Liquid Electricity that in a way resembles the water upon the Earth plane.

It is quite transparent and is everywhere, in its air-like quality it is very easy to breathe it in, apart from actually nourishing a person it stimulates all of the electrical molecules and fibres that **go to make up that persons interior 'workings'. Do not read that word as if it means 'solid' parts, all workings as it were are by 'thought' and are 'not' a per**manent fixture as it were!!!

Here as in many of the unknown Planetary constellations, Thought is the paramount instrument of eventual objective creation, of whatever is desired at that particular moment! And can be completely altered by there again, Thought!! So to a great extent permanence is not the main objective, unless desired to be!!! This main Electrical ingredient is virtually the building blocks of Life itself!!

We spoke of 'air' another aspect of it is not just as a food, but also as a liquid to be imbibed, for it is very palatable and refreshing. There are, shall we say Oceans of this particular facet of electricity, in fact beneath their 'earth structure' lie vast reservoirs of this liquid!

Now in other parts of the planet under examination there are still more reservoirs, but this time the liquid is not transparent but of a 'heavy nature' and is used for, shall we say constructive practices! For example 'mechanical appliances'!! No! Not your sort of mechanical, they are used for vapour beams, highway's, paths of navigation, that are in a way like your corridors in 'Air Space'!

People travel as they wish, providing their own thought mode of transport. But! First they have to 'lock on' to the beam that will take them to their desired destination, once this has been established, their vehicle with the appropriate code within it can then proceed. Variations in speed are left to you, but once 'locked on' you cannot leave the beam until your destination has been reached!! No moving parts! Just complete relaxed comfort. No noise, just you and your companions enjoying the views and talking amongst yourselves as to what you are going to do when you reach your, shall we say holiday resort??!! Everything regarding the flying is controlled by the beam and NO fear of accidents, which are, incidentally unheard of here!!!

In some respects these inhabitants resemble the Spirit that Earth people associate with themselves. They are Highly evolved beings that work in complete harmony with their surroundings. They too, **are a form of 'human being' and come within the orbit of Identifiable aspects of what is thought of as 'The Humanities'.** But remember that just as upon Earth when the cycle of evolution began there were Seven Root Races, with more waiting **as it were 'in the wings'.**

So those inhabitants that we have been speaking about also **have their form of 'Root Races',** which have many subsidiary offshoots so to speak. **Their Root Races are allowed to 'come and go',** in other words when a particular Race reaches its intended height, they are then ready to proceed to and even higher grade of distinction upon an adjoining Planet. With the intention that what they will learn will eventually be of extreme use to those upon their previous plane of existence. And so they will once more rejoin their Particular area of the Root Force as Highly **evolved Teachers of their, shall we say, 'descendants' that are now** in the place vacated by those others that had reached their zenith of near perfection!!

The plane that they originally transferred to is the equivalent of one of your Higher Spirit Ones that you upon Earth know about!!

Before we leave that episode we have to inform you, that their Form or Aspect of the Creator is NOT the same as yours!! Another aspect, Another facet! All part of the Unknowable Force that pervades not just Your known Universe, but All others that have their place in the Space that is Forever a part of that Immutable Force that some would say is The Breath of God, That Unknowable One or Ones (?) that are responsible for All Life Manifestations of whatever subject you care to mention!!!!

Use your Intuitive Insight when reading these narratives or discourses. For Not everything is what it may seem or appear to **be!! Your World is 'Your' responsibility as Theirs is Theirs.**

You have no right to expect other forms of Terrestrial Beings to be waiting with open arms to welcome you to 'Their World'. They already know more about you than you could possibly realize!! They witness the Turmoil you are creating for yourselves and do not wish to be a part of it. At present!! They do not 'see' what you are doing but are aware of the trauma that it represents, they can sense all of the various disturbances upon your globe. For the thoughts that are generated by these occurrences form a dull vaporous cloud around your earth, which prohibits any form of erstwhile contact with those of a Higher nature than your own!!! Just remember you are 'one amongst many' and by comparison you do not come out of it with glowing colours!!!

The next step in your (that is your World's) evolutionary stage is to rid your Earth of all the unhealthy toxic elements that You! Yes You! Are responsible for polluting the very ground you walk upon. And the oceans that lap your shores and the Skies above where you have created for yourselves a monster that feeds upon those polluting gasses that you send up, and yea even your own thoughts that add to that form of pollution!! For thoughts are positive reactions to negative and undesirable elements that you are in danger of becoming addictive to them. Not all drugs are the ones you are familiar with in this present age, drugs are insidious and disguise themselves very well until it is too late to change the habit!!! So learn to pause before you actually think, for a thought once thought cannot be withdrawn from the reactions of it if it is one of those vindictive unhealthy specimens that we can see floating around in your atmosphere!

Evolution spells Change, so make sure your change is in the right direction, Forward and NOT Backward, where stagnation will set in!!! As we have constantly said to you, 'Put Your Own House in Order' before you think of entering another's Space!!!

As Earth people you have a tendency to look at everything with a human viewpoint and understanding. And this we find is your main stumbling block to any form of either unification of your own species, not to mention what your attitudes would be should you encounter a species not unlike yourselves. But of a far superior attitude towards all other forms of Creation, regardless of their origin and their so-called place in the Destiny of this tiny Planet called Earth!!!!

Keep an open mind when dealing with anything to do with **either the Spirit, an 'Alien' life Force, or even Space itself!!!** For Space and Time are well known for their eccentric behaviour! Or perhaps we should say, Your comprehension of what those two commodities represent!!! Remember in other discourses we have **stressed the form known as 'Illusion' that pervades ALL living** animate or inanimate Creations of those most High!!! You cannot be party to their Divine knowledge, just onlookers and not participants as it were!!! Remember also your own limitations, set **your sights on what you feel you can attain and don't be too** critical of yourselves if you cannot at first accomplish the feat you set your mind upon!! But do not be daunted by what you may consider as failure, for very often failure is the stepping stone to future accomplishment!!

And here we beg leave of your friend the Scribe to once more bid you and him a Farewell. And may your God bless you in your searching and seeking after the truth or should we add The TRUTHS, for there are many of them before the Ultimate Truth can be discovered.

We bid you Farewell.

And Brother we embrace you in love and true companionship! **Farewell little ship upon life's Ocean, one day you will find your** anchorage that is awaiting your coming. Farewell! Farewell! God go With You!!!

Chapter 25

July 30th 2008

PERCEPTIONS OF THE MIND!!!

Life!! What does it really mean? To most people it seems to be a series of Ups! And Downs!! Very rarely on an even keel!! And yet if it wasn't for these so-called 'ups' and 'downs' don't you think that life would seem rather dull and predictable? Well I suppose some people would be quite happy for that situation to be their lot in life, but to the majority of folk they seek something more not exactly exciting, but shall we call it challenging? For it is the unexpectedness of Life that is what is loosely called the Spice of Life!! Well now transfer all of those sentiments to the period you tend to call The After Life!! And you would not be far wrong.

For Life, upon whatever sphere you may be dwelling and we are speaking of the Spirit Life!! Life really does continue, perhaps not at the pace you have been accustomed to but nevertheless it does continue, and here we add with all of life's Ups and Downs!! Contrary to what many people tend to think, that the Spirit World, or Heaven, one of them at least! All things suddenly become perfect!! Not so little brethren of the Earth! Perfection does Not come easily, one has to work for it and at it, for it to become a viable positive form of life expectancy!!!

The Worlds of the Spirit, and there are many of them, and if we say to you 'Perceptions' perhaps you will understand the meaning of 'Worlds'!! Think about it and know that within each and every one of us we dwell at times in various Worlds! You may say of the imagination! But that is not such a bad thing really, for from the imagination much can be achieved of positive and lasting value!!! Just because you become your real self at the transition period you have not lost your powers of the imagination, in fact they are enhanced as you learn to progress in your new life.

But upon the worlds or Spheres of the Spirit, you can take an **imagined thought 'form' to a positive conclusion!!** In other words you learn the art of creativity!! But here again we stress those two **words 'Ups' and 'Downs'.** Not everything to do with the next phase in your evolutionary existence is as predictable as you may think!! As Spirit you do not live in isolation unless of course that is part of your chosen way of life!!

As part of the community, just as upon the Earthplane, you **have to contend with other people's points** of view, and believe me everyone has them in one way or another!!! So Life isn't so different upon our realms after all, is it? But!! We learn the art of toleration! That does not mean agreeing, just to be sociable or even trying to get on with each other!! You learn to adapt, you did upon earth, and the same applies here!! We are trying in our **way to prepare you for this change in life style, 'your life style'**!! So much of our life upon this first plane of existence almost mirrors the one left behind upon Earth when you vacated it!!!

Familiarity is what you find at first and that puts you in the right frame of mind, you come across situations that remind you so much of earth life and so you are not at a loss regarding how to cope with them!!! Gradually, yes very gradually you find that the **old familiar things that you at first remembered and yes, 'clung on to' begin to fade, for now the situations and life style has taken** on quite a different phase!! You are learning that the Spirit side of life has so much more to offer you, now that you have become accustomed to it. For after all, this is Now your true life, unless of course you intend to return once more to the Earthplane for another round of experienced learning! In which case you will most probably go to an area, where you will be in the company of others awaiting their return to their next round of the re-incarnation period!!

Here, is where you are able to view what this new Earth life has to offer you, and the journey you take, which is of a mental one is one that you will eventually be living, and is Your Choice Entirely!! So remember, whatever you decide you will have to abide by it! There again Thought comes into this, as it does with everything. So make sure your thoughts end in Positive actions and not the negative variety, which may seem attractive at the time but nevertheless are a backward step and most probably in **the wrong direction!! And here dear travellers upon one of life's** paths, we bid you Farewell and may your God guide you and keep you safe.

And to you Brother we also bid you Farewell, which in your case is just a word and not a reality, for we are always near you in thought.

Your work does matter little friend, and one day you will see the fruits of your labours!

We bid you Farewell.

And May Allah be praised and look kindly upon thee little brother.

Chapter 26

August 17th 2008

CREATION! HEAVEN! = EVOLUTION OF THE SPIRIT!!!

We are going to talk to you about the world of the Spirit. 'Our World' and the one that you will return to when your transition takes place and you leave behind your garment of flesh and put on your Spiritual garb of understanding and enlightenment, which really means your heightened perception of not only where you are but also your relationship to this particular Sphere and its cosmopolitan population that you are now a positive part of!!

And by 'cosmopolitan' that is exactly what it is!! Populations are just the same here as they were upon the Earthplane! In other words you have exchanged one venue of Life for another one, albeit upon a different vibrationary plane of thought, but still one where life really does go on. You will have such a lot of re-adjusting to do, especially of your mental awareness of the life force all around you!! In a way it is settling back into your familiar, we cannot say routine, because it is not, you have **recently left a lifetime's experiences upon Earth and so you are** Not the same Spirit person you were when you embarked upon that form of re-incarnation!!!

Even your remembered perception of this first sphere adjoining the Earthplane has altered, as it should when you think back at what you were like all those years ago!!! Change! Change! Change! All part of your evolutionary spiral, You may well meet up with friends you had made upon your previous passage of time upon this realm, we are not talking here of your relatives of the Earthplane that perhaps have preceded you, with their own transitional period!!! No! We are referring to the group of friends that you belonged to! Both them and you will have a lot of catching up to do.

And then you will have to make a decision as to your future role within your previous group!! For remember they will have advanced upon the Spiritual spiral and you on the other hand have been, shall we say somewhat **'restricted' while dwelling upon the Earthplane!!** Though you do have a wealth of experience and knowledge that they would be anxious to hear about. The **outcome may well be that there isn't so much catching up to do** as you at first thought. And so you can now resume that place that was left vacant, is awaiting your return!!

Life really does go on, and your group of like-minded travellers takes on a new pattern of thought awareness. **Now don't imagine** that as a group you actually, shall we say live in a form of commune, though there are many such communes, all studying various aspects of the continuation of life and its expectancies!!! You are your own person and you live as you feel comfortable with, there are no set rules and yet there are universal guidelines, which all Spirit people are pleased to abide by and work within!!

If you and your group are sufficiently advanced regarding **Spiritual Matters and by Spiritual, please don't think of that word** in a Religious connotation!! Life here is not one devoted entirely **to what many people think that that word Spiritual involves!! It's** part of your life but not exactly the be all or end all, of it!!! This first Spirit Plane is the one of adjustment, to keep you in touch **with Reality for this plane is even more 'Real' than your previous** one.

There's so much that you can achieve in so many areas that offer you plenty of scope to use your 'gifts' is a misnomer, for no one but no one is handed out so-called Gifts, in whatever direction they lie! Gifts are hard 'earned' – hard 'learned' if the truth is known!!! We mature because that is our aim in life, and with maturity and here we are speaking of the mind, there comes the rewards that go with that effort of will, on your part!

Your 'private life' upon the Spirit plane is just like the one you lead upon the earth one! What you do with it is all up to you. You are not subject to scrutiny by anyone. Though as you do progress in whatever you have set your heart plus Mind upon, it does not go unnoticed. Your whole Auric colour vibrations are witness to your personal evolutionary progress. We state a fact and a truth believe that. We are trying to tell those who perhaps are apprehensive and under various assumptions regarding life on the Spirit planes, that being a Spirit is its own reward.

You are here where you belong and your life is what 'you' make of it, there's plenty of advice and help if and when you need it and ask for it!!! If your sojourn upon this first plane is, shall we say permanent and not transitory, then your life ahead is a truly remarkable one. Full of expectations and yes, realities, positive ones as you progress, and this one is only the first of many that in due course are awaiting your entry upon yet a further rung of the evolutionary ladder of Yes! Spiritual advancement, and this time that word does denote where your capabilities have brought you too!!!

You progress at 'Your' own pace; no need to hurry for Eternity is a long way off as far as you are concerned. Though here we pause and say not everyone wishes to leave a Heavenly Sphere of comfort and familiarity, and they are free to do just that, that is their evolutionary pattern and would obviously suit them, until perhaps they wished to broaden their horizons!! Such is progress, slow or fast, makes no difference to the final outcome if you follow our line of thought!! I suppose we should say to you that each Sphere or Plane of existence is more beautiful than the previous one, shall we perhaps add 'In Your own perception' and we leave you to be the judge of what we are implying!!

Quite often people discover that they have capabilities they never knew they had while dwelling upon the Earth plane. Some of those capabilities are shall we say, inherited from your mortal partner of your lifetimes liaison that have lain dormant in your memory pattern.

Until circumstances have awakened those memories and you can now feel grateful for that partnership that was a two-way unfoldment of both of you. Your character as we have said before in other discourses has been moulded by that lifetimes partnership, even if at the time you were unaware of its growing as it has!! It's only in retrospect that you can begin to evaluate what that Spirit and Physical's joint venture upon life's path has brought to your now Spirit life. And you can now see that your choice that you made regarding your intended birth in your re-incarnation period, was the right one for both of you we must add!

Life really is a wonderful experience is it not? And then there's the continuation of it upon the Spirit plane! Where you can really see what that time spent upon the Earthplane has taught you, you are where you are now because of it. And that was principally because of that choice you made and the mortal body that you chose to become your physical partner for that lifetime's experience of living and learning!!! Such is the wonderment of God's creative Thoughts that gives to all of us these ever-ongoing lives of discovery.

Be conscious of that privilege of being Spirit and Physical, Mortal and Immortal that leads us back to our Creator Genius, the one we call upon as God our Father in Heaven!! Whatever race colour or creed, GOD is the GOD of all peoples regardless of the name HE maybe called in the different areas of your globe!!

As you progress so you begin to alter your perception of the Creator.

You see things differently, in fact you see them as they really are and perhaps not as you have always imagined them to be!! Upon the Earthplane you think of God as you are brought up to believe in Him, but when you are upon the Planes of the Spirit your understanding takes on a different perspective. For you are more aware of what Creation really stands for, you know you are part of it, but you now begin to accept that creation is part of you. What affects one affects All, and that goes quite literally for 'everything'!!

You can marvel at the fact that as a Created being you really are a part of your Creator, a living part as He is a part of you!! As a living vibrating Spirit essence you are no longer on the outside looking in as it were, you are now on the 'inside looking out'!!! You are 'Creation' in its finest form and from here on your perception, your inner spiritual perception is gradually being heightened so that as you proceed to the Higher planes of Esoteric knowledge and participation, which means you are now directly involved with everything that is going on around you, and yes even within you!!! Creation now takes on quite a different meaning; you can appreciate and sometimes understand what are the Complexities of Forms of Creativity. They vary greatly from sphere to sphere, or if you prefer from 'Heaven to Heaven'!!

The vastness of what Creation is capable of is simply so astounding and mysterious that just to know that you are a part of it is all the reward that you need. You are without perhaps knowing it a Co-Worker for and with, your God. And there is no better way of showing what this means than giving your Love for everyone and everything.

For it is Love that not only binds us together but creates a bond that grows in strength shall we say, 'day by day' or should that be, from age to age!!? And when you consider that time is timeless then your eternity is ever present in all that you do!!!

And here is where we bring this treatise to a close and bid you our customary Farewell and may God bless you in your endeavours.

And to you Brother Scribe. Our love and continued support in **what you are doing, don't be disheartened little friend for all is well**, believe that.

Farewell but never Goodbye.

Chapter 27

August 30th 2008

THE CHOICE IS YOURS!!

We offer you a speculative proposition and it is:
The Many faces of God! Or, The Face of many Gods!

The choice is yours, for to tell you a truth either could be the right one, and when we say 'the right one' we are saying to you 'For You'!!! Your whole life is made up of 'choices', which way to go? Shall I stay put? What will happen to me? The choices seem to be endless, yet each choice can be seen either as a stepping stone towards a new discovery, or a stumbling block that anchors you to the past! And here we are talking metaphorically, and though its mainly aimed at the mind, it undoubtedly has repercussions on the physical body, and yea, even its Spirit companion who shares very much in the mental activity of the mortal being of its encumbrance!

So then, what will be Your Choice? In this conundrum of Gods Singular or Gods multiple?!! And why are we asking you this you may wonder, well whatever you choose to accept will no doubt influence your future, that is the physical future of your bodily companion! We do not include the Spirit at the present time, because the Spirit already knows what the answer to this conjecture is all about!

When one has been brought up by ones parents, a child usually absorbs what it has been told and educated to believe and accept. But with the onset of adulthood the mental challenge of what has always been seen as, shall we say the Gospel truth, the challenge turns out to be sometimes quite mind shattering, figuratively speaking. And can sometimes result in complete abandonment of all pre-conceived ideas about God and 'His' place in this World's History, nay in the whole Universe's would be more accurate!!!

And now you have to think about that prospect in the broadest of terms and that is no mean feat if you are seriously considering what that outcome may be. Should you find that all of your previous ideas about God have to be challenged as to their authenticity and their very existence of verifiability, which we have to tell you, to a human being that is well nigh impossible! And you will have noticed we have expressed human being and NOT Spirit counterpart!!!

For as you progress upon the various upward spirals of Spirituality, your whole perception of the 'Creator of Creation' takes on a completely different outlook!! You notice we have said 'Creator' in the Singular and that adjective pertains to the Unknowable Essence of Life Force that has Always been but never Understood! And that is as it should be, for 'we' that is All of the manifested Spirit and Physical aspects of Creation that go under the heading of Mankind in All of His various 'disguises' upon all of His various planes of existence, are 'aspects' of that Unknowable Life Force.

This is generated and created by those as yet Unknown or should we elaborate and say as yet unidentified 'God Creators' whose names are 'Legion' and who Exist in Reality but 'NOT' the reality associated with humans!! They are in Dimensions of existence that cannot be understood by present day mankind!!! Dimensions can be represented as of the mind and the imagination, and from those two they touch upon the fringe of the reality of the 'unreal' that is nevertheless a Reality of a sort that mortal Man cannot comprehend!!!

Reality can also be called '**Illusion**'!! And yet it has its base in the 'Real' make no mistake about that, but what is real upon one plane of existence may have no visible existence upon another one!!! There may well be similarities but that is all, the actual substance that goes on beneath the subtle exterior of these various planes has no relationship to physical substance at all!!! Accept that fact, and then go forward with us as we proceed with this treatise of the Unknown and to some, the Unbelievable existence of what cannot be proven either for or against, it just IS!!! Whatever 'IS' may be!!!

Now your Earth is composed of dense heavy matter or substance if you like, that is the cause of all of your catastrophic **upheavals, which is the 'natural' existence of unstable matter. The release of all of the pent up energy that exists beneath the earth's** crust must have an outlet somehow, otherwise the whole globe would explode Cosmic debris once more! To be part of another planet of life force and substance!!!

But the other Dimensions that we spoke of earlier they, and here we qualify and say not all of them, for they vary in degrees of vibrationary force! Well some of these other Dimensions, and we say to you call them Planets or Planes if you wish, are composed of Elements that you have no conception of. They almost defy description! For instance, where you have earth that is what you walk on and live off! Theirs is of a translucent (not a substance) a translucent form of, how shall we phrase it? Solid Water like substance, that is equivalent to your earth, it can appear just like your earth in many respects, depending upon the locality!

There are elements of growth tissue that can be used as food when required. There is no form of deterioration of their substance, it merely returns to its original, and re-growth then starts all over again! No waste whatsoever!! This water-like substance is very pliable and walking upon it is very easy and pleasurable, there's a spring to it and so one step is probably equal to two or more of your earth ones!!

The 'Sea' and 'Air' are likewise very buoyant and effortless either breathing or swimming or sailing. At night there is a heavy dew, which descends like a transparent vapour, it is a nourishing substance for all kinds of growth and so there is no need for what you term as fertilizers!! As this planet that we are discussing has beneath its surface a fluid-like substance that keeps it constantly balanced in its correct cycle of positioning in its orbital belt. The movement of this planet is smooth and rhythmical, and so the seasons come and go with hardly a change in temperature, except for the two poles.

North and South, they remain constant neither hot nor cold just moderate. There are also two more poles, East and West, that so far as we know have no immediate impact upon either the weather or anything else, but they are there for a reason we are **told, they seem to be a form of 'reserve' if they should ever be** needed. They could override any form of interference with the other two by releasing powerful waves (not sea waves!) of magnetic energy that would counter balance any disturbance, either from within or from without, of their globe of habitation!!! Now all of what we have said, can be multiplied a million times over and over, such is the complexity of Creation and Those who Create!!!

Call them what you will, it does not alter the fact that God's (if you wish to call them that) exist everywhere. And they are All, **facets of that Unknowable Force and yea, answerable to 'IT'!!!**

When you see the staggering wonders that are being created all of the time upon and within all of the Universes in Existence, You can appreciate that with all of the diverse creations, they need more than just One Creative Genius to perform the feat of practical Creativity. If Creation is to continue on its pre-destined course of perpetual Evolution that does not end with the word

'Eternity', for that word heralds a New BEGINNING. A re-birth of what 'was' and is now what is to be!!!

This discourse started off with 'Your choice' did it not? Well dear friends of the Earth this is where we will leave you, for the choice is yours!

We have made Ours Long, Long ago as has the Little Scribe only at present he doesn't know it!! Oh! We stand corrected He says he does!!! Brave words little friend Brave words!!

We bid you all Farewell and may the God of Your choice Bless you on your path of discovery!

Little Brother!! Peace we leave with you little soul of the Earthplane. Journey nearly over! Fare – thee – well. God be with You, is our parting wish for you dear friend.

Chapter 28

September 13th 2008

ANCIENT AND MODERN

Welcome Brother, we greet you in the Name of Jesus the Christos Peace we bring you little Brother your world that is your personal world, you need have no fear about it for we are with you at all times, even when you may feel at your lowest ebb! We watch over you for you are very precious to us, believe that for we speak a truth, and now let your pen speak for us!!!

What is it that we can say to not only you, but to those others who may read what is being written? You long to hear of something that you have not heard before, sadly to say we cannot perform a miracle that will astound you, but! We can perhaps give to you a new slant upon an ancient truth, that has eluded your inner perception, the one of the Mind, where all things have their beginning, and sometimes they get lost or are pushed to the back of your waking consciousness, until!!! Yes! They are once more awakened, perhaps through just a word in a conversation, or even a sentence on a written page!

Ancient manuscripts are usually couched in the vocabulary of the age in which they were written, and so some of that ancient language maybe hiding a truth that could well apply to this day and age. That is, if you the searchers after the esoteric mysteries are reading with an open mind and do not take the exact wording 'too' literally, so to speak!!

The subject that is now to be under discussion is God in His Heaven or Heavens **and what our relationship is to 'Him'**, and shall we add **'His'** to Us!! All of Us!!! In the past, the ancient past, Heaven and indeed even God were talked about almost with a reverential form of speech. As if Heaven were somewhere up in the Sky just awaiting our arrival, that is if we merited it! And as for God the Creator of all this wonderful place we are to go to, He according to legend would be sitting upon a throne in all of His seen Majesty, with the Archangels and Seraphs and cherubims gathered around him to do whatever he wished them to do!! And we, poor mortals would be in that Divine presence awaiting judgement on our past life upon the plane of Earth!!!

Well that might have suited those people then, but what about Now? Today!! Are there still people in this rather materialistic world who still go along with that rather over simplified version of God and His Heavenly abode? We say, Yes there are, so those Ancient scriptures on fragile pieces of parchment have quite a lot to answer for!!! If that is really the case with some people, then we say to them in all sincerity and yes Love, Please think again. And think seriously about what you seem so anxious to hold on to in your beliefs about God, and Creation, and what it really does **mean in 'Reality' and not just in a cosy satisfying, comforting,** and nostalgic version of the past!!!

We hesitate to take away those things that mean so much to so many of you and if we did succeed then that would leave a large vacuum that must be filled, but with what?

We are told to say that now is not the time in this Earth's Epoch when that can come about!! It will take time, but eventually attitudes will have to change if you really and truly want to see, What Creation and the Creators of it really mean!! It would mean a fundamental change in your whole perception of what to **many people is their 'Religion' and their 'Religious faith'**!! Religion in a way is like the scaffolding that surrounds a building that is in progress, once the building has been completed structurally then the scaffolding can be taken down, revealing the constructed building in all its shall we say, 'beauty'!

But that is only the beginning of its life, its inner life to be precise. For until it is furnished and the interior decorations are as they have been visualized by the architect completed. Then the building is ready for occupation and it comes alive!! Now think back to the scaffolding, its job has been done no need to keep it up, so equate that scaffolding with the word Religion. Do you follow our line of thought; Religion like the scaffolding had its place, but now is the time to move on. Scaffolding gone and what was it hiding? NO! **Not a building, Not a Church, but a 'Temple' and that Temple is 'You'!!!** You are God's temple and now you can begin to see that within that temple dwells that part of the Almighty that we call our Spirit!!

And now we are in a position to see where it is that we, the Spirit fit into this wonderful piece of Creativity. We can appreciate the Wonders of Creation that are endless, for Creation in one way or another never ceases. And we, both our Human companion upon the Earthplane and our Spirit counterpart, are witness to this ongoing Creativity.

By not one, or two, but by Many Creators that are all Aspects of that Unknowable Essence of Life Force that has always existed and always will!!!

'Our God' like us, is an 'Aspect of that Life force' in all its abstract glory!! We are allowed to as it were, view God as we wish! **That is through His bounty of the oft mentioned 'Free Will'!!** Which in spite of what is said of it, it does have its limitations! And that is for our own good!! Believe that for it is a Truth! For without a so-**called 'brake'**, unleashed free will could cause havoc, and Man in his present stage upon the evolutionary chain just could not cope with it!! And why? Because **Man does 'NOT THINK in a COHERENT FASHION!!'** That is something that in the future He must do!!

And here we are speaking of Man generally and not those in the minority who are the true seekers and searchers after the truth, even if that truth may, in the light of reason cause those searchers to question it!! Yet that in its self is a good sign, for to question is to learn, and to learn is to begin to understand the **complexities of what that word 'Creation' really stands for!!!** For Creation is the manifested aspect of the Divine Unknowable **Thought, of that 'Life Force' that permeates the Whole of Known** and yes, Unknown Existence wherever it may be!!! And think upon that in the broadest of terms!!

You humans marvel at the varied creations you observe upon your **little planet, yet 'they' are but a fraction of what has and yes,** IS still being in the stages of Thought Creativity!!

If those who have read this treatise and who perhaps had thoughts in another direction, have now changed their minds regarding those ancient doctrines, we hope that we have been able, in some small way to begin to fill the vacuum that we spoke of some while back!! And now it is Your turn to carry on filling that vacuum with your added knowledge and you may be agreeably surprised at what your thinking is telling you. **Don't** dismiss it as your imagination, for the imagination is a wonderful tool when properly utilized for the benefit of not only yourself, but also of others!!!

We have only touched the surface of what we would have liked to talk to you about, but that need not stop you from putting your own interpretation upon what has been written by our friend the little scribe. Just THINK about all that you see around you from the humblest to the highest forms of Creation. And know that what may appear as a simple construction, when seen through the eyes of a magnifying glass can actually show you the intricate, amazingly detailed formula that animates that created **aspect of the life force! And 'WE' are part of it all!!!**

Be humble and give thanks to that Unknown Creator Genius that we all call by the name of 'God'. Singular or Plural, makes no difference we 'All' are Aspects, whether viewed in 'Abstract Form' or as a 'Personalized Being' that we call upon as 'Father'!!!

We leave you upon that note. Peace be with you and we wish you all, success in your searching for the Truth, in one of its many aspects and disguises!!!

Farewell Brother. **We leave you in God's hands.**

May Allah be praised

May Allah be praised.

Chapter 29

September 14th 2008

ANOTHER DIMENSION, FOR WHOM?!!

These are going to be just my thoughts!
At least that is how they are going to start!!

I was thinking about 'Beings'!! Those Beings that exist in another dimension than the one that we are in! And yet 'They' can also function in Ours, when they feel it is necessary or needed. Though I do believe that certain 'Ones' have a duty as it were, to be responsible for 'Elements' and that word is to cover a multitude of what we might call 'Natures habits'!! I think I read, oh! a long time ago, that there were Four of these 'figures' that had control over this planet of ours, but I can't remember what their 'duties' were!!!

Why I've been thinking along these lines is because in my 'inner screen' for want of a more appropriate word, I saw a 'face' a very, very large one, only for a moment or two, but it was enough for me to set this train of thought into action!!

By way of explanation, I have in the past and yes, even now been 'aware' of these Beings, these figures of Gigantic proportions, and only very rarely have I been aware of them in their entirety!! Usually I 'see' shall I say, sections of them, for example, A face, A hand, A foot, and this is usually shall I say, by 'accident'.

In other words I was not consciously shall I say, searching for verification of their existence outside of my 'imagination'!!! And sometimes one of these Beings seemed as surprised as I was that I had seen them, or rather part of them to be precise!! I've written about one recently that I saw when the 'clouds parted' and I beheld this wonderful looking enormous head and face. And this giant of a figure looked straight at me with twinkling eyes and shaking his head so that his locks of hair moved from side to side and I 'heard' Him laugh as if to say, 'Now you've seen me, what are you going to do about it? And before I could utter a reply, the clouds came together like a curtain obscuring my view!!!

Now on two or three other occasions, either in my deep dreams or when I've been on a 'mind travel' with my Brother guides I've come face to face as it were, with one of these Figures and when I say 'Figures' I do Not mean a sculptured figure, but a living Being, either seated upon a throne like structure or Standing in front of me!!! Now I've written before that I never feel at all, how can I put it? Intimidated by their size. Even though I must appear like the size of an ant in comparison!!!

There again I have written that communication with these Beings has been through Thought and so the difference in size as it were, is almost irrelevant! as far as I was concerned!!! And I presumed that also went for the Being I have mentioned! Or am I being presumptuous! I hope not!!

Well this sort of brings me to what I started about.

Are they these extraordinary beings that dwell in another dimension are they part of our World's make-up, as it were?? Are they Aspects of the Creator God or Gods' and are they sort of custodians of this Planet of ours, monitoring its 'goings on' by which I mean Natures behaviour patterns as well as our own, I should add!!! And also another thought has just crept in, Where do they reside? Is there a Planet that caters in size for these enormous figures?

We upon this Earth have I suppose 'human size' vegetation, even if some of it may be enormous, we still feel shall I say, 'comfortable' with it. The only 'things' that cause us to feel shall I say, 'awe struck' are usually 'Man Made'. Skyscrapers for one thing, but that's only the actual 'outside' building so to speak. Inside, the size of rooms or apartments or offices etc. are usually acceptable regarding their size in conjunction with the humans that use them!!!

So then 'size' must also be part of where these Beings dwell! Though I've just thought That as they must have 'Powers' that would astonish us with their abilities of creativity, perhaps by their powers of Thought they can if the situation warrants it, reduce their size to that of an acceptable one when dealing as it were, on a one to one (or many!!) basis of we as human beings!! That perhaps come under their form of jurisdiction!! They may even be among us even now and we know it not!! Perhaps they may appear as 'Super Human' beings, either in form or in mental awareness, in other words 'Highly Intelligent' with knowledge far in advance of those around them!!!

I suppose with Creators and those who do their bidding Nothing is impossible!! And so we shouldn't be surprised at anything that may seem to our so-called logical minds, as fanciful almost impossible situations that defy description upon this planet, that in itself defies logical explanations regarding its very existence and construction. Even when scientific people come up with plausible explanations as to the origin of not only of this planet but the whole Universe that houses it and millions more!!! We know 'Nothing' when it comes to trying to fathom out what has originally stemmed from the Thought Creation of the Unknowable Source of Life Force in its untamed essence of Primordial Chaos, that only works within the boundaries of its Laws. Its Universal Laws upheld by those Beings of Light that is the Hierarchy of Elected Gods of Creativity.

Where on Earth have my Thoughts taken me? Good question little Brother and that should answer your unspoken thoughts, need we go any further in explanation? NO! I don't think we need to!!! And so perhaps we had better bring this treatise of yours... **and ours to a close, and one day we will pursue this** subject of yours regarding those Beings of Gigantic proportions that intrigue you so!! And to Us? Well we know all about that subject and that is all we are going to say on that matter at this stage!!

So we bid you little Brother with the inquisitive mind, Farewell for the time being, and do not be surprised at what may transpire in the near future!! We depart dear friend, we depart. Farewell and God be with you and with those fellow travellers upon the path of life. Farewell.

Chapter 30

September 18th 2008, Morning

EVOLUTION!! FORGET DARWIN AND THINK FOR YOURSELF!!!

I begin this writing with a form of explanation. I shall start with my personal Thoughts upon the subject I am going to try and write about. Whether or not those thoughts of mine 'get taken over' by those who have far more knowledge than I have on every subject I may touch upon and so I leave that explanation there. And proceed with what I want to write about and that is: 'EVOLUTION' and how it affects Mankind and all of the other created aspects of shall I say, the Divinity? And leave you to think your own thoughts regarding that expression!!!

The other evening there was a programme on the television that I looked forward to with anticipation because there were going to be various well known and famous people from the world of Science!! I honestly hoped I was going to learn something from their collective thoughts from such eminent men. Was I left disappointed or elated at what I had been told and shown? Well you might have guessed it, it was the former!!! These scientific brain boxes all have their various theories about simply everything! They have blackboards upon which they furiously chalk equations (I think!) and end up by saying, 'Well you can work it out for yourself can't you?'

And then they wipe the blackboard clean!!! And of course I didn't understand any of it, let alone 'work it out for myself'!!

Now I come to what 'I' think and actually I've written something similar in one of my books! And it is this! Scientists waffle on about Evolution and Darwin's theories and NOT ONCE do they mention the 'Spirit side of Man'!! It's as if it's either a taboo subject or perhaps they don't even think it's worth a mention as they can't see it, or weigh it or hold it in their hands and say, 'Ah! So this is the Spirit is it?!!!' And of course up to a point they would be right, you can't do any of those things, at least the man in the street cannot and that includes those scientific bodies I've been talking about!! Though I'm sure they do not equate themselves with the 'Man in the Street', at least not mentally I presume!!

Now regarding the evolution of Mankind! He it is who is the only Created species who can shall I say, 'instigate' his own evolution!! He thinks, he has free will, and I say here 'only up to a point' contrary to what he may have been led to think!!! And I add also that up to a certain degree 'He is Programmed' just like all of the other created species. More about that later!

All of the other species of Creation, i.e. The beasts of the field, The Birds of the air, The 'fish' of the Sea! And all of the other, dare I say subsidiary? Created life forms!!!

They are 'Programmed' and that goes under the heading of Nature or Natural!! They do <u>NOT</u> evolve of their own accord.

Their form of Evolution begins upon the 'Plane of the Spirit' where all forms of experimentation takes place in those areas that are designed for this form of experimentation or 'evolution' if you are bold enough to accept that premise!!!

We are, that is the shell we call our Human body of temporary habitation, we are basically of Spirit Substance part of the Life Force that is literally 'Everywhere'. Whether you believe that or not, makes no difference. 'The force of Life' is what makes us what we are, Humans are one aspect of it, Spirits are another, and there are other aspects of it that, up to now we know nothing of, and yet They do exist in Reality! At least that is what I believe! And we do also little brother! Pray continue!!! Well that was a nice intrusion, thank you.

Upon those realms where experimentation is really a continuation of the creative aspect, all the life forms both animate and inanimate, yes even 'inanimate forms' have, or have had life within them!! Well those realms are where 'Blue Prints' that cover this Evolution process are formulated, prior to them being put into practise in reality i.e. upon an existing species upon this Earth of Ours (though the procedure is 'NOT' confined to this Our Planet only! (Food for Thought there!!)

And when you really think about it logically you surely will come to the conclusion that what I have written does make sense!! Just look at it, how on Earth would a created species have the ability to change either itself or part of itself by its own thought will power?! Impossible unless....!

It had been programmed to, after a certain period in its cycle of life expectancy and predetermined duration of that particular species!!!

Now Man!! That's a different evolutionary subject altogether! He creates his own evolution, by consciously changing his circumstances, and life style, by which we mean His Dietary habits! They contribute greatly to his form of evolution. Witness the difference in physical structure through the ages and how today even you can notice the change in the bodily appearance even in a matter of a few years! Then there are 'Wars', which have a great impact on not only people but also the inventions that stem from the conflict. Things that were created for War, can be re-designed for peace time and can make the life style of the various populations much pleasanter, though as usual there's always another side to progress and a price has to be exacted, not always welcome, but nevertheless it has to be taken into account!!

All of the above contributes in no small way to Man's growth and Evolutionary stature!! The Inventions, the Artistic creations of Music, Literature, Sculpture, Painting and not forgetting Medicine, and those people who have what they call 'a calling', the Nurses, the Doctors, the Physicians of not only of the body but also of the Mind!! I suppose I should add Religion or a form of Religious Culture or Faith, though to my mind Religion as such needs a thorough overhaul as to what it is that People feel they 'need' but not necessarily want!!! Now that's an anomaly and no mistake!! Does that signify that something is lacking and has that 'something' to do with the Creator we call GOD!!?

Most people I'm afraid have some very peculiar notions about the Deity and yes, I even include those of the Religious orders themselves!! Many of them secretly question themselves as to what they are expected to preach and teach!!!

No wonder that this world seems in a rather chaotic state at present, and I'm not referring to Nature's bizarre behaviour even though she is not entirely to blame. For Man must also share in this criteria of what is seen to be happening to this once beautiful planet of high expectancy! And by 'Whom' I feel I must add!!!

When the Scientific bodies discuss Man and His place upon this planet and the planets place in the Universe, they give all their glowing theories about what a wonderful creation he is. And then they come to what to many people seems to be an untimely end to their sojourn upon this Plane of Destiny. And what do the scientists and their followers say about the demise of the mortal body of flesh? Is it the END?! Logically speaking it would appear like an irrational ending to all of the effort expended in not only keeping the body alive, but all of the accrued knowledge, and it's no good you saying, 'Well it's passed on to the next generation!!

I find that very cold comfort, when regarding what I think of as ME! But then I'm fortunate for I know that this Mortal Me is but a facet, a dwelling place for the Real Me to exist in, and by

Real Me I'm referring to my SPIRIT! That we ALL have, whether it is accepted or not.

Eventually the Man in the street will I was going to say, will come face to face with his spirit counterpart, but by then he will 'be' His Spirit and will look back upon that physical vehicle he inhabited for that lifetimes journey upon Earth as a worthwhile experience. For it has taught him much about the realities of life upon the dense sphere of Earth that he needed in the furtherance of his evolutionary cycle upon the spiral of ever lasting LIFE!!

The death of the Mortal body is the necessary door that leads to the opening of Spiritual awareness of just what Mankind means in the scheme of, once again I say the word, 'The Almighty.' And you must put your own interpretation on that Statement, for I am sure mine would not go down too well with the majority of people. Because I am very open minded about all things to do with the Esoteric Mysteries of this 'Our Universe' and what it holds captive in its strong embrace, that to many seems like Eternity! And that word needs a lot of thought and explaining, for Eternity is just a thought, of 'commodity' on the part of that Unknowable Essence of Life Force that is held as responsible for 'All' that there is, or has ever been or ever will be!!

And I say to those Scientific sceptics, 'Put that in your pipe and smoke it!!' I don't give a fig for your explanations that do not include the Spirit side of Mankind. Look for what you cannot explain with your noughts and your crosses, use your Inner Feelings of Intuition the ones you have acquired during your constant re-incarnations upon this and other Planets of visionary instruction and learning.

Don't be blinkered by your own, or other's thoughts, just remember NOT everything needs an answer, accept a feeling and you won't go far wrong!! Even if I cannot give you any physical viable verification of what has been written down this day of September 18th in the year 2008!!!

The Little Scribe

I believe what I've been privileged to write, because I know of the source from which these thoughts have come and I accept their authenticity without question!

Think what you will dear readers of this treatise, accept or reject that is your undoubted privilege. I bid you farewell, a fond farewell.

As do We little Brother Scribe. Farewell, a very worthwhile excursion into Thoughts from Near and Afar!!!

Farewell and God bless You.

I add a postscript to the foregoing treatise!
Regarding Man's Free Will.

I did say He also is programmed just like the animals that he calls his brothers!! Well this Free Will we hear so much about, what **exactly is it and where does it reside? You can't see it and** yet it is so often said, 'Use your Free Will'! as if it is a gift bestowed upon us!! So what is it for? Is it to tell us what is right and what is wrong? Is it another word for our conscience? Is it something to do with the Holy Spirit that Jesus spoke about when he was returning to his heavenly abode?

We tend to think that the words 'Free Will' covers many areas, but does it? I think that 'Free Will' has its limitations, there are boundaries that it is not allowed to go beyond. In other words, if you attempt to circumvent that freedom of Will and go beyond what you know is your real limit. Then I feel somehow your other half, your Spiritual side would put a brake on what you were endeavouring to accomplish, and that implies that you were going against what your Free Will was telling you, to Stop! Before it is too late for a retreat!!

There must be a lot more gradations about what the Spirit can **do and can't do regarding the mortal bodies activities, it can't** perform miracles, though we think it can. But after all it's (the Spirit) it's only a form of continuity of the human self is it not?

And as that is an area that I cannot go into, as everyone is an individual in their own right and so I'll end my postscript right here!!

Farewell and thank you for your patience, that is you dear reader!!!

Chapter 31

September 20th 2008

TO BE! OR NOT TO BE! IS THAT A QUESTION?

The above is an oft quoted expression at least the first part is!! The first part is from one of Shakespeare's Plays. The second is just me asking 'Is that a Question?' And I should add a further line 'Is that ME? or NOT ME? and I suppose I can go further and say TO be ME, or is this Me NOT ME at all???! We are such a complex being of the Almighty's Creation it is difficult to come to terms with the fact that this Mortal being that I say is ME is really only a facet of the true Me! and where is that one to be found, and when it is, is that the true one, or just another aspect of the original? And who or what can that be? I venture to say 'The Soul' or should that be the 'Soul Essence'?! and if that is the case then I am an essence of What? Or Whom?

And that poses a very awkward question that needs a straight answer. For we have been informed from ancient scripture that we, that is, Mankind was created in the image of that Illustrious Deity that man has labelled **'GOD'**! So does that make us a part of that sublime One, Meaning are we a 'part' of God? Or are we but a reflection of the Creator, another aspect, another facet, but not actually 'part' of that Deity, shall I say, 'personally'!!?

Have you, the reader of this treatise that I have embarked upon, have you at sometime in your life caught a glimpse of **yourself in a Mirror's reflection and just for a brief moment you** do not recognise the person looking back at you from shall I say,

'A glass darkly?!' For you behold the reflection but the surrounding details seem to be obliterated!! And then, the moment has passed and it is 'You' who is your reflection and the other one is no more!! Quite a conundrum is it not? Who was that reflection that stared back at you with almost a look of unbelief!! As if it was you the onlooker who should not have been visible to the mirrored image!!

Was that stranger another You? from perhaps another dimension? Was he who you would one day become, upon your cycle of the stairway of Evolution?!! And stairway implies steps going up and shall we also say, 'down', or perhaps a better expression would be 'behind you'!!! for you may well be quite a long way up upon that stairway to the stars and beyond!!! If you were in a position to observe this metaphorical stairway, would you perhaps see even more of you?!! And perhaps not even recognisable as who you now think of yourself as ME!!! And yet if, like me you have experienced this brief meeting either in the dream state or in a flash of inspiration of another aspect of yourself, accepted and acknowledged to yourself as 'You' and yet not the same in appearance as you think of yourself as!!!

This other 'You' most likely is from a Higher plane and perhaps you to him might seem as what he knew he once was, and he may well feel of wave of nostalgia for the past!

And if that were so then are We upon this Planet called Earth, are we now in the Past and do not know it!! Is this life that we assume we are living now, are we just shadows of what was, and will one day be no more? Or is it just the minority of those of us who are the seekers and searchers of the mysteries of the Esoteric. Are we the ones who will one day step out from the past and take our rightful place upon what to us may seem like the future but in reality is the NOW! For those other 'YOU' who are in that dimension of the mind that only now and again gives us an insight into what can be, and yet in reality already IS! For that other one of ourselves, that lives not in our imagination but in the Real World of the Spirit!!!

Cast your mind back to the beginning of this treatise and read those words again, 'TO BE! or NOT to BE,' and the answer must come from You. When you have given it earnest thought and your intuition plays its part in helping you to come to a conclusion, that may as yet not be verifiable in shall we say, the orthodox way of thinking. But then, seekers and searchers can never be classed as being of the 'orthodox persuasion'. That is the complete opposite of what you are endeavouring to accomplish. Unravelling the tangled skein of Esoteric knowledge that will guide you along the inner pathway of Spiritual realization and advancement! You have chosen because you have been 'chosen' and we leave you to think about who it might be has done the choosing!!!

We bid you Farewell dear Students for that is what you are in this classroom called Life and we add Which Life??!

And to you dear Brother, We have kept you busy on this fine and sunny morning, and as you so rightly said to yourself out loud. You are indeed very fortunate to be where you are and yes, Who you are!!! And we will leave the rest unsaid, dear, dear, little person, we embrace you as a treasured one of us.

Farewell.

And yes, May Allah be Praised.
May Allah be praised.

Chapter 32

September 21st 2008

SPACE, ILLUSION, REALITY, WHAT IS IN A NAME?

Take up your pen little brother and leave the rest to Us!!! We also say welcome to those of you who maybe the readers of this mornings foray into the realms of Fantasy and Illusion, in other words The Realms of the Worlds that you know of as 'The Spirit'!! A word that to some means occult occurrences that they have heard about but as yet cannot be verified to their satisfaction!! Quite understandable and we accept that form of criticism, but with reservations, and they are, that 'We know' what we say is the Truth for we have verified it for ourselves by the mere fact that 'We Are Spirit' and do dwell upon the planes of those Worlds!

And yes, they are Worlds, though perhaps not as you upon Earth think, that Worlds are all the same, in shall we say, Constructive of Cosmic Matter!! You at present dwell upon one of dense heavy matter, yet that is Not the heaviest of Cosmic matter by any means!! There are many degrees of matter, that cannot be pigeon holed into a certain formula of what your Scientists would call 'Primordial Chaos' before it has been shaped into a visible form known as Planets. And even then Planets as such can vary in their density as to be, we were going to say, invisible to the naked eye and we add 'of Man', that is the Human variety, if you follow our meaning!!

For Man as such is also variable in His construction and that is depending upon his natural place of habitation!! Earthman has been constructed as it were to function in a natural way upon the plane of Earth, while we, to give you an example, are of the Spirit essence that has a natural affinity with the Worlds of the Spirit. And yet we can also 'function' as it were upon many other planes, yours included, but we do not dwell permanently shall we say, upon them in a 'natural fashion'. Meaning that we can adapt and yes, adopt a likeness of a human identity when we wish, and that could come under the heading of 'Illusion'!!

That is for those who can 'see' us via their mental awareness of psychic abilities!! And if we say 'Clairvoyancy', read that in its broadest of terms to cover all of the phenomena of the Esoteric senses!!! You follow? Good!! We proceed. Now there are other 'forms' (another loose expression!) other forms that come under the heading of the Humanities and yet they are also of a High Spiritual nature, which allows them to fluctuate between many spheres that are quite different from their original one!!! By actually becoming through thought manipulation identical to those indigenous populations of the sphere that they are visiting!!! More 'illusion' but with a strong sense of 'reality'!! They blend in and are therefore accepted without question!!!

There are so many variations of the created species you upon Earth could identify with!! But you may as it were, suffer from 'comparison'! Man it would seem is Not as He thinks He is, the Highest form of Creation, and if we add of the 'Animal Kingdom' and we state a fact not a criticism!!!

For after all We who are inspiring the writer of this treatise were 'once' the same as you are!!! But with countless incarnations we are Now entirely Spirit Essence and there are even more shall we say, 'Essences' that we will become as we progress upon the Spiral of Spirit Evolution!!!

So there is much for you upon Earth to sample as you grow into maturity and yes that you are 'heir to'! By the grace of, we shall say 'GOD'!!! Such is the complexity of 'Overall Creation' and the Many 'Creators' that have their part to play in this Your Universe of Evolution and Experimentation! And do Not despise that word, for experimentation is all part of the cycle of growth and its ultimate objective.

'PERFECTION!!!' And you already know of our previous thoughts on that subject!!! When Man has learnt to accept the fact that This World is not the only one that he can and will eventually inhabit, it is the natural and pre-ordained destiny of all forms of Creation, if they are to progress and not stagnate because of their inability to see 'further than the end of their nose'!! Another fact and not a criticism!!!

Just remember, you 'DO' have a place in the overall scheme of Created Creativity regardless of who the 'Creative Geniuses' may be!!! Keep an OPEN MIND, regarding just about everything, and do not be frightened of Questioning what you may not quite understand! You may not get the answer you are hoping for, or even an answer at all, but don't let that stop you from your searching!

For that is progress in its subtlest of forms, so don't be daunted or put off by what others may tell you that you should know about! You are your own Judge and Jury, keep it that way, you probably know far more than you give yourself credit for!!! And also bear in mind That illusion can pass for reality and reality quite often has an air of illusion about it!! Keep your feet upon the ground even when your head metaphorically speaking, is in the Air!!!

We think that this may be a good time for the little scribe to put away his writing implement and relax for awhile!! And so here is where we depart, but not for long we have been told!!!

Yes I am back, with my pen in my hand and ready for the inspiration that I know will be forthcoming!!

We started off this discourse with the words 'Fantasy and Illusion' and we cannot get away from those two words when we are discussing Creation and what it means! Upon Earth, Man looks around him and marvels at what he sees! That is what he says 'God has created'. And we find no criticism in those sentiments, But 'God' (if you like) God did not just stop there, and by 'there' we are talking of your World in general!! What about the Space that surrounds all of those Cosmic identities? The Stars, The Planets, The Cosmic Debris resulting from the formation of those Planets and Worlds etc!

And what about the deep, deep Space that has so far alluded your attempts at forthcoming what it contains and we add 'If Anything!!!' So much of what could be termed as 'visible' to your Scientists, actually is not even there!

It was, but not now! You perceive what your senses tell you should be there and in a way it is!! But the reality of that statement is that what is seen is a photographic mirage of something that Was and no longer IS! Just a memory upon the Universe's canvas of Illusion, that remains to tantalize scientists and their colleagues until they find that the reality of what they think they see is not a reality at all. But a Cosmic imprint upon the Mind of the Universe and like all things of the past will one day be not even that!!!

Some of those hidden Suns and Moons and Stars in their galactic splendour, that at present are beyond Man's comprehension will one day come forth and be revealed and take the place that was at one time vacated by those other Cosmic Identities, leaving just a memory and nothing more!! But be not deceived by what Space allows you to see, for 'Now you see it, and Now you do not!!!' Look not for what you can see, but look with the inner sight of Intuition and feeling, and the reality of your efforts could be exceedingly rich in understanding what 'LIFE' really is and what it means not only to you but also to the Creators of it!!!

For they really do weald the Power of Life and Death in all of its multiple faceted Illusion of, yes!! 'Reality and Illusion.' You have been warned, so be on your guard when you think you have solved one riddle for there's always another to take its place!!!

Some things dear friends upon the Earth are best left alone until the age when Man can accept His Destiny and not be shattered by the knowledge of it!!

And that will be a very, very, very long time coming to Earthman and Woman!! And here really is where we say we will depart from this excursion into the thought pattern of that little person who is called a Scribe!! We've known of Him for a very long time, even though he is unaware of when and where we were once companions upon a very different voyage of discovery!! And one not of this, his present World!!!

We depart and say Farewell to you the students of Esoteric Knowledge.

And to you Brother it is not Goodbye or even Farewell, but just a parting until next time!!!

Chapter 33

September 24th 2008

THOUGHTS! THOUGHTS! THOUGHTS!!

These are going to be My thoughts at least that is how they are going to start off! And here I am going to give you a sort of warning!! Reason being that some people might call them 'Heretical' and yet that is Not my intention. Please believe that for I am sincere in what I write and after all they are only my thoughts, and no one else is to blame if they cause offence to anyone who has positive feelings about certain events that have shaped the Destiny of this Planet that we call Earth!!!

I've often thought that we are perhaps rather insular in our feelings and thought patterns regarding Our place in the Universe. And if we really are as important as we tend to think we are, taking into consideration that we have no other world like Planet that we could compare ourselves with! That is why I say we are very 'insular' because without a comparable Planet that boast a habitable population of Human like beings as ourselves, we just cannot use the word 'compare' justifiably, can we?!

What I am getting at is that Our Historic past, present, and hopefully future is all that we actually know with positive verifiable evidence about Our World.

And so we seem to be Blinkered as it were to the possibility that somewhere Out there in Space there maybe Worlds of habitable existence with perhaps a species similar to our own, but of a far Higher Intellect and Spiritual awareness that would pale us into insignificance in comparison!!

We talk about God, as if 'He'! is the Only creative force in this Universe of Ours and 'Ours' is not the correct word to denote our position in it! For it is 'NOT' 'OURS' by any means, we are only but a fraction of Created Life Force in the form of a Planet and what it holds!! So we cannot legitimately call it 'Our Universe' we only dwell within its confines like all of the other life forms that I firmly believe Do exist in the so-called 'Space'. Which if you could really 'See' it as it is, you would be amazed at what it contains, and by contains I mean 'Visible and Invisible' creations that we are totally unaware of!!

Thinking of what our Ancient scriptures and Religious Cultures have handed down to us regarding this World and the visible Heavens above it with the Stars and Galactic Stella like objects. That we label as Meteors, Cosmic Debris, Meteorites, and all sorts of dubious appendages that go to 'make up' this Section that our World occupies. But what about those as yet Unexplored Avenues of Space that beckon the Scientists to try and infiltrate with their rather crude and definitely outdated methods of motivation that could so easily end up as even more Cosmic Debris! If they only knew it!!!

To put it into today's vernacular 'There's another World Out there' Metaphorically and Theoretically speaking!!!

We are but amateurs in this discovery business of Cosmic identity!! There are 'others' 'out there' so far advanced in their knowledge and Thinking capacities, that 'we' are really hardly worth a mention!!! And that is the crux of the matter, we are insular not only in our habits but also our 'Thinking'!!! We have Brains! But are they used to their full ability? I venture to say NO! they are Not!! Perhaps though, we have not been programmed to take into account those areas that Man has given labels to in the hope that one day He will be able to tap into what for now, seems like forbidden territory!!!

Now I come to what might be considered as Heretical **thoughts by someone who doesn't know what he is talking about**!! A valid criticism I grant you for I have no verifiable evidence to back up my Theoretical thinking. Still I shall plod on in my endeavours to try and understand my thoughts on the subject, of whether Our God who we can only talk about in an **abstract fashion, Can 'He' be the 'God' of the Whole of this Universe or perhaps just a part of it?** And is 'He' an Aspect of that Unknowable Force of Life creativity that we just cannot put a name to let alone offer up a description of what this Force really is!!

It is beyond our Mental capacity of comprehension and that is probably our salvation if we really knew it. For to acquire such knowledge would I fear result in complete annihilation of our very life force, we would no doubt be absorbed into the very force we are endeavouring to penetrate. Our identity no longer, to **behold, we are but 'nothing' just a part or particle of that Force** that cannot be identified as anything we will ever be aware of.

A Force that IS! That Was! And Ever Shall be!!

So does that mean that in some way we should reconsider our pre-conceived ideas about God, or Gods, or as some would have it NO GOD at All!! And I for one most certainly do NOT go **along with that assumption for Creation to be Created 'Must'** have a Creator, whatever name you wish to identify that Creator as!!!

All I am trying to say is that we should try and think in the broadest of terms and not be held back by what we have been told to believe and accept. The idea of GOD and Creation and **Life or rather Lives must not be confined and labelled as 'such and such'!** Life in all of its complexities is so Vast and the Vision of it so hampered by pre-conceived notions, that we must step out upon uncharted territory and accept, I was going to say, the 'unacceptable', but that would be wrong, only accept what 'You' feel is right for 'You'.

And if you think I have left out things of great importance, then I say to you What I have left Unsaid is what is really important, for I have left you to fill in the Blanks with your own interpretations. And that way I feel I have not knowingly or **willingly upset people's feelings** upon subjects that perhaps cannot be explained with words but wi**th feeling's 'Inner feelings'**. And to be quite truthful I myself have not allowed my deep, deep inner thoughts to surface, because I would not know where to go from there if they did!! I accept my own limitations and know that when the time is right I shall know what I do know, yet hesitate to acknowledge it now in this life!

By which you may infer that it will be in my other one that my Thoughts will be awakened as part of my ongoing evolutionary spiral of Spiritual awareness!!!

I leave you there and wish **you God's blessings in your** searching after the truth, which no doubt when you find it, will lead you to even more facets of that illusive commodity Truth, in its many disguises!!

Farewell, Farewell it is now my turn to voice that sentiment!

And dear Brother we say to you A fond Farewell for your earnest endeavours, which dear friend have been entirely Yours with no added help from Us, just a thought participation of **genuine endearment for your brave efforts** upon this morning's treatise.

Farewell dear Friend and Brother, Farewell.

We are joined by many others who wish you well and also call you Brother!!!

Chapter 34

September 27th 2008

THOUGHTS THAT COME AND GO!!!

I'm sitting here in the sunshine enjoying a very pleasant Autumnal day, and not thinking about anything in particular. And then I started to think about one of my previous incarnations, not exactly the whole of it, in fact only a brief aspect of it. Namely a Knight in Silver Armour who was larger than life (meaning my present day size!) and who in the course of conversation with me (via my mind) turned out to be 'Me' and he couldn't quite understand why I was so small and of no importance! I won't go any further than that because I have written that account before in one of my books!

But it has set me thinking about those other aspects of me that have, shall I say 'Had their day' or rather 'life' and are now just a cosmic memory and 'surface' as it were every now and then!! But I feel I'm wrong in thinking that, and I'll give you the reason for that turn around in my thinking pattern! It's probably all theoretical on my part, and I'm not sure how I'm going to write about it so we'll have to wait and see what this pen of mine puts down on this paper!!

Well, I know that the Soul (that is Mine I'm talking about!) well the Soul does create for its own purpose of knowledge and understanding several 'facets' of Spirit substance.

Each an identity in its own right so to speak, and each one for a different plane of existence that culminates in the one that interpenetrates with this Earth of ours! Now I believe that not all of the 'Spirit identities' are shall I say of 'Human like' form. Some I believe are in a slumbering embryonic Aura surrounded state, awaiting the time when they may be called to assume an identity that the Soul feels it needs for a particular purpose!!

Those Spirit Identities that I have mentioned that have a 'human like form' I now think live an almost parallel life to the one I live upon this Planet!! A life not in the least like my earth one, but one that is compatible with its surroundings upon which it dwells!! I keep saying 'IT' though I know its another aspect of Me, but I can't keep saying 'Me' when I'm speculating on their various existences!!! And 'speculating' could also be theorizing because I can't give you any verifiable proof only what I get through feelings!!

And here I'm presuming that some of the spheres that these various aspects are upon, are of a 'Spirit Nature' and not a material one like our own, and yet I feel that the life that 'goes on' on and within these spheres does have some sort of affinity with ours!! I wonder if some of these 'spheres' are 'perceptions' of the mind? 'Theirs' not mine!! I hasten to add! Now that seems strange as I write it. Do Spheres (not all of them!) do they have 'areas' upon them that are in a way an extension of the original and where 'One' may either visit or stay, mentally or 'physically' shall I say? Depending upon the degree of Spiritual advancement.

'Life' I am being told, surpasses anything I can possibly imagine, their spheres of Existence are on the Spirit Level, ranging from, shall I say the one we are aware of, to those much Higher that culminate at the Soul Plane. Where after that they are so High that very little is actually known about them that could be passed on to we who dwell upon the lower plane of Earth! For we would not be able to comprehend what it was that we were being told or Shown!

As for the 'Spheres below' the Soul plane itself their degrees of Plasticity are almost beyond belief! One of them is so ethereal, it is like living in a dream world, for it is governed as it were by **'Moons' and Not Suns.** And so the quality of life is more upon a Mental plane, life is one of exquisite harmony for all around above and below there is an air of tranquil beauty. People and animals and Birds have an air of fragility about them, as if a strong breeze would blow them away. They are almost translucent with an Aura of subdued colours that reflect the Moons rays of Silver and palest of Gold.

Time here is devoted to the study of the Mind and its intellectual powers of intuitive thoughts that can be as it were, passed on to the adjacent spheres that form the evolutionary chain or Spiral that goes down, as well as up depending upon your degree of understanding!!! I wonder which one of Me is upon that plane of endeavour?!! And how long will it be before I become Him?!! **Further 'down' there is another sphere of** comprehension that resembles the earth in many ways, but has not the heavy matter that governs our Planet!

This one has many beautiful cities of cultural attainment, where experience is one of reality, by which I mean if for instance you were viewing a beautiful picture, you would experience what the artist felt when he or she were painting what it is you are viewing. You would if you wished become almost a part of the picture. **And the same applies to everything around you, you 'are'** part of what you see, you belong as it were to not only the seen Creation but to the Creator of it as well. For that is what this sphere is all about, it is to show you that you are literally part of All Creation and what affects you affects it!! and Vice-Versa!!

Upon this sphere the physical you is not like the physical you of the Earthplane and yet you are aware that there is a link and a very strong one. This plane is one whose predominate colour is Gold in all of its multiple shades from deepest to palest, and here **the Sun's, for there are three of them, never sets! When one** sleeps, the other two are alert and so it goes on and night-time is but a reflected glow, Life is one of gentle awareness of everything that exists.

And the combined thought waves of the inhabitants surround this plane with peace and harmony. Here dwell the Thinkers, the Artists, the Creators and those with the highest ideals and their aims are to help those upon the lower spheres to try and see what God is all about in their lives!!! Wonder who I will be on that plane? Oh, it's just occurred to me 'He' has influenced me in my artistic endeavours!!

I've often wondered about who inspires me in my paintings for I know 'it' can't all be down to me, because I'm very surprised when I see the finished picture!! I haven't painted for a long time so what I've written pertains to the past!!! There are more, I am told Spheres that is or should that read perceptions? For some interpenetrate with others and are looked upon by the indigenous population as a form of Dream state or world and yet they are a reality, though I believe they (the spheres I mean!) come and go!

In other words at times they become invisible and I don't know why! On these spheres there is One, NO!! Two of ME that know of each other and also of Me upon the Earth, but they put this down to the Dream state, meaning to 'them' that is what our World appears to be!! I've never thought that before!!!

I have seen one of those 'Me', but I don't know which one He is!! Then there's another Spirit Plane adjoining the one we know about and there is a Spirit Version of Me dwelling on that plane, He seems to Mirror my life pattern, But! With one big exception He never does the wrong thing, He always does the Right and Good things, where I would dither about right or wrong, this is Never an issue with Him. I think He influences the 'Spirit side' of Me who in turn tries to do the same for me, not always I'm afraid with a satisfactory result!! On my part that is!!! Trial and Error, it's a great way to learn about life, even if it's hard at times and it's only in retrospect that you perhaps see the error of your ways! That's 'Me' I'm talking about not You!!!

So what has all of this thinking and writing taught Me? That there's a great deal I don't know about not only Life but also about Me! as a person or should I qualify that and say, Persons!!! I wonder just how many of those Spirit Aspects of Me that the Soul has created will survive intact. Or perhaps I presume as I get Higher I'll exchange the one I am at the next stage, for the One who is waiting for me to step out of the old Me and enter the more Spiritual One?!! Well done little Brother!! You're getting there eventually so go on with your 'Soul searching' and you do know what we mean!!!

Well!! I think that means I had better give my Thoughts a rest for the time being, and as it's now my bedtime it's a good enough excuse to say Goodnight and Farewell. And yes, God bless!!

Ron the Little Scribe!!!

It's now Sunday morning the 28th of September!! I've been 'wandering' and not really thinking, What exactly do our lives upon all of the various spheres of reality, and also of comprehension, What do they mean to the 'Creator' of 'All of This'!!? And by 'This' I mean All of Creation in its Entirety both here and Elsewhere and that really encompasses not only This Universe but all of the others that we have no knowledge of, at least I suppose I should say that is Mortal Man!! For I do believe those upon the Higher Realms of Spiritual awareness have access as it were, to 'Realms' beyond our Universe's outer perimeter!!

And when I say 'Realms' I have a feeling that there are Realms or Worlds, or Planets if you like that exist in the Space that is beyond that aforementioned perimeter, but are NOT in a particular Universe of encampment if you can follow me!! In other words they exist in that Space that is Everywhere and yet they are as it were, anchored to a particular 'Orbital Belt' just like the Planets etc. that are in our Universe! These 'Free' shall I say, 'Spirits' and here I'm referring to the Realms or Spheres and 'Not' to the indigenous populations to be. They are 'Not' as it were, confined to a Universe's Law of procedure!!

They are Embryonic Nuclei of what they are to become when they are harnessed to their allotted Universe of Expectation! And so the Higher Spirit Forms that I previously mentioned become the Forerunners as it were, of the New untried Souls that are to populate the various Realms I have hinted at!! They are to be of a much finer and highly Spiritual Species of Twin Soul personalities, each separate and yet truly One!!

They are literally to be the 'Gods' in the making, the Future Creators of Many, Many different species of Semi Human like beings that will find their way to various Worlds and Planets on multiple Universes! And here I'm told to say that Not All Universes are the same in Size or content! Some may only hold shall I say, 'a handful' of Planets, but those Planets herald the Dawn of a completely New Form of Creation and here I am told, No Further little Scribe, For all of the previous information is in the 'Lap of the Gods'!!! And we and you are not privy to their as yet Unborn Thoughts on any of the subjects aforementioned!!

We encourage you little scribe to cease your writing of those thoughts of yours that have wandered into unknown and forbidden territory. We know you understand and we bid you Farewell, let this be the end of your thinking for today and yesterday!

Farewell dear little soul, we bid you a loving farewell.

May Allah be Praised!!

We also leave you in His Care little chela, be content and know that you are known, so be it!!

Farewell!!!

Chapter 35

October 9th 2008

WHAT DO YOU NEED?!!

Well little Brother, you have at last decided to pick up your pen and wait for inspiration!! And so we bid you welcome, and now relax your mind and let us take charge of it for just a little while!! Are you ready? Then here is where we begin and you, shall we say, mentally take a rest!!!

So much about your World at this time needs explaining, but explanations are not always to the liking of those who are listening to them! But they need to be aired and viewed as it were, **from an outsider's point of view.** You have, it would seem to our way of thinking gone a little too far in your universal pursuit of what you call happiness!! To be quite frank your whole idea of what that word encompasses needs to be re-evaluated and put into its correct perspective!! What constitutes happiness? You will **no doubt look around you at 'things' of a material nature, in other words 'possessions'.**

Now of themselves that is not a bad thing, but! It all depends on what effect they have upon you as a person!!! You may feel, well they give you a sense of security and pleasure, but do they? If you really think about it and yes, look at these worldly goods in the right perspective!! To most people they have to work hard to **achieve what they believe is the right 'life style' for them and yes,** also for their family!!

Credit must be given to those who are the 'breadwinners' for so much seems to rest upon their shoulders, but is all of this worry and instability the price that has to be paid, for this so-called Life Style?

Do those worldly goods and chattels really bring you peace of mind and complete satisfaction? Or are they just temporary stepping stones to yet more acquisitions that are to fill the gaps in the ever increasing vacuum of 'Must Have'! Do you really <u>need</u> all of those 'props' to create a sense of happiness and well being? Well do you?!!! And if you are really truthful in your answer to yourself you will have to admit that No! they are not 'All' needed. In fact 'need' is completely the wrong word you attribute to those possessions for more than what they actually warrant, when it comes to what is really important to your well being, which includes those around you in your immediate family circle!!

You are if you have not already realized it being 'Brain Washed', by those little and not so little screens that seem to dominate your lives, whether of leisure time or even at your place of work!! So-called 'progress' has a very heavy price to pay for what it produces! You do know what we mean, You Don't NEED a quarter of what those insidious adverts tell you you should, by rights have, to give you a liveable lifestyle!!! In a way it's pandering to your insatiable appetite of 'must have'!! It's another name for GREED!! And think about that word!! It's probably one that you have never thought applies to you personally, but never-the-less it is GREED!! Whichever way you chose to look at it!!!

And has it produced lasting happiness?! Think about it and think hard!! You'll probably find that the answer is in the negative! For it isn't lasting, it's forever in need of 'topping up' and that should make you think about those words again. Do you really 'NEED' this and that to satisfy your craving for a life style that mirrors those that are shown upon your television screens as the only one that should be considered as acceptable!!! And you know very well that to try and ape those 'life styles' is <u>not</u> very practical when it comes to the reality of 'real life'!!

What with 'Designer labels' upon practically everything you see in the shops, as if having something with a 'Name' attached to it makes any difference to the article or piece of clothing. It's all for 'SHOW' and it is you who is doing the showing and that is mainly to impress others with your ability to afford these so-called desirable objects!! And just how many parents have to scrimp and scrape to oblige those who are following the current trend!!

We are all 'individuals' and we ought to be proud of that fact and not try to be one of the 'Herd'!! Be 'Yourself' and no one else! Have the 'guts' to stand upright on your own two feet. It may be hard but it's the right thing to do, if you really want to live your own life and not be a meek follower of others with stronger wills than you think you may have!!!

And now we come to this 'Financial Crisis' that is affecting the whole of your Planet. Perhaps this is very necessary if you did but know it. Your Monetary institutions that you call Banks and Building Societies have for far too long been run on a basis of 'Risk'.

They take risks in a fashion of pure 'recklessness', there again 'Greed' rears its ugly head!! The same applies to these 'Stocks and Shares' that pander to that same word, regardless of any moral obligations of the instigators when feathering their own nest at the expense of others!!! Words written on Paper and what do they signify? Nothing when it boils down to it.

It's all a form of 'game' a hideous charade of make believe, and that very often with the lives and livelihood of shall we say, the 'gullible sections' of society who wish to believe what they are being told, or should that be What they are being SOLD!!! And the price is definitely not peace of Mind for anyone!! Least of all those whose savings are put at risk, and for what? To get something for Nothing!! But it doesn't work!! At least not for those who are doing the speculating!

There is always a price tag associated with this idea of something for nothing! You get what you pay for and though you are lending your money, even your savings in the hope of getting a good return for the effort, it's one thing to get what should be considered a fair amount of interest and that should be acceptable. But to expect more than a 'fair amount' once again that ugly word 'Greed' creeps in!! For to get and expect more than a 'fair amount' means that the risk you are taking is bound to be just that, a Risk!! For all parties concerned!! And you are now witnessing for yourselves what that risk involves!! And to be quite honest with you, 'Is it worth it?!!

This global shakeup of this whole system is to make you, that means All of you, to reconsider what this form of 'Monopoly' game is all about!! It all boils down to what it is in life that brings peace and security to it! And though we accept that the monetary system is a necessary part of what you consider is a 'decent life style' in this day and age, there will come a time when the idea of money exchange will no longer be the 'order of the day'!! You, that is those who are running this system will have to 'come up' with a viable alternative, a system that is 'Fair' for All concerned. The Labourer must be recompensed for his 'Hire'.

Whatever the alternative may be, and that should go through the whole system from 'start to finish!' From 'top to bottom!' Your Nations will come through this present turmoil but they will have to have a completely different outlook, nothing is going to be the same as it was. And that dear friends will ultimately be your 'Salvation'. Believe that for it is the Truth that we tell you. Your whole form of 'Priorities' must be overhauled.

If you must continue with this money system then 'Get it Right!' Do not seek an easy way out of your present dilemma. Your whole world is metaphorically speaking, 'Shrinking'!! You

The Little Scribe

cannot isolate yourselves from your neighbours. For what affects one indirectly, affects all eventually, can you not see that? Put this 'House of Yours in Order!' before you seek to explore parts of your Universe that are out of your reach, and will continue to remain so, by the 'Keepers', of what we shall call the 'Stability of Multi Unification of all Planets of Physical Habitation'!!!

And read into that what you will! You cannot alter 'their' decisions regarding Mortal Man's feeble endeavours of what he calls exploration of the Cosmos!! When he has proved to 'Them' that he is worthy, morally worthy in every sense of the word and can be Trusted! Then, and only Then will be given the facilities and knowledge of how and 'where' he will be allowed to pierce the Curtain of Cosmic Density that will reveal to him untold Wonders of Creation. 'The Creations' of the Gods of Creativity of which he has no knowledge of at present, though there are some upon your Planet who have pierced that curtain and returned but have sworn to remain silent about their discoveries. Until they are told the 'Time is Right' for them to divulge what they have been privileged to observe!! Their knowledge will be passed on when their transition takes place. So that the secrets will not be lost to the future generations!!

We feel that we will now cease this discourse, because we have been asked to do so. Take heed of what has been written and know that Those who need to Know how to resolve your present problems are being inspired from above and within to put into place, at least for the time being, plans that can be worked upon for the benefit of All.

We will now withdraw from the Scribe's thought mechanism and thank him for his endeavours on our behalf. We bid you brethren of the Earth, Farewell.

And to you Brother, Farewell and much love from those who have your welfare at heart. Farewell little friend, Farewell.

Chapter 36

October 12th 2008

IS THERE AN ANSWER?!!!

God, = God's, and then = God!!! So then Creation equals Creations, equals Creation! And that last word 'Creation' is synonymous with shall we say, The overall Creator? Or the Creator of all that there is, and we add 'Visible' and also 'Invisible' and all of the 'in-between areas' that may well encompass both of those aspects!! For there must be in-betweens, that we have no prior knowledge of, and shall we say, at present!!!?

The word 'GOD' seems to be the one Universal word that is understood by all peoples the world over. Even when a name other than that one, is used by different cultures to denote the Deity that they believe is responsible for all of the seen aspects or facets that they associate with that unknowable One!! Though in some cultures they do aspire to create shall we say, a 'physical' or 'material' likeness of identification for their own personal reasons!!

While in other cultures the Deity of their choice is represented in an 'abstract form', because of their feeling of reverence for what to them is an unknowable force of Life personified. And therefore should remain as it were unattainable and unknowable and also remain a source of mystery that should not be even attempted to be explained!!!

And if you care to think about it, who are we to even venture down that avenue of thought that might lead us not only to a derangement of the mind, but also to our own destruction as a mortal human being!! There are 'things' that we are not intended to know about, or even to question let alone expect an answer!!! We are but mortal, even when we return to Spirit with our cloak of immortality, we just cannot comprehend the complexity of what The Eternal Unknowable Life Force consists of!! We have absolutely 'Nothing' with which to judge it by!!

And yet! We are given and allowed to 'see' as it were, An Aspect a facet of that incomprehensible Source of All that there is or ever was, or ever shall be, in our 'God of our choice'. We 'see' or understand our God through not only our inner sight and feelings, but in the many wonders that exist around us that we can consciously attribute to our 'God'. Perhaps a scientific person would endeavour to, as he would no doubt say 'Put you straight' upon the subject of creation and the so-called evolutionary process that has resulted in Man / Woman, beast, bird and fishes to name but a few of those wonders we spoke of!!!

Science says it deals in logic and verifiable circumstances, but logic can sometimes become quite 'illogical' when trying to explain Mankind and his place in the Universe. That is the one we see with our telescopic lenses and outlandish probes! But! They seem to ignore completely the immortal side of Man, and we speak of 'HIS SPIRIT', and that is exactly who 'we are'!!

All of us, even those sceptics who will one day find out just what the 'Real Truth' is regarding those two components that go to make up who we are!!! For without our Spirit partner and guide to carry on with what has been learnt by mortal man during his life's journey upon earth, then it would appear almost like a waste of effort on his part if all of that learning would become as naught. When Death overtakes the physical image and releases the immortal Spirit to continue the life's journey upon another plane of existence!

And we are putting aside in this treatise the argument regarding offspring and their part in perpetuating what the parents have contributed to posterity! If anything!!!! We are dealing with the individual here and not with the mass of humanity at large!!!

When dealing in the broadest of terms with Mankind you just cannot ignore the Spirit side of this joint venture upon this plane of Earth!! All religions it seems have this desire to believe in the existence of another world that we go to at the transition of the mortal body of flesh!! So why do most people fight shy of expressing their inner thoughts on the subject of the World of the Spirit and 'those' who inhabit it?!! If they really believe that one day they will go to this other world, this 'after life' as some will call it, why not try and find out more about it while they are still upon this physical one? If you go abroad on a holiday you try and find out as much as you can about the country of your choice. And that, regarding the holiday period is usually only a matter of a few weeks or even months!

Well, if you do that for a holiday, doesn't it make sense that where you are going to when you leave your physical body behind, you ought to try and find out more about it? For let's face it, This will be 'your new life's pattern' whether you believe that or not, it makes no difference, you are 'here' upon the Spirit plane for the foreseeable future and there's no going back to the Earthplane. At least 'not yet', but we do not intend to pursue that avenue of thought in this treatise. There are many books upon that subject so visit your libraries and see for yourself!!

So where has all of this thinking taken us to?! We started off with GOD = GODs = GOD!! And that is where we will end this treatise. Whether you believe in One GOD, or many GODS or NONE AT ALL! It doesn't alter the fact that CREATION has to have a CREATOR, to make it work, doesn't it? So it is now up to you, either go forward with your thinking or if you wish do not think at all! Makes no difference to the outcome as one day you will find out for yourselves. Just as We have done! Though not all of us needed to!!!

And so we bid you a fond farewell and hope that we have given you something to think about!!

Little Brother Scribe!! Need we say it? Yes we will, Farewell dear friend, farewell and may God bless you and your thoughts. Farewell.

And yes, May Allah look kindly upon you little friend of both worlds!!

Chapter 37

October 17th 2008, Morning

THOUGHTS! ABOUT WHAT?!!!

I am sitting outside in the warm Autumn sunshine and what follows is, how shall I put it? A journey? Well, not exactly, my eyes were closed and then I became aware that I, that is me, not the physical one I must add and yet I was aware of my 'body' but it wasn't my usual one! I was standing upright and in front of me was not what I thought I was going to see, I was expecting a 'tunnel', like people describe when they have a near death experience!!

What I beheld was not a tunnel but an archway with a vaulted ceiling that extended into the distance, the ceiling was blue and covered in what looked like diamonds. But they were tiny star-like incandescent lights almost like living glow-worms and the aroma of attar of Roses mingled with sandalwood made me feel quite heady. And then I was aware of two figures, one on each side of me, but to describe them I cannot, for there was an Aura of such brilliance that I could barely see their form. Somehow I felt a gentle pressure on my arms as if they were escorting me along what now seemed to me, like an aisle in a cathedral.

At the far end I could see a golden glow and as we approached it, I could see that the glow was from outside.

And the pair of doors which were of a glass-like substance covered in a golden filigree of ornate leaves opened and we were then outside of this temple, and beholding a breath taking view of what I took to be a garden. But it stretched so far into the distance that I thought I was mistaken. There were trees that seemed to bend and sway gently as if being caressed by a breeze that didn't exist as far as I could make out. They looked like umbrellas of palest green leaves that shimmered and sparkled and turned to emerald green and then back again. And all the time I could hear children's voices and laughter, but I only sensed them I didn't see them, though I felt they were playing at hide and seek and it was they who caused the trees to almost dance when they swayed back and forth.

The light was so bright yet quite soft to the eyes and it had a quality of almost healing about its gentle rays that I could feel upon my skin! So I must have had a body of sensations but was it mine?! Yes it was, but one of the many others that go to make up the original me I've just been told!!

My two companions were still with me as we seemed to glide over the moss-like earth that my feet touched every now and then, and it was like deep piled velvet and most pleasant. I glanced down at my 'body' and found that I too, had an Aura of translucent vapour, I feel it was partly from my companions and not all of my own 'making!!' We left the area of land and glided over a lake of palest lavender in colour, towards an island that seemed to be suspended above the water!

I later learned that this island which was a Holy Sanctuary of Divine Thought, actually moved about in a gentle circular rhythmic pattern, covering the whole of the lakes surface. And when night fell it could be seen glowing and leaving a trail of luminosity behind it, and the lilting sound that emanated from the island's Sanctuary seemed to linger upon the luminous trail that was left behind!!!

I must now go back to when my two companions and I alighted upon the floating island. We were greeted by saffron robed monks and escorted to a small building where we were given robes to put on, and our feet washed and sandaled and then given what I thought was water, but hardly had it touched my lips than I went into a deep dreamless sleep. When I awoke my two companions were sitting beside me smiling gently, it seemed that they had not had the same drink as me. For they, I found out later, were the assigned companions whose mission was to care for those whose transition from mortal to immortal had been arranged, but I was not told by whom!!!

I said I fell into a 'dreamless sleep' but I feel I was wrong, because though I didn't think I had 'dreamt' every now and again I get a faint remembrance of 'something' that had happened to me. It was to do with the saffron robed monks and someone or something else that was Bright with Light, and what else? I wish I could remember. I've just been told it was to do with your future and we are not allowed to say anything more on that subject dear friend.

And so I suppose this is where I have to end my glimpse of something I'm destined to experience, but when? I wonder!!

So I will end this morning's thoughts and questions that have no immediate answers as far as I am concerned!!! So shall I say Farewell? Might as well, even if this is all about me and I don't think it will be part of another book! But there again Who knows!!!

After reading this over I've a feeling that it is my transition from one dimension to the next! Home at last!!

Chapter 38

October 24th, 9 p.m., 2008

SPECULATION!!!
IS THERE AN ANSWER?!!

What are my Thoughts? For as yet I haven't decided to have any!! And yet if I sit here with my pen in my hand, then I'm bound to end up writing something, even if at the close of, shall I call it a chapter? It will probably turn out to be thoughts from outside of myself, it usually is!!! I'm glad to say!! Well Brother, you are quite right, so prepare yourself to relinquish your thought mechanism and allow us to take it over once again!!!

And so here begins our treatise for tonight. And we shall call it Speculation!! And the speculation is to do with Mortal Man's desire to know more about what to many is called, 'The after life'. The majority of most of earth's populations have very varied ideas about this so-called other life that carries on when this one comes to an end, that is for the mortal being whose cloak of identification is his garment of Flesh!!! And that garment is not needed upon this next sphere that you call the Spirit World. In fact it could not even exist upon that sphere of enlightenment, unlike its Spirit companion of this life times incarnation!! For Spirit has the ability to be able to function upon both planes of habitation, and it would seem both at the same time if it wishes!!

So how is that possible you may ask, if the Spirit can do that, Why cannot the Mortal being called Man have the same ability? Well, you do know the answer to that don't you?! Man is Mortal and his garment of flesh is only suitable for this dense Planet upon which he resides it is only programmed to last for One lifetime, and no more!! However much he may wish it could continue, and yet you know, it does! Via the Spirit connection **that has been the mortal man's** constant companion for his whole physical lifetime!!

Spirit is the guiding force for both itself and its protégé, even if to many people that idea does not seem feasible to them, and why? Well physical man does not as yet have the ability to **actually 'see' his** lifelong companion, he perhaps sometimes has a feeling, an inner feeling that there is more to himself than he is physically aware of. But to be able to say with certainty that this feeling can be equated with an entity that he cannot see, but only **'sense' if pressed upon the subject by an observer who has esoteric** knowledge of the Occult and the Real World of the Spirit!!! He would have to say, 'I just don't know.' And believe Us, the Spirit World is a reality, as we ourselves are, in fact, its far more 'Real' **than what you may call, 'The Real World'.**

There are so many dimensions to life, that to try and limit them to just the Earth plane and perhaps one Spirit Sphere, is just not possible. For Dimensions or Vibrationary aspects, can intermingle with each other, shall we say 'overlap' at certain times, when conditions permit!! By which, you may understand that the cycles of evolutionary progress, is not always understood by 'the layman in the street'!!!

We all progress at the 'pace' that is suitable for us, and so what is 'available' to one may seem to be withheld from another!! There is always a reason and that is usually in the comprehension of the individual, those who are the searchers after the knowledge of the Cosmos, and how Mankind fits into this vast complex that also encompasses his Spirit side. They are the ones who are the spearheads of the New wave of life forms that are to bring a higher understanding of what Creation is all about and also what it is for!!!

Man has always been aware that he has an unseen side to his being, even when he does not exactly understand how this has come about and so he on the whole does not give it too much thought until…!! shall we say, he reaches an age when he feels that he would like to **know more about this 'After life' that people** keep telling him does exist, but where?!! And that is a question that is never going to be completely understood by the majority of people. Unless, they are open minded about what they are **being told or even what they are 'Not' being told!! Isn't there a saying 'Sufficient unto the day…'!!!** etc! etc!

One day perhaps, when Man and Spirit are, shall we say 'One' then all will be revealed. But not yet we have to tell you, for Mankind would not know how to handle this Occult knowledge. In any case when the transition does take place and the Spirit is released from his erstwhile companion of the Earth, he will know for himself. For he will be once more upon the plane that he had been upon many, many times and so those questions of the past will have now been answered and yes, verified!!

But sadly that will not be a great deal of comfort for mortal man in his present stage of development.

Just accept that 'Life' does go on, and on, and yes, and on!!! It never ceases, for that is what Creation is all about. Speculate by all **means, but don't be surprised if the answers you are expecting to** the questions that you postulate have very ambiguous sounding replies!! And all for very good reasons we can tell you!!!

And so we will end this night's treatise and let the little Scribe prepare himself for bed!! We thank him for the use of his mind and his pen hand.

Farewell little friend we are never far away, believe that for it is the truth!!

And to all those who are indeed the seekers and searchers of **Earth**'s mysteries we say to you carry on, for you are the lights that brighten up the dark corners of man's deepest thoughts of, 'Why' what is It all about?!!!

Life is One big Question Mark, and that's what it is All about!!!!

We bid you Farewell, and may the Blessings of your God be with you now and in the days and years to come!!

Chapter 39

October 25th, 10 a.m., 2008

HOW DO YOU 'SEE' GOD?!!!

There are many thoughts chasing each other around in my mind and the one that seems to be uppermost is the word GOD!!! And if I'm wise (which I am not!) I should leave that word there and go onto something else, but knowing me, I'm bound to come back to it, so I suppose I may as well think upon that illusive subject of GOD!!

Well, to start with it is only a word, and yet it causes a lot of speculation and sometimes quite heated arguments as to whether there is a God or not!!! I suppose it all depends upon your circumstances and Religious beliefs, which many people accept as gospel and not to be tampered with!! But surely we are allowed to question the, shall I say, 'validity' of the being we have given the name of 'God' to?!! Of course in various cultures they will also call their God by another name that 'they' feel is a suitable appendage to the word God!! But they are only words of dubious appellation.

Words are just thoughts that are put down on paper or parchment as the case may be, and are only for the benefit of, shall I say, other human beings and not the Deity in question!!! Who I should imagine does not need words **to crystallize 'His'!!** thoughts!!! For Divine thoughts would result in positive activity not needing words to explain what was intended!

I believe that upon certain planes (and here I'm referring to the World of the Spirit) Thoughts supersedes the written or spoken word regarding conversation!!! Would that be in the form of a 'mental picture' that conveys what that person wished to be 'said' or rather 'understood', would be a more appropriate word I feel!! To have that command of ones thoughts and be able to project those thoughts for another person to understand what was meant, would I am sure require a great deal of mental ability of coherent manipulation, on the part of both parties I should think!!!

I wonder if we mortals will ever be able to muster or should that be 'master'? our thoughts so that the spoken word would merely be another form of communication if required!!! Now where has all this writing brought me to regarding the word 'GOD' and the rather speculative thoughts on my part?!!

Well, if you must know, I personally feel that I cannot envisage God as being somewhat like a Super Human being type Creator. And yet I do talk to Him and say 'Father', so I am humanizing 'Him' aren't I? But that's only for my benefit and not 'His'!! My word 'Father' cannot alter the fact that it in no way explains the reality of what GOD really is!!! If I venture to use the word 'Essence' or 'Aspect' or even 'Facet' do I know what I'm talking about? And if I'm honest then my answer is 'No, I don't!!!'

I can't express my thoughts in words for they are not thoughts but 'feelings' – 'inner feelings', and somehow they explain to me what is really 'unexplainable'.

But if ever I do in some strange and wonderful way understand what that word 'GOD' really represents, I shall not be disappointed, because I don't think mentally I'm bound by any pre-conceived ideas of what I should believe. I'm very open-minded upon most things, so to find out that God is not how I physically am supposed to see Him, would not cause me any distress. But rather elation to think that my thought that borders on the abstract with regard to the 'Make-up' of God does have some semblance of truth about it, as far as I am personally concerned!!!

When you think about it God is very 'personal' to everyone who believes in one. So probably no two people actually 'see' or experience God in the same way. No wonder that in many cultures there are a multitude of different aspects of the One overall God, and so in those cultures you can pick and choose the ones that suit you and then everybody is happy, at least that is how it seems to me!! And who am I to judge the merits of these worshipped Deities?

There's no doubt about it Mankind / Womankind are complex creatures of Divine Creation. And if worshipping certain God like Deities gives them a meaning to life, then that adherence to a particular culture is to be applauded and not criticised in any way. Especially if the adherents put into practice what their Holy books of Divine inspiration commend them to live by. Loving their neighbour, respecting their parents and those of the older generations.

In just living a good life, a 'God' life in fact, is all that is required of anyone who is trying to observe those tenets that go to make up the reason why we are here upon the Earth plane in the first place.

That is what Life is all about, it may not be perfect but it does **point the way to that illusive word 'Perfection'**. And Perfection is another name that you can add to the word <u>GOD</u>!! Well I think I've done quite enough thinking for one day, thank you!! And so I'll bring this, my so-called treatise on GOD to a close and bid you the reader (if there are any!!!) Farewell and may Your God bless you, as I know He does. Farewell!!

It's now 2.30 p.m.! Though I did have a lunch break in between the start and finish of this discourse!!

'The Little Scribe.'

Chapter 40

October 26th 2008

JUST THOUGHTS

Just Thoughts on my part to be explored at a later date!! That happens to be Now!! And I didn't expect that!!! We talk about 'The Spirit World' and we know about 'Our World' and we understand about its various climatic conditions. And the vagaries of Nature, i.e. Earthquakes, Volcanic eruptions, Tsunamis, Lightning Strikes and anything else associated with the Natural behaviour of Nature upon this Dense Volatile Planet that we call Earth. Now that pertains to this World and we have to accept what happens, this is to do with a Planet.

Well, what about the 'Spirit World'? Is it also a 'Planet', a World of construction similar to our own? But actually in 'No Way' like our own as far as I am able to judge by what little we are able to glean from the 'occupants' of that Sphere, that we are told is 'invisible' to we, upon this lower Planet. And yet 'it' is a reality to those who dwell upon it **and to where 'We'**, that is All of Us will go to when our transition from mortality to immortality takes place. And the physical shell we call our body disintegrates in various circumstances While the Spirit, that is the Real person (though not always accepted in that light) is now free to resume its 'interrupted' life back upon the Spirit Realm!!

So as Spirit we will be living upon a sphere that is suitable for us as 'Spirit entities'! if so, is that 'World' made of the same 'substance' as we as Spirit are? It must be a reality, though not a reality in Human like terms!! So! Does the World of the Spirit have 'Weather' as we upon Earth understand it? And if so, do the conditions that go to make it what it is have 'Climatic conditions'? i.e. Natural phenomena, like the ones I've written about at the beginning of this narrative?

But as we understand it, the Spirit World to us upon Earth is 'Invisible' but to 'them' NOT!! It's real, even more 'real' than our World is to us poor mortals!! Do those upon the Spirit World observe our weather vagaries, but are not affected by them? We, that is our World is not invisible to them even though we must be on a different 'vibrationary wave-length' than they are!! So exactly what does Invisible and Visible mean? Are they aspects of the same life force? And here I'm talking weather wise and not 'physicality' or 'Spirituality'!!

Is their World of such finer vibrations that any deviations to do with, shall I say 'Natures Natural behaviour' is somewhat 'modified', and so anything catastrophic in Natures peculiar habits cannot be transferred to the Spirit Plane?!!

Those Spirit beings that we are allowed as it were to view or rather be aware of, have abilities to alter not only themselves but also their 'immediate surroundings'.

And by 'immediate' I'm thinking of 'locally' and not 'generally', and that I presume is if and when circumstances warrant any local change!!! There's so much that is to do with their personal lives and yes, their overall form of existence that we seem to be unaware of, or perhaps we haven't asked the 'right questions'!!! And that goes for me as well! It's only just occurred to me during this writing that I've never asked mentally about the weather conditions, but I shall rectify that omission pretty soon I think. That is if I haven't already been told in thought that I will be given as much information on the subject as 'they' think is necessary for me to come to terms with!!! I can't wait! Now that my appetite has been whetted, I'm anxious to know more!!!

The Little Scribe

Patience little Brother, Patience! All in good time, carry on with your thinking, we are well aware of it, to be sure!! Now where was I? Oh! Yes! The weather and its affects on the, can I say, the 'indigenous populations' And I have said populations and that should cover All forms of, should it be 'Nationalities'?? The more I think about it, it seems the less I know!!!

We seem to imagine that the Spirit Realm or sphere that we first go to after the demise of the physical body, is a sphere of wonderment and, shall I say delight? Where all things are possible (if you think hard enough!) or in some cases no thoughts at all just an acceptance of what is happening! It's a good job that it's our Spirit that will be the one who has to come to terms with the fact that you are here (on the Spirit plane!) you are here to stay and for the time being there's nothing you can do about it!!!

I'm not being pessimistic or pedantic, it's just that I feel we ought not to put on our Rose coloured spectacles, but to see things as they really are and NOT what we perhaps expect them to be!! But let me hasten to add This realm, this Spirit World, is a beautiful and wonderful place to be alive in, make no mistake about that, it's just that there is a lot of readjusting of ones previous thoughts regarding this first Heaven that you come to. By which, you can understand that there are many, many more that will eventually be your dwelling place on your evolutionary cycle that is to take you back to the Godhead of your Creation!!!

Well, I feel that I've just about exhausted my thoughts for one morning, but I am looking forward to When my Brothers take it upon themselves to enlighten me upon this subject that I've been thinking and writing about. So I suppose I'd better close this chapter and give my thoughts a rest!!!

Farewell! There! I've said it! So you have little brother, so you have!! We also say Farewell till next we meet in mutual thoughts And until we do, we say God bless you little one. God bless you!

Chapter 41

October 27th, Morning, 2008

HUM!! AH!! NOT WHAT I EXPECTED TO HEAR!

Yesterday I put down on paper various thoughts that had been milling around in my mind. Well today I'm going to try and collate what I had written and perhaps condense it somewhat!!!

Well my thoughts were to do with the Weather! No! Not ours but upon the realms of the Spirit!! I don't think I've ever asked them about their weather, it just hasn't occurred to me to do so. But with all the strange weather patterns that are going on, on and around our Earth plane, it set me wondering if upon the Spirit plane they experience similar aberrations in Natures behaviour! We know that the Spirit sphere of comprehension does impinge upon ours, I don't know if that is all the time or just occasionally when circumstances warrant it!!

We are also aware that the Spirit entities, which of course includes our dear departed loved ones, are well aware of what is happening not only to us but also to our Planet! They are for the most part, shall I say invisible to the majority of us mortals and here I am excluding those gifted people we call clairvoyants and mediums, who it seems are the 'go between' between the mortal and the immortal!!

So, then our world in visible in every respect and must also include all that is befalling it at this present time. Their world is one of reality to them as ours is to us, but as their world is on a different vibrationary wave length to ours, hence the invisibility that is a form of illusion in a way. We are real and can be seen, while they are real and cannot be seen!!! At least theoretically speaking!!

Now we come to a difficult phase that needs explaining and I am not the person who could do that explaining other than to say whatever I do say will of a necessity be Hypothetical. And yes, theoretical, for I cannot personally verify any of my comments upon those subjects that come under the words of Occult understanding!!! So please bear with me if you will and reject anything that you cannot go along with!!! Well here are my thoughts regarding the Weather patterns upon the Planes of the Spirit!!

As their world is on that waveband of 'invisibility' as far as we are concerned their weather, must it would seem, be governed by their 'vibrationary field', now we are told that 'Spirit beings' have completely different 'powers' to us, and can manipulate 'things' to suit their purpose. All within the 'Universal law' I hasten to add. I do not envisage them being able to alter the weather, so I'll proceed with other thoughts that are popping in and out of my head!!

I have a feeling, and it's more than just 'my feeling' that the weather patterns upon the Spirit plane are much 'softer' than ours.

For example, I think the seasons are more flexible, they as it were 'merge' with each other and so you couldn't stipulate seasons with Winter, Spring, Summer and Autumn! The seasons are 'blurred' though, as there is not a great deal of difference in them it really doesn't matter if 'Winter' turns out to be 'Spring' or even Summer!!! It would seem then that there would not be any violent changes, for example, Storms, hurricanes, and suchlike. As the Spirit realms are mostly harmonious in their activity, there are very few what I would call surprises weather-wise!! Though I'm being told that their Poles i.e. North and

South, and yes, even East and West are somewhat different to the rest of the Planet.

The North and South have a lot of 'Electrical activity' resulting in Storms, that by our standards are quite 'mild'. Though people do love to visit them and enjoy the spectacle which is something like the Earth's 'Northern Lights'. These Electric vapour fingers of light can sometimes envelope those people watching and it gives them a sense of heightened awareness, mentally, they feel stimulated and with a great sense of wellbeing and being part of the Creative process of all Creation. The effects lasts for a considerable time and their Auras are magnified with outstanding colour vibrations, so that when they go 'back home', their friends and neighbours love to be near them, for the 'colours', which are in effect 'life particles' benefit them as well!!

The East and West Poles are surrounded by not water, but a liquid essence that people bathe in and also take in as a form of 'drink', which is not only nutritious but also stimulates their 'Higher Spiritual Awareness'.

This doesn't happen to everyone, only those who are on a higher cycle of evolution, they are in fact preparing themselves to ascend to their next period of re-incarnation upon a different sphere of comprehension!!! All to do with their weather patterns or so it seems to me!!

I'm told that they do have a form of 'rain' but it's more like a heavy dew, and does not last for very long and if you get wet, it dries almost immediately!! Children love to splash about in it because it is warm and even tastes quite nice!!

Nighttimes are really like twilight because of the two moons and are quite magical to walk about. Quite often people gather together and it becomes a real social occasion with music and laughter, most enjoyable for it becomes a real family treat with the children allowed to stay up for as long as they want to!!

The Little Scribe

And all of this started out as a hypothetical journey of finding out about the weather!! So life really does go on and by the sound of it a most satisfactory one to be sure!! I wonder just how near the truth I may be, or perhaps I'm nowhere near it, for I did say Hypothetical and also Theoretical didn't I?

Well little Scribe, all that we can say to you is, your theories are interesting, but as for being near the truth well!! You'll have to wait and see won't you? We can tell you that, Weather, regardless of whatever Sphere you find yourself upon Spirit or Physical, Weather is completely unpredictable.

Mother Nature always has the last word and that is a fact and we will leave that right there!!!

Hum-Ah! I wasn't expecting that!! So it seems I shall have to wait and see just like everybody else!!! Brother!!! You won't have to wait much longer for your answer and here we really will bring all of this to a close!

So once again we bid you our dear, dear, friend and fellow Brother in Christ, Farewell, and May God bless you little one, God bless you!!

Chapter 42

October 31st 2008

IN THE BEGINNING. THEN WHAT?!!!

Random Thoughts on my part!

Creation? What is it for? Now that's a strange question, you would think that the answer would be obvious, but is it? I'm not sure, still I'll persevere with my thoughts and see what comes out of them! I expect what I do write will seem to some people as 'Heretical', and as I don't as yet know what my thoughts are on the subject let alone what my pen hand will write down, I'm as much in the dark as you probably are!!

Alright then, Creation!! What's the point of it? And has it always been in existence? or was there a period, I was going to write 'a time', but I feel that 'time' as such didn't exist if what I'm about to write is anywhere near the truth!!! Well was there a 'period' when Creation was lying 'dormant' waiting perhaps for the 'One' (who we know absolutely nothing about!) waiting for this Unknowable Essence of absolute Life Force, to jolt that dormant creative urge into positive activity?!!! And was that first act of 'Creation' by that one the Creation of an Hierarchy of like minded 'God Creators'! imbued with attributes of that Unknowable Creative Genius, who gave to them astonishing powers of Creativity!! And just Who would these other Created Creators be?

Of Spirit Essence? Another word for 'Life Force'? and would these Creators be for want of a better word on my part, 'Beings' of 'adult construction'? Not as adult Human beings I think, but of an essence of 'Mind Substance', capable of carrying out what had been programmed into them from the original 'Life Force or Source'.

So what 'they' created would of a necessity be aspects of that First Divine Thought Intelligence, and once established would then be 'free' to pursue their own ideals and ideas, all within the shall I say, the 'Universal Law' laid down by that 'Master Mind' of Unknowable Source!!!

So then we have what can **be called 'Space'**, which I presume was Always an element that existed even before that 'Unknowable Mind substance' came on to the scene!!! Could 'Space' have been the unknown source of Energy, that brought that Original Mind essence into Existence?

Now 'Creator' and 'Created Gods' could use their Mind Power of Thought creation, to, as it were, create abstract elements of 'Life Force' or 'Life Forms' and see how they behaved when coming into contact with other thought created life forms of unknown capabilities!! A gigantic jigsaw of 'Trial and Error'. That must have been taking place in what I visualize as a transparent **Globe suspended in Space** and observed by the 'Creative Gods' from the outside so to speak!!!

Each God monitoring their particular aspect of thought creation, which would eventually result in an amalgamation of All feasible aspects that could be controlled and become forms of Life sustaining elements.

By which, I mean the 'stuff' that we call the 'Building Blocks' of all known Life. There would **need to be shall I say 'Houses'**, where created elements could bond together and thrive or not as the case may be. And by 'Houses' I refer to 'Created Universes'!!! Which of course includes our very own Known Universe!!

I just cannot begin to calculate the millions or trillions or zillions of what we call Earth years that all of this creative energy would take, for these unknown 'as then' elements of Life Force to become viable possibilities of habitable construction. And by 'habitable' I am not thinking in terms of Mankind or Spirit-kind, but of unspecified forms of life that preceded all of those fossilized remains that the archaeologists find, and try to date. These other forms have left no trace whatsoever and yet they did exist in reality at one 'time'!!!

So then what are my conclusions upon this Hypothetical speculative foray of mine into the realms of 'Creation' Creators, Gods, Universes, Space, and that 'Unknowable Life Force and Source' that is beyond our comprehension?!

I don't really expect anyone to agree with my theoretical interpretation of Life before it became known as a reality and 'Those' who took part (and still do!) in its 'seen' and partly understood Creation!! I expect I've only uncovered just a small corner of life's tapestry, but somehow I feel quite satisfied with what has been written.

Though whether I shall think the same after I've read this mornings treatise, is another matter, and yes I'll record it on a cassette and see how it sounds!!!

Further Thoughts to my previous ones! And these are to do with the 'Hierarchy of Creator Gods'. Those that the 'Unknowable Essence of Divine Thought' Created as partners in the scheme of what That Creator visioned for all forms of sustained 'life force'. That were to be the ongoing aspect of Creation, evolving once again in a never ending cycle of manifested thought creations!! Each God Creator a Creator in His own right.

There would be those who would Create Entire Universes, while others would be the Creators of Planets, Worlds, Stars, Cosmic effulgence etc. Others of equal stature would be responsible for all forms of Creatures, Man included!! The aspects of Creation are endless, until such times when certain Created

Creations are put into a form of Slumber to re-emerge at a future date as a newly created species!!

Those Gods of the Hierarchy nearest to the Sublime God Creator are the only ones who as it were, are on 'intimate terms' with that 'Force'. They in a way are a safety valve for that Divine One. For the Life Force of that One is beyond Any Description for the Force Power defies any kind of definition, but the release of that untamed energy can be channelled through those Creator Gods aforementioned and so stability and equilibrium can be maintained!! We have no idea of what magnitude that Force Power is capable of.

For where Those Gods dwell is unknown to any other beings save for just a few who are in a way liaisons between the Higher Aspects and those on the Lower rungs of the evolutionary ladder that encompass all of those abstract facets of creation. That we as **Mortals and Immortals see as manifestations of the 'One' or 'Ones' that we are allowed to perceive in our own individual way as <u>GOD</u>**!!! And that is why we as Spirit and our companion that we are allowed to be part of upon the Earth plane, are forever striving to once more become Unified with that Godhead that we know we belong to. Even though we had to leave the presence of that Deity and then find our way back through countless incarnations that would ultimately fit us for that final journey of re-unification with our Creator God. To know, as we are known!!

Not the end but a new beginning on the path of Eternal opportunity that will take us Where??? And here I am being urged to bring this final chapter to a close, and so this is what I will do. You may be very surprised little scribe at what to us makes real sense, and we congratulate you on your mental awareness upon what to many is a forbidden subject!!!

We wish you well little friend, and do NOT worry, about what you cannot as yet do anything about! But All is being attended to on your behalf, Believe that. Fare Thee Well!!

Farewell. Farewell, and I feel that I have completed what I set out to do this day!! Though I'm sure I have others to thank in the process!!

Post Script to the above!
I have thoughts regarding the Appearance of those Beings of the Hierarchy, but I am keeping them to myself, for I feel it would be too presumptuous on my part to speculate via the written word upon such a personal subject.

'The Little Scribe.'

Chapter 43

November 2nd, Sunday Afternoon, 2008

THIS ONE IS DEFINITELY NOT FROM ME!!

It's just occurred to me that when we, that is 'we' upon the Earth plane think about things to do with the Earth, the Worlds of the Spirit, Planets and other Worlds, which we are endeavouring to ascertain if they are or ever were, inhabited by beings like ourselves, and then of course to cap it all, GOD!!! And our thoughts always seem to hover around the, shall I say, the human like stature? That is of course, because that is all that we are acquainted with. 'Humanity' and all that that word implies!!

We even try to associate God in a human style, as if He is a **Super Human Being and that also goes for the 'Angels'**, the Arch-Angels and any other form of Angelic type being that we perhaps do not know anything about, other than in an abstract form, so to speak. **It's as if our Brains or Thoughts are somewhat restricted** when it comes to trying to explain, or understand anything that may not be, shall I say, under the influence of that one word 'Humankind'. And by that word I am not just referring to human beings!!!

It is understandable, because we do not know any better!!! But is 'everything' especially the unknown 'everything', does it have to be understood as being of the Human style variety?

Or can our minds stretch a little further and say that Man and all that we associate with him is NOT necessarily the Only form of Creation that has been Created. And by 'Creators' of unknown proportions, who in themselves may not actually resemble Human or Spirit Beings that we seem to imagine is the 'be all' and 'end all' of Created figures of recognisable features!!!

There well maybe, shall I venture to say 'Beings' that if they were to come across 'human beings' in their travels might find it difficult to associate themselves with that strain of 'Created creatures' who they would consider as an outdated species of perhaps, antiquity that they had thought had ceased to exist long, long ago!!!

Now! Ego inflated Man, does that make you feel that perhaps you've got it 'all wrong' when you think of yourselves as the Highest form of creation?!! I was going to say of the 'animal species', for after all we do come under that category do we not, considering our basic structure i.e. Skeleton, bones, blood and skin tissue etc! And here I'm going to write something that some will throw up their arms in horror and say Heretic!!! Are we the products of the God or Gods that we have been told about? And if so that explains why we are shall I say blinkered, when it comes to thinking about 'anything' or 'anyone' that we do not consider comes under the heading of 'Human' taken in its broadest sense, I hasten to add!!!!

It may well be that our understanding regarding 'Our God' and His Hierarchy of Angelic beings is our error of judgement!!

We assume that 'He' and they are of the Human type variety of identification, but are they? And if He and they are, is that all for a purpose? And the purpose being that our form of Human beings are, for want of a better word, upon the lower rungs of the Evolutionary ladder of expectation!!?! And that upon 'other rungs' there are Other God Creators and their cohorts of creativity that could be called 'Varieties' of the Basic principles of created 'Life Force'!!!

And please understand that 'All God Creators' are Aspects or Facets of that Unknowable force of 'LIFE UNIFICATION' that pervades all of LIFE SUBSTANCE everywhere!! And so they (The Gods) are all of equal stature and have their chosen place in the Scheme of that Unknowable Force of Life Energy. And yet they have been known to, shall we say, 'exchange places' and so bring forth New and exciting phases of growth in the form of Created creations of outstanding virtue and capabilities. And even of unheard construction that defies any description that we are capable of!!! That is 'We' of the Human / Spirit variety!!!

DO NOT limit your thoughts to what you feel is expected of you, or to what you feel you have been 'brought up' to understand is, shall we say 'Sacrosanct' and must not be altered in anyway whatsoever!!! Just remember that You are of This World and This Universe. There are Others, believe that, and you are not necessarily confined to this particular one in your evolutionary Spiral of Life's existence!! More for you to think upon. You are where you are because of your own efforts to those who support you. We speak of those of the Spirit-world.

And so if you wish to progress further, then shall we say not the World, but the Universe itself is your 'Oyster'. And from Spirit to Human and then back to Spirit and from there, Where?? Forward and Upward dear friends of the Earth, and always keep an Open Mind about everything and use it to open the doors of discovery. The discovery of yourself and the part you are destined to play in this ever changing game of Life and Lives to live and be lived!!!

We depart from this strange encounter with the earthling who wields His pen like the sword of Damocles!! More power to you little one, we await your coming to our part of your Thought World, which is one of Reality and you do know it!!!

We do say Farewell, though the expression is Alien to us!! Farewell!!! May Your God be with You!!

Chapter 44

November 4th, 9 p.m.–10.30 p.m., 2008

VERY QUICK, VERY BRIEFLY IN MEDITATION.

The Colour was Amethyst and then purple, deep deep purple with gold.

The whole Air seemed to be full of a Mauve, or pale Lilac Colour, a Vapour like mist, yet it didn't obscure anything. It parted and there standing, was a figure in White.

It was 'Jesus' he smiled and held out his hand towards me and as I approached he moved gently away as if inviting me to follow him!

Follow in his footsteps!! I felt I was not worthy and as Jesus turned to look at me he said,

'I am only a Man and not a God!!'

This startled me and I lowered my head. But I understood that what he was saying was that I was able to follow Him just as his followers did. Because to them He was a Man and not yet thought of as God, which he is Not which I think will upset a lot of people's thoughts! I'm getting used to the idea now, so I can accept it, if He wants me to be a follower of His Ideas and not to put him on a pedestal to be worshipped. That is NOT what was intended when He took upon himself the Role of Teacher / Preacher / Healer and Scapegoat!!

Not in the sense of washing away the Sins of Man but being an example of what Man can become when he lives as a

Godman!! With all that that entails!! Even when He was misunderstood regarding his mission upon this Earth at that time, and this was NOT the first time that He had incarnated upon a Plane that was in need of Spiritual Guidance!! And it will not be the last one by any means!!!

'Jesus' is the name that we know Him as, but there are many identificationary aspects that we have no knowledge of in other words, the name of Jesus is 'Legion'!!! and Legion means many not just ONE!!! They are Aspects of God but they are not God!! But Beings of the Highest form of Creation, with powers of supernatural excellence that cannot be comprehended by Mortal Man. Even though their appearances have the semblance of physicality and seen by some as having Auras of extreme beauty that cannot be explained by any normal occurrence!!!

The road to God realization and acceptance of what that would mean if one was to be granted that rare privilege, is a lonely road and not to be envied by those of faint heart!! The complexities of Creation in all of its variability is one of perpetual mystery and likely to remain as such, until decreed otherwise!!! What is to be known will be known when Man and Spirit are once more United as they were in the very beginning, when Time was but a distant thought yet to be born!!!

And here I leave this strange interlude of mine that started with a form of unintentional meditation on my part and developed **into this written chapter that I don't fully understand!!!**

Then it is now our turn to say to you dear Brother the inspiration was from our side of life and was instigated by a fellow Brother not as yet known to you but one of great antiquity!!! We bid you **goodnight and leave you in God's hands.**

Farewell little Scribe.

Farewell.

Chapter 45

November 7th 2008

IS FACT A TRUTH?
AND IS TRUTH A FACT?!!!

What is a Fact? Is it a Truth? Or is it someone's version of what they have either been told or even read and they are expected to accept that Fact at face value? Or can they question it, either in their own mind or as the case may be, ask the person who is stating that Fact to verify if at all possible, the validity of their statement!! So often 'facts' so-called have been somewhat embroidered over the years and perhaps in the repeating of it, the original meaning has become obscured. And the stated fact takes on the garment of folk-lore, and all shall we say non intentional by those or the one stating this fact, that must of necessity be 'second hand' so to speak!!!

In other words keep an open mind about everything that you are either being told, or what it is you may be reading! And here we are really speaking about what some people call 'Esoteric knowledge'. For anything that comes under the heading of 'Occult information', needs to be carefully evaluated if perhaps 'you' are intending to pass on that information to an avid listener. Always stress the point that it is your 'personal view' that is being expressed and the listener or listeners, must make up their own minds as to whether they wish to accept your version upon the subject in question or reject it, but shall we say 'not out of hand'.

For if what has been said results in a discussion and not an argument, then you may find that what was at first, shall we say not accepted, but questioned, can sometimes result in a complete 'turn around' by the listener. And even the one who first put forth that fact for discussion may see 'things' in a different light!!! Such is the power of 'words' either spoken or written. They can change a person's complete life!! And we hesitate to say in 'what way' we leave that to, shall we say 'Fate' or even 'Destiny'!! So 'words' are 'tools' that must be used with care and yes, with conscious thought we will add!!

The people we often call the 'Searchers and Seekers' who are trying to find answers to age-old questions that somehow never seem to have, shall we say 'straight – forward' answers, very often the reply may seem to be 'ambiguous', it can often be taken in more than 'one way'. Now that is because whoever it is that is doing the answering be it mortal man or immortal spirit, is that they are giving the answer as their 'personal' opinion, which quite often cannot actually be verified by either subject!!

Though when the question is being answered by the Spirit entity, you can be certain that they are expressing what they know of as a 'truth'. But you the mortal being, have to take that answer on 'trust' or as some might say, having 'Faith' in the one that is giving to you their learned knowledge of their experience upon the Spirit Plane!! Such a lot has to be taken on trust by Mortal Man, when he ventures in Thought and Mind when dealing with Occult complexities that are from a different vibrationary sphere of habitation!!

What is perfectly 'Normal' to a Spirit upon the Spirit plane if spoken about in, shall we say a 'matter of fact' way, could quite easily get misunderstood in the translation period of what is taking place. Either in the mental exchange of the questioner or perhaps the 'go-between' of perhaps a clairvoyant and the 'sitter'.

We know that you do understand what we are saying. And that is where the word 'complexities', becomes a 'fact'! and a Truth!!

Nothing is as 'straight forward' as it might appear, for a 'lot' has to be done behind the scenes so to speak, before anything of a coherent nature can be accomplished!! But it is!! And that is the wonder of it all, This interplay of Spirit and Mortal!! If only it <u>was</u> understood by shall we say, 'The Man in the Street' and he could accept this union of those two elements, God given elements. Then he would find that Life with all of its 'Ups and Downs' really does make sense and the living of it is the most natural thing in the World and Yes, beyond it!!!

For life does go on, regardless of the Sphere you find yourself upon! One day perhaps those two elements Spirit and Mortal Man will amalgamate into the 'One Mortal Being' that was originally envisaged by the Creator of all that we can see around us. And yes, even the unseen creations that do exist in reality, even if Mortal Man is unaware of their existence!! We upon the Realms of Spirit 'do know', for are we not a part of this 'unseen creation' that is a 'reality' but in a different vibrationary field to yours?!! A Fact!! A Truth!! The choice is yours! 'Trust or Faith!!' Two words with a wealth of meaning!!

And here we depart from this morning's discourse, which the little scribe had no idea what he was going to put down on this paper when he picked up his pen and said to himself, 'I wonder if I shall get any inspiration?' Well He has the answer and the writing to prove it!!!

Thank you little friend, thank you!! We will bid you our usual Farewell and we trust, you the reader, will accept our parting thoughts of Farewell and God Bless You All!!

Farewell Brother. May Allah look kindly upon His little servant. Farewell.

Chapter 46

November 8th 2008

THE WATERS OF THE MOON!!!

The waters of the Moon! Now why have I written that? I don't know anything about the Moon, in fact I don't think I even took much notice when 'They' put a Man on the Moon!! It didn't strike me as very relevant, at least as far as I was concerned!! So what am I going to write about it? I could say 'Heaven Knows.' So perhaps something will come to me if I wait long enough!!

Well, 'waters of the moon' I suppose should make me think about the effect the Moon has on our seas, our tides and I believe it also has a benign effect upon certain vegetables. I think that there is amongst farmers a strong feeling about the planting of certain vegetables when the Moon is in a certain period and if they do, those particular vegetables benefit in some peculiar way. I don't know if it's the size or the nutriment value, but it definitely is an advantage to those crops that are planted when the Moon's cycle is propitious!!!

Also I believe a lot of people who take the moon very seriously, are greatly influenced by its somewhat mysterious magical kind of aura of what is not quite understood. It's as if at times the Moon can as it were 'see' the unseen things of the Earth and can influence them.

It's almost as if 'She' is guarding them against unknown forces of, I hesitate to call them 'evil', perhaps 'unhealthy' would be a more appropriate expression to use when trying to explain the unexplainable!!!

I find the Moon a very, very fascinating object of curious intention. It's almost as if the outer contours are hiding something that is 'going on' beneath the surface and that one day that surface will, like the shell of an egg, crack open and reveal a glorious interior of such stunning beauty that will be breathtaking to behold!! And I wonder if there will be a form of ethereal life force that will amaze us upon Earth, Civilizations of beings that have slumbered for countless millenniums and can now be released from that torpor that must have seemed like death!!

What are my impressions regarding those populations that inhabit the interior now 'exterior' of the Moon? Well, my first thoughts are that they (the inhabitants) are above average height, with a skin colouring that resembles 'spun gold'. They have an aura of exquisite tone colouring that alters with the change of mood. Their hair varies in colour and texture but it is mostly of a fairer tone, some very blond almost white, while others are a beautiful golden glow as if the hair is alive with light. I did not see any dark shades, though I believe there are some with an auburn colouring tinged with gold. They (the people) come from a distant part of the Moon and are considered as very special. I believe they have strange occult powers that they can use when it is considered necessary.

They originally came from another planet of very highly Spiritual quality and it was with the intention of starting a new race of intelligent Spiritually advanced Beings. But the problems that beset the Moon at that time resulting in what we see of it now, cut short that enterprise! Perhaps it may be again revived when the eggshell crust has disappeared. But that will not happen yet I'm told!!

The Earth has first to be cleansed and altered and then the Moon's surface will be shattered, and once again there will be a form of intercourse between the two planets, they may even become as 'One' eventually!! The Moon I feel is Our (the

Worlds) Spiritual counterpart, that is why it has such an effect upon our Planet. And those people who at certain times seem to be affected by the Moons various cycles, have a longing (but they do not know why) have a longing to shall I say, Return to their place of Birth!!!

They feel at those times a highly charged Spiritual affinity with that mysterious Orb, almost as if they could float along one of the Moon's beams, They are virtually 'Moonstruck'!! But they are NOT lunatics by any means!!!

Now where has all this information come from? I can remember when I was a child about 6 or 7 years old, I woke up in the middle of the night and the window was bare and there covering the whole of it was this gigantic face of the Moon, it was of course outside. But I thought it would come in and I screamed and screamed and screamed, and Mum and my Sister rushed into the room to see what it was that I was frightened of!!

Mum pulled the curtains shut and she calmed me down, I can still see that Moon's face even now, but it doesn't affect me, though when the Moon is full I do like to look at it, it fascinates me I almost feel 'I know it!!!' Now that's something I've never thought of before!!!

And I think that perhaps that's a good note to finish on, and close this chapter on the Moon and my Hypothetical conjectures about its past and its future!!!

I say Farewell!!

Chapter 47

November 9th 2008

WHO ARE YOU?!!!

Some while ago I was looking through previous discourses and one of them, or rather a small section of one caught my eye and I started to read it, it dealt with 'one' of the other shall I say, ME's?!! About coming face to face with him, well I won't go into the details regarding Me, I feel I want to, in a way talk about 'generalization', in other words what may affect everybody!! If that's possible!!

So here goes! You understand the principle of shall I say, multiple identities that go to make up who we are, and that will encompass mainly those of the Spirit. Though later on I think I have to **include another aspect and that is, one of those 'identities' are of the human variety, and I don't think I have to stop at 'one'** of them!!!

Well as you are already aware of the various Spirit forms that the Soul is permitted to create for the purpose of gathering information, upon the various spheres that show the distinction between Perfection and Imperfection, that the Soul needs to understand. But as it is already that aspect of the Divinity that is Perfection, it has to be made aware of what that actually represents, hence the Spirit essences of its creation.

Not all of those creations are shall we say, of 'Human identification' and some are in an embryonic stage encased in a vapour like aura, and these are in a slumbering state, awaiting shall we say, **the time when they may be needed by the Soul's** thought desire of extension! We will leave those for they are not required in this particular discourse!!!

As you are also aware of the various spheres or planes of existence that all play a part in the growth of not only the Spirit essence, but eventually the Human being upon the Earth plane. And here we have to say that not all spheres or planes are 'realities' in the sense of being viable places of habitation. They can be Mind or Thought perceptions, which never the less can become ' Thought realities' to the one to whom they are being thought about!!! We move forward and say that some of these spheres that are realities, have upon them Spirit creations that resemble those humans that they are a part of! If you follow what we are saying.

They 'resemble' but are not necessarily identifiable as the one upon the Earthplane, and yet if they were to be seen by that one they would be known as an aspect and accepted as such!! In perhaps a deep dream sleep they might encounter the Spirit one, and they both would know that they shared the same identity!!

Though the Spirit one has a life of its own upon that sphere where it remains!! But it is a Higher form of shall we say, Spirituality? And does or can influence that one upon the Earth plane through thought and yes, through dream encounters, which is via the 'Earth Spirit' for want of a better word!!

Who then influences the mortal being who is its lifelong companion!!! We have given you one example, but of course there are more and their life styles vary as they the 'Spirit essence' approach the Earth plane's existence and influence!!! We have up to now only dealt with the Spirit Aspects, we now proceed to an even more, how can we put it? A more unusual and difficult to explain 'aspect' and that is, that this particular aspect or facet of the Earth bound human being is A human being, not recognisable as one would have thought. But a completely separate identity of their own, in other words, shall we say, a stranger? whom you have never met before and yet...!!! They are linked to you in some strange way.

When first you encounter them there is an 'instant rapport' between the both of you. A feeling of having met them before, one of knowing them! And yet both of you know that this has not been so!! You might even say of this encounter that you are 'Ships that pass in the Night,' for it is just as likely that you will not meet again, and yet neither of you ever forget that you did meet and it has left you wondering, and there is an explanation but of course you are unaware of it, both of you!!! And the explanation is that you both are YOU!!! Separate beings, leading separate lives, but joined together by Spiritual forces that you can never quite understand!!!

You may not even be of the same sex!! When you both meet up again it will be upon a Spirit Realm, and recognition will be instantaneous and so the jigsaw begins to take shape. You know that you both belong to each other and now comes a very strange but touching part of this narrative.

You are now confronted by the Higher Aspect of you both, the one that you will now become upon this evolutionary journey that is to take you to realms that await your coming!!! It has been known that this form of unification can occur in ones lifetime more than once, depending upon the degree of Spiritual advancement.

Here we are speaking of those people that you may well call 'Saints' and those of mystic persuasion! Some lives are very complex and cannot be taken as the normal run of expected life evolution!!

There is so much that we do not understand about ourselves and our other 'selves'. Eventually though all things are made clear, when as enlightened Spirit we are reunited with our Soul Creator to once again set out upon our final journey of self discovery, where the end turns out to be a New beginning!!!

We have moved have we not, from the One to the Many that go to make up the 'One' who we really are!! And so we feel that perhaps this is where we should depart from this treatise of the many facets of what it is to be a Created Being whose lives mirror those of shall we say, the unknown Creators of our Destinies?!!

We leave you in peace and to you little Brother you may return to your place of rest; your work for this night is over.

Farewell and May God bless you for your endeavours. Farewell.

Chapter 48

November 10th 12.20 a.m.–1.45 a.m., 2008

THE BLACK HOLE CORRIDOR TO WHERE?!!

We greet you Brother.
The subject for tonight's discussion is SPACE!

We begin!! Space is not what you think it is. It is Not just an empty void filled up to overflowing with Planets, Worlds, Stars. Galaxies and Debris, in fact all that your Scientists can observe and 'More'!!!

Now Space is made up of many different elements of unseen 'matter'! And Matter itself is also made up of various elements **that fluctuate from being almost like a form of 'clear soup' to a** thick stodgy almost solid form of impenetrable force, and there **are many more gradations of this Elusive form of 'Spaceness'.** For instance, on the Outside of this your Universe it is floating in a translucent almost transparent Sea, where it is anchored as it were **by an invisible 'chain',** so that it is allowed a certain amount of freedom of movement, shall we say, back and forth and hinting at side to side!!

Now Space within the Universe is shall we say, trapped and confined in this shell like creation. Though it is always trying to escape and return to its original place of origin Outside!! We are **interested at present with what it houses within its 'prison' the** Universe to be precise!!

In the 'beginning' the Universe was an Empty void awaiting the gestation of all of the Planets, Worlds etc. that were being created by those Unknown forces of 'Mind Creativity'.

The Creators in fact, the Created Aspects of the 'Original Life Force of Unknown origin'!!! Your scientists have speculated on what they like to call 'Black Holes' that exist in Space. These Holes are not just holes or tears in the space's fabric. They are in effect 'Pathways' or 'Corridors' that are dotted all over the place, waiting for the right impetus to shall we say, bring them into activity! They have at their 'top' so to speak a sort of 'criss-cross flap' that when agitated opens up revealing the passage way through the aforementioned space. It is 'hollow' but has a pulsating effect like the pumping of a gigantic heart. And now we come to the strange part, this vortex sucks in whatever it is that comes near to it, it in a way neutralizes if it is a planet, its gravity field and so it becomes helpless in the vortex like grip.

Now this corridor is filled with a vapour that wraps itself around the object under discussion, in a way protecting it and then it transports it along its whole length until it reaches its destination. Sometimes it's only a matter of a few million miles and then the Planet in question is 'spewed out' into its New orbital belt and none the worse for this encounter!

Now! There are Black Holes, which incidentally are not black at all, but are multicoloured and these extend much, much further through this semi-solid space like sea, and here we will tell you of a phenomenon!

They, whatever it is that is being transported or should we say, transferred? Through this corridor, 'come out' not to the inside of the Universe but to its 'Outside'!! Into the vast, vast ocean of Primordial Space in its translucent form of Sea-like 'matter'! Virgin Space in other words, and whatever it is that now finds itself outside of its former home of habitation is for the time being left as it were, to its own devices!!! It is virtually 'lost' and must somehow seek a refuge. And it does, Within a companion Universe that is in the vicinity.

As it no longer has its original field of gravity, it picks up this **New Universe's force field of gravitational pull, and** so it is now absorbed into this new Universe and becomes a permanent part of its evolutionary cycle!!! And all that that implies!!

If for instance it was a Planet housing Life Forms of all descriptions they would have been automatically put into a form of Hibernation, until this transference had been completed. Then this awakening heralds a new round of Life incarnations of which we are not at liberty to comment upon in this treatise. For it would need many volumes to recount their new life styles in their new environment and the many different species of Life forms that they will now encounter.

New lives, New beginnings, so you see the so-called Black Holes can in effect be the start of New life and not the end of one!!!

But this is where we are being told to bring this discourse to a close and so we will bid the little scribe Farewell.

Perhaps one day we may be allowed to pursue this fascinating subject of an Unknown Universe, and what it has to offer to a traveller from another World, another Universe and another 'time'!!

We bid you Farewell Brother, quite a lot for you to think about we feel!!!!

Chapter 49

November 12th 2008

COLOUR AND ITS NOTATION!!!

Sitting outside enjoying the Autumn sunshine my thoughts turned to the word 'Colour' and just thinking about it sent me on a journey of nostalgic memory about a little old lady that was a friend of a friend, and we were invited to tea one Winter's afternoon. The lady's flat was on the top floor of a rambling late Georgian or early Victorian house that had seen better days!! Well to cut a long story short, around the walls of her flat were a series of not very big pictures in watercolour, and I can't remember what the subjects were. I have a feeling they were sort of abstract, not modern abstract it's just that they didn't represent anything in particular, but the colours were soft, not pastel, more of muted tones. They were about 10 inches by about 8 inches I should think, and there were sixteen of them and one more that was different.

They interested me, and the lady told me that each picture represented part of a whole symphony each colour being a note or notes, and the sixteen could if you knew how, be played as the complete work! But the Key to how to do it was the Seventeenth picture, without it, they were just pictures of interesting colours!!!

Now I move on for a couple of years or so, having lost touch with the lady in question! Well in an old Antique come second-hand shop in the Old Town of Hastings, there upon the walls were those very same pictures, all sixteen of them. So I asked the proprietor did he have the Seventeenth one and he replied, No! he didn't know there was one!! So I told him that the sixteen all together could be 'played' as a complete symphony if the Seventeenth one that was the Key, could be found!! Somehow he didn't seem very interested in what I had told him and I left the shop feeling rather sad that that lady's cherished pictures that represented a Symphony was now lost and would probably never be found!! Well so much for my saying I'd make along story short!!

But it has brought me to what I'm going to write about! And that is Colours and their respective musical notations, not as a colour being associated with a particular piece of music that may appeal to a certain person, which is quite a different matter!!

No! I'm thinking along the lines that each colour actually resonates with its particular note of identification. Even if to our physical human ears we are unaware of these invisible to us sounds of collective harmonies shall I say, of the 'spheres'? I'm thinking of all the aspects of our colourful surroundings i.e. Flowers, Trees, Birds, and yes, even inanimate objects like rocks, stones etc. and the very earth we walk upon. **All of these 'sounds' that are there but perhaps are only noticed by the few, who are in 'tune' with their surroundings!!!**

You know yourself how certain colours appeal to your senses, **and how you 'feel' better in certain garments that you 'know' suit you, and others that are just not you!!!** I feel that colours give off vibrations and if you have an affinity with them, then you register that feeling of rapport and can if you wish build upon it. Without realizing it you are absorbing those harmonious vibrations and feeling better for it!!

While another colour, even when you may like it, somehow you are not on its wavelength so to speak and so it does nothing **for you and I add, 'spiritually'.** For a harmonious form of living physically speaking, is bound to have an effect upon your Spiritual life of inner perception. I believe I either read **somewhere or heard, that some people can actually 'see' through** parts of their skin, colour! I wonder if it is not 'seeing' but 'feeling' they perhaps without knowing it, are picking up the vibrationary wavelength of whatever it is that their skin is in touch with!!!

We know that certain colours have healing properties. I think but it's only what I think, that the stained glass windows in churches and cathedrals and other places of worship were originally intended to be of specific areas of healing qualities. Especially when the rays of the Sun shone through those windows and anyone who was in 'line' with those coloured rays, would benefit both physically and Spiritually!! There is so much that we need to know and be aware of regarding those hidden qualities of even just the ordinary things that we take for granted!!!

Put yourself in touch with your own inner sense perceptions, give yourself a few moments each day of quiet contemplation or even no thoughts at all. And hold in your hands something that has your colour vibrations and yes, it's musicals notations within it and see how much better you will feel after your union with that other you, of Spiritual persuasion!!!

Also if you have difficulty with your sessions of sleep, put that same something under your pillow, after holding it for a little while and see if you don't get a better night's rest!! You are your own physician, you know that, but a little 'outside' help does not come amiss!!

And here is where I think I will close this subject on colour! And hope I haven't bored you with my reminiscing!! I won't say Goodnight because it's Good Morning, and it's a glorious one!! Farewell!!

Chapter 50

November 15th 2008

MAN!!!?

Do we really know what being a human being is all about? Or are we just kidding ourselves that we do matter and to whom? Ourselves? Our Family? **Our Nation?** Well haven't you forgotten someone? Could it be the One we call our Creator God?!! Have we left anyone else out of this our speculative equation??! If I said the word 'Spirit'!!! What does that evoke in your innermost thoughts? That is if you are one of the people who believe that we all have a Spirit! I expect many will just think of that in a abstract way!

Spirit is not exactly a familiar form of personal reference, for how often could you say that on a personal level you are fully **aware of your Spirit companion of this life's cycle that you are** upon?!! We may very well believe that having a Spirit companion is true, but speaking in a logical fashion, that's something most of us have to take on trust as it were. Though some do have a feeling, an inner feeling that amounts to a certainty even if, shall we say, it requires confirmation from an outside source.

For example, a medium or clairvoyant, who has this ability of 'contact' with those in the world of the Spirit!! There again that word 'trust' has to be applied, depending it would seem if the medium or clairvoyant is either known, or even not known personally!!!

So much that is talked about, and yes, written about, regarding esoteric situations that it is no wonder that the majority of people, view such things with a sense of, not exactly disbelief but one of speculation. For after all they are expected to accept things that are in a way 'second-hand' knowledge, with, how shall we say, 'no concrete proof' in a physical sense to bolster up their statements?

Trust! That word crops up again, and yet it is a significant word, and does not include 'Blind Trust' or even 'Blind Faith'. It is all up to the one who is seeking answers to age-old questions about the meaning of Life and 'Lives' that stretch further than the Earth Plane to Worlds, not of the imagination, but worlds of reality, in fact Worlds in another dimension to our own!!!

And when we speak of worlds in other dimensions and vibrations you can include the Dream Worlds, the Astral Worlds, the Worlds of the Etheric, the Worlds of the 'sources' etc. And some of these 'Worlds' are 'perceptions', though do not dismiss them on that account, for perceptions are from the intuitive strata of the inner life of the individual. And what starts off as a 'perception' has its roots in an unseen and perhaps unknown reality, that does have an existence in an unknown dimension!!!

Such is the complexity of 'Life Creation' by which we mean 'All' Life Creation, for all such creation does impinge upon All of Life whether we realize it or not!!!

And those of you, and indeed those of us, Who are thought of as 'sensitives' are influenced by the unseen forces of 'Nature' in no uncertain manner!!! And we should add the 'Super Natural' as well!! And read that as it is meant to be read and not as 'supernatural', which seems to have a different connotation to such a lot of people who 'dabble' in things of Esoteric sensitivity!!!

And 'complexity' is just what the idea of Creation is!!! For it cannot be analyzed, pigeon-holed and labelled and put onto a shelf with all of the other labelled, shall we say, eccentricities of Nature and her wayward behaviour patterns!!! There are 'things' that defy the 'logical'! explanations that Humans try to use in their exploration of the Cosmos and what may exist beyond our understood, or rather 'misunderstood' Universe and what it holds within its tenuous grasp!!!

Each step that Mankind takes, is a step into the Unknown. And sometimes the Unknown is best left alone until such times as Man is in a position to understand his 'Place' in the Cosmic History of this Universe and its 'Planetary inhabitants'. And we are not talking about the Life Forms that take refuge upon said Planets!!! And if you have read that correctly you may well come to the conclusion that 'Life Forms' of 'all' descriptions have a tendency to 'wander', in other words 'migrate' from one Planet to another!!! They are not conservative in their behaviour patterns!! So our advice to those of you who are in a position of 'Global discovery' – 'Expect the Unexpected' and we say no more on that particular subject!!!

We started off this treatise by saying 'Do we really know what being a Human being is all about?!' Well, let us quantify that statement by saying No! We do not think we do! And here we are speaking in the broadest of terms regarding Physical Human Beings!! And the reason we say that is because present day Man (who incidentally goes 'back' many millions of years in your calculation of 'time'!!!) Is not the only known species that comes under the heading of 'Mortal Man'.

Contrary to popular belief there really are other 'variations', shall we call them? Of what comes under the heading of Mankind! You understand about Planets and you hope that one day you may come across a species of your own kind. At least one that can be safely recognised as belonging to what you consider 'your own kind'!!! You at present label them as 'Extra Terrestrial Beings' or as you seem to prefer to call them 'Aliens', which somehow makes them sound 'sinister'!!

But had you thought that to 'them' if there are any 'THEM', you could well be considered as an 'Alien Species' of an unknown life form!!! Think about that, has it deflated your 'ego' just a little bit? NO?! Well it should, for Man is 'not' the highest created species that has been created!!! He maybe while he dwells upon this Earth planet, But should he eventually discover other Planets that are inhabited by 'Created Life Forms' he may well have to alter his previous assumptions of being the 'superior' species created for this 'Planet'. And notice we have said 'This Planet' and draw your own conclusions as to what we are implying!!!

And now we move on just a little further along the chain of 'Evolution'!! You may not be aware but there are dwelling amongst you people who in your ignorance you would probably consider as 'Aliens'. They are NOT! They are a higher more spiritual form of Earthman! In other words they are the forerunners of a new Root Race, One that has been awaiting the time when they will be called upon to incarnate upon this lower dense planet, they are part of a well thought out long planned form of experimentation!!

They will be monitored during their various 'lives' as to how they can adapt to this plane of heavy matter, for in the far off distant future of this Planet it is to be altered, made less dense and more like a Spirit plane. The one that adjoins this Earth and the one that many of the 'seekers and searchers' of the Esoteric mysteries are aware of!!

Your Earth will be 'upgraded' as it were, and Man in his present trapping of Physical matter, i.e. Flesh and Bone, Blood and tissue, will take on the garb that is usually associated with those who dwell upon the Spirit World. And who from time to time need to incarnate upon the Earthplane for lesson learning and life experience. This will no longer be the case as it is today and always has been!! Mortal man will become 'Immortal Spirit Man'. No longer a liaison of the two facets of the Created aspect of the Divinity!! Physical Man will have served his purpose well. This part of the ongoing experimentation of Spiritual growth of the Spirit will have culminated into this joint union where the original two will now become the 'ONE' as it has always been intended that he should!!

You will then be able to join all of those others, (unknown to you at present!) upon the Evolutionary trail back to the source of the 'Pure Created Life Force'. That is the sustaining element of 'All Life' Everywhere!! And that really does mean Everywhere, within the boundaries of your Universe and also outside of it, in company with all of the other ongoing Created Universes that have their places of origin in Outer, Outer, Space!!

We have come to the end of this treatise about Man and his place in the scheme of the Universal Mind of that Unknown Force of Life, that is Everywhere and always has been and indeed always will be. Ponder upon what has been given to you, you students of life and its hidden meanings, and we bid you a courteous Farewell.

And to you our Brother in Christ, We thank you for the use of your mind and your pen hand, both invaluable instruments of learning. **We bid you a special Farewell, and say to you 'All is Well.'** Do not fear for the future it is being taken care of. Believe that for it is the Truth.

May the Blessings of the Ones on High sustain you in your work upon your chosen path of service. Farewell! Farewell!

May Allah be Praised!!

All Praise be to the God of the Universe!!!!

Farewell.

Chapter 51

November 17th and 18th 2008

TIME – IS IT RELEVANT?!!!

TIME!! What is it? Is it to do with the gravitational pull of the Earth's core? Could it be neutralized on a personal basis? For example, is there something within us that has an affinity with the concept of the magnetic pull, which is part and parcel of what we think of as Time? So if we could eliminate that gravitational pull that bonds us whether we like it or not, would we then be able to regulate the idea of time to suit our personal requirements. Ignoring shall we say, what maybe 'going on' around us, for example, other people who are in the grip of this time factor? Is it all to do with the 'Mind' and our perception of how we 'see' time as it affects us personally?

Does that mean that no two people see or experience the same time scale in the same way? Does time depend upon everyone's perception of it? So is Time to be calculated as a commodity that if, for instance, work did not come into its jurisdiction a person could theoretically ignore the passage of time, for they would be in a way, be the Master of it and not its servant!!!! And yet Time would be ticking away regardless of how an individual decides to use it? So is Time an immutable substance?

Or does that just apply to this Earthplane of dense matter, where to get from A to B, literally has to take Time because of the denseness of the 'matter' that makes up the life force of this Planet? I.E. Its gravitational pull that we cannot ignore because within our human body gravity has an ally an affinity that at present it cannot control with its power of Thought?!!!

So is it our Thought mechanism that is our stumbling block that prohibits our power to actually control Time, by attempting to ignore its very existence?

So do all Planetary forms of different Matter or Substance also have there own form of gravitational pull, and does gravity 'vary' depending upon where you are in the Cosmos? Could that account for the erratic behaviour patterns of Stars, Meteors and all other forms of Stella activated Substances of existence?!!!

It's now 5.30 a.m. and I'm going back to bed for another hour or so!! I'll continue this writing later!!

Well it's now 9.20 in the morning and I am back with pen in hand ready for whatever thoughts of mine or 'otherwise'!! may come to me regarding this thing called Time!!!

Well the Thoughts that so far is uppermost in my mind is the one called 'The NOW'!!! We are told by those who know these things that Past! Present! and Future! Are viewed (at least upon the realms of the Spirit!!) are viewed as the 'Eternal Now' in the thoughts of the Creator and Creations!!

Does that mean that what was past, and now even the present and the future, have all 'happened' and are in a way like a carousel, a merry go round. And if one hops on to it at a certain place then that theoretically speaking, is the evolutionary period that one finds oneself in! And here we are not speaking of 'One' as a person, but 'One' as the 'Whole' of the Planet concerned!! In this case Our World!!! And that part of the Now, remains until such 'times' as it is decreed otherwise!!! Could that also account for that feeling that sometimes comes over a person that all of this has 'happened before' and yet one cannot actually account for it physically. It's just a feeling and then dismissed because there's no proof to the contrary!!

Now taking a leap into the imagination, could all of this have happened to certain members of the population, when they were upon another planet? Is that what some people say is a Parallel existence?!!! Such a lot of conjecture regarding what could be, and what is, and what very well might be!!

We have said before in other discourses that Creation as such is so complex as to be beyond Man's present comprehension, as indeed Man himself is!!! We are NOT GOD, and can only feebly speculate on the Deity's thoughts, so no wonder we find that we are in error of so many 'things' that need an explanation. And sadly we are not likely to get one that can satisfy our longing, some 'things' are best left as they are!! Do you not agree?!!

Another Thought! Can it be that the 'worlds' or realms of the Spirit are also part of this strange concept of the Now?!!

We are told by the inhabitants of that world that time as we view it upon the Earthplane is not relevant upon the spheres of the Spirit! A day! A month! A year!! Just words that don't seem to mean anything!!! Now this has brought on another thought, as we are told that there are Worlds of the Spirit does that literally mean a 'World' or are they Perceptions of the Mind? That would seem to mean that 'they' are not shall I say, 'realities'!!! And yet we are told of the 'Evolutionary Spiral'. I know that that pertains to ones mental awareness and yes, perception, but if that word 'Spiral' denotes also an actual advancement of the Spirits Spiritual evolution, then to my way of thinking that implies a (for want of a better word!) a 'physical movement' in an 'upward' figuratively speaking! Direction!!

And if that is the case, would another Realm or Sphere or whatever you wish to call a named place, would that one be in the same 'Time Scale' as the lower one for instance?!! There again 'Time' is being quoted as if it does matter!!! Quite a lot of quiet thinking needs to be applied I feel when trying to unravel what seems an anomaly regarding Time and the Now!!

Just so little Brother!! Quiet thinking is being recommended, for you have embarked upon a very emotive and oft misunderstood aspect of the Creative process!! Namely 'Creation' and all that that word implies!! We feel it is now time for you to relax and so we are returning your avenue of thought back to you, with sincere thanks for the use of it!! We bid you little Brother Farewell. This joint effort has been very worthwhile for all concerned!!!

We also bid your fellow students Farewell, and we are including those from Our Side of Life!!!

Farewell dear friend. Farewell, do not get despondent for All is being taken care of in All areas of your life!!

Fare – Thee – Well.

May Allah be Praised

May Allah be Praised.

Chapter 52

November 18th 2008

NOT WHAT I SET OUT TO WRITE!!!

Further to the previous discourse on TIME! And the Now! How does Space! figure in this equation or concept of Creation?! For after all as far as we know Space has always been in existence and dare I say it, even before Creation as we have come to understand was even contemplated and contemplated by...!!? We cannot say By Whom! Or By It! or even By That Unknowable Life Force! That really is Unknowable to those who think deeply and sincerely about the Origins of All forms of Creation, and the actual Means by which Creation and all that that word encompasses came about!!!

It would seem, and this is only my way of thinking about it, most people want to accept that Creation Per Se is by the God of their choice and no other!!! And who can blame them when those ancient manuscripts and books of Holy Virtue have made it very clear that GOD is 'THE CREATOR' of all that can be seen and yea, even unseen!! Even though the name of God is not always recognised as the same in various Religious Culture!!!

Quite a paradox is it not? I personally feel that man has a lot of re-thinking to do regarding his concept of what he thinks about 'God the Creator'!!! Do we have to go on thinking of just One Creator God? Why not more than ONE, maybe Two or Three or even many more.

If you remember correctly, in the Bible of Christian origin it does state that God said, 'Let Us Create Man in our own image,' or words to that effect and **by 'Us' surely that must mean Beings of a similar nature to the aforementioned God!!** 'Aspects' of that Deity, created by Him as partners in this ongoing venture of Creation of All known and unknown forms of life, in fact of Everything that is!!!

When Scriptures were being read and shall I say, only partly understood by the laity, and the question or even hint at disagreement with those scholars of Esoteric wisdom was unheard of. And if voiced would bring about dire consequences for the unfortunate person who had the temerity to put forward an argument contrary to what was an accepted fact by those scholastic minds!!!

Not like today, I'm glad to say, when there are so many books, fiction and otherwise that encourage the reader to Think for themselves and question what they perhaps do not understand. Today Space travel is almost looked upon as a normal experience. Men on the Moon, and talk of Mars perhaps one day being 'invaded' by Earthman!! Now that does sound like Science fiction. But sometimes fiction comes first, quickly followed by Fact!! Verifiable fact, and yet still there is so much that has not **been yet uncovered or understood and here I'm thinking of the 'man in the street'**, and not necessarily the dedicated scientist **with an 'Open Mind'.** For you do need an open mind when you are discussing the Universe and what it holds and more importantly, what or Who, it is that keeps it going!!!

What with Atomic explosions and Natures repercussions to **Man's onslaught upon her cloak of Earth, and the seas that cry** out for deliverance from the toxic waste that is poured into her once clean oceans of discovery! And the blue, blue skies above your earth that one day will turn Blood Red with your deadly pollutants that seep into the atmosphere as if by stealth, to one day reappear as Acid Rain!! What then?!!! We dare not hazard a guess.

You have advanced with your technological achievements but at what a cost? Your Planet is Dying! Yes Dying, for it is not being given the time to recover from the ill treatment you give to her. Remember you do NOT OWN THIS PLANET, it is only on Loan to you and can as it were, be taken away from your poor stewardship!! As you Sow, so then shall you Reap!!! Take heed of our warning.

Put your House in Order and don't look Heavenwards for a solution to your troubles. Do you really think that there is a Planet a Virgin World just waiting for you when you need it?!! Wake Up!! Wake Up!! You have no one to blame but yourselves if this World one day ceases to become a viable plane of habitation, but a dead orb, floating listlessly in Space awaiting a Cosmic Death where Debris is your epitaph!!!

Think again Brethren of the Earth. The keepers of the Flame of Life that illuminates your Earth are losing patience with you, and if they ever do! Well...!!! Need we spell that out?!!!

You know the Answer and we leave you to ponder upon what turn your Nemesis will take!! We shudder at the thought of that prospect.

And now we leave you!! Your little Scribe is somewhat bewildered at the turn his treatise has taken since he started out upon it! Take heart little one none of this will apply to you. **We leave 'you' in peace and with our appreciation for the use of your** pen hand. God bless you and keep you Safe is our parting gift to you.

We do not say Farewell. We say Goodbye!!

Well Brother, what can we say to you, all quite unexpected **'they' whoever they were, had permission to use our line of** thought transference, which ended up with you and your pen hand!

We bid you a fond farewell little one. Farewell.

Chapter 53

November 22nd, 3.15 a.m., 2008

HOW DO WE VISUALIZE GOD?!!! AND HAVE WE GOT IT RIGHT?!!!

Welcome little friend, let your pen do the thinking for you!! In other words, put yourself into our hands and we will be your guides for this nights treatise about Man, the Cosmos and God!! And just what is the relationship of these three?!! Where do we start? Well the logical position should be 'God' shouldn't it? But we are going to start with the Cosmos! Which incidentally is the manifested body of God, the aspect that is the starting point of this discussion!!

You wonder how can the Cosmos, this Universe be the body of God. The seen aspect as it were!! And then Man!! What is his position in this treatise? Does he have a place in our story or is he just another facet of that Deity that we cannot seem to get away from?!!

All right then God the Cosmos, God the Universe, God the Creator! We could go on and on enumerating the various aspects that go to make up this vision of the God consciousness. We strive to understand the reason, the meaning of what this life and all of the others really mean not only to us, but also to that Unknown Deity. That Creative genius that is the instigator of not only who we are, but also Why we are who we are!!!

Rather a conundrum is it not? Why should the Creator even bother with a being that is called Man? Is it because we are in essence part of that Creator?! And is 'Man' the only Man-like being in this created universe that we find ourselves in?!! Are we just one of the many facets of the Almighty? Are we a sort of **replica of that One? Or is Everything that is created 'replicas' in different forms and yet all part of the original 'Whole'?**

So, are we so important? Or do we just think we are, because we are told via those ancient scriptures, that we are made in His Image? And so we must be the highest form of Creation? But wait a minute? How do we know that we mirror the likeness of God? Has anyone seen this Creative genius? This Deity that we **sometimes call 'Father'?!** Are we part of His Creative Thoughts, or did we just happen to be cast in the mould of a human being of doubtful lineage? Is everything that is created, created for a **specific purpose or does that purpose come about by 'accident'?** or as some would say, by the process of Evolution?!!

If all that is created can be considered as aspects or facets of the Creator, then we must all be linked together in some way. In other words, we that is Man, could quite easily have become **'something else'**, if we are all part of the same Creative Mould before it becomes separated into these various compartments. For example animals, fish, birds, trees, flowers, animate and inanimate extravaganzas such as Mountains, rocks, and the **suchlike?!! Was 'Man' consciously decided upon as the created** essence that was nearest in likeness to the Creator?

And so he was almost by accident made the Highest form of Created thought made manifest?!!! In other words, one of the **other 'forms' of creation could easily be likened to the likeness of** the Creator. And so we may be quite wrong when we try to visualize our image of God as being like ourselves in an abstract **form of 'Physicality', or should that be of 'Spirituality'? or even another 'Ality' if there is such a thing!!!**

So then have we, that is Man in just one of his many disguises been singled out as the most promising of all the created forms of manifested Life Force? Or could it be that an aspect yet to be

Created will supersede Man as the Highest form of Creation?! Would that imply that the God, the Creator is forever 'changing', for creation we are informed is an ongoing sensation, never standing still, in other words, 'evolving'? And what does that word actually mean? That 'we' also are evolving? And evolving into 'What???!'

Do 'creations' in their broadest sense, 'come and go' as it were? In other words 'a season' and then what?! But what of 'Man', and here we stress the various aspects of him that go to make up the 'whole'. For we know that Man that is Physical Man, the human being that we know of as ourselves, is but a reflection of the true created being of 'Spirit Essence'. And as such is given the status of 'Immortality' just like His Creator!! So with our programmed evolutionary period upon the cycle of lives, for example, re-incarnation as a human entity, for a set period and then once more back to our original created conception of Spirit essence and continual evolution.

Because of the cycle, do we as Spirit continually change? And yet remain essentially our original created Spirit self?!! To one 'day' be returned to the fountain head of All Creation? But as what? Still an entity of personal identification, or are we to once more become absorbed into the original chaos of created thought energy or essence? Do we have a choice? Or has our outcome already been decided on our behalf? So the question is, perhaps not all created entities retain their individual identity in a personal fashion!! That may well be a question best not answered in a discourse of this Nature!!!

We seem to have left out the Cosmos that was mentioned at the beginning of this discourse, yet have we? For the Cosmos is another name for the Universe, and Man is a microcosm of the Macrocosm in other words, he is part of the fabric of the Universe, which is the manifested aspect of the Thought Creator, so we haven't left it out after all have we?!!

But we do feel that perhaps this is a good note upon which to close this discourse for the time being at least!! The little Scribe is beginning to wonder what he will make of all of his writing when he reads it in the morning! So we will let him return to his bed of rest though it is nearly morning as far as the time goes!!! We bid you Farewell dear friend we meet again in thought later.

Farewell and God bless You.

P.S.

An appendage to the above treatise. I've now read what I wrote in the early hours of this morning and it's made me think, and this is my thought!! As we are aware, or perhaps that should read 'As we presume' that GOD or even GODS created all that we see around us, Just what could His likeness be? We naturally assume He in some way has a Physical (wrong word!) likeness to ourselves, or the other way around if you like!! But as 'The Creator' He could 'pick and choose' whichever likeness of any of His Creations that He wanted to!! And perhaps Man need not be His only permanent choice of character!!!

Now that smacks of Heresy some will say!! But take a look at some of the Hindu Gods in sculpture and that then is food for thought, and no mistake!! So I think I will leave you the reader or listener, to come to your own conclusions regarding how You see the Deity of your choice!!!

End of appendage!!!

P.P.S.

And How about the Egyptian Deities? Just a thought!!!

Chapter 54

November 23rd 2008

TO BE 'COLOUR-BLIND' COULD BE A BLESSING!!

Could the 'Original Root Races' have been created by Individual Creator Gods? And if so could this account for the various different coloured pigmentations of the skin that seems to be a stumbling block to the Unification of the various races? The Basic Structure of the human body is the same regardless of race or colour, so is it just the outer covering of skin colour that seems to separate the races from even trying to understand that it is only that colour that makes them appear different? It is this very colour distinction that makes for variety of the human species, and we should glory in this colour variation and 'NOT' think that any one particular colour is of more importance than the others!!

Don't think that when the transition of the Mortal body takes place and the Spirit within is released, that it suddenly takes upon itself a Universal colouration. For the Spirit of that mortal body that it occupied during the lifetime of both of them, chooses to remain for quite some time upon the Spirit realm as a complete replica as far as bodily features are concerned, as its mortal companion upon Earth was when alive!!! So colour wise there is no difference unless the Spirit wishes otherwise!!

Which of course it does as it becomes more used to being its true Spirit self, which is a form of iridescent luminosity, an Aura of translucent beauty that houses the Mind essence of Spirit awareness!

So colour as such is not one of peculiar distinction, it is the Universal Spirit garb of an enlightened being, and the colours that are visible are the colours of true spirituality that are continually changing as the Spirit evolves upon the upward Spiral of understanding and heavenly virtue!!! If only man when upon Earth could be aware of this Aura that emanates from each human being on a lesser scale than when in Spirit. He perhaps would be less hostile in his outlook regarding his very own species of God created matter of human substance.

We all belong to the same family of Humanity, so why not get used to the idea, instead of trying to find fault where none exists?! Accept God into your lives, and that means use that Holy Spirit **that is part of all of us, we can't all be Saints, but there's no harm** in trying to be is there? And understanding each other makes for a more harmonious existence, and you know it does, so why the delay? Your neighbour is your Brother and in this day and age your neighbour will be maybe several thousands of miles away, **but he's still your Brother.** So accept that fact and treat him kindly.

And just remember about that word 'Karma! cause and effect!' as you sow, so shall you reap! Those words though ancient are **still applicable to today's living!!**

Confrontation is never a suitable answer to any form of not **understanding another's point of view! So why not change** yours? You maybe surprised for it may turn out to be just like the other persons that you are criticising!!!

Time for me to say Farewell and this I do in all sincerity. Farewell and may your God bless You.

Chapter 55

November 24th 2008

JUST RANDOM THOUGHTS!!!

These are just random thoughts on my part, at least for the time being they are!! After reading what I had written yesterday and what I did write were my 'inspired' thoughts and I cannot take any credit for them!! Well it got me thinking about GOD, GODS, and RELIGION! That is Man's contribution to what he thinks must please GOD! And that leaves me wondering! For the precepts in I think all known forms of Religion, if they were adhered to and more importantly practised, dare I say 'religiously', then they are good guidelines for a satisfying life style.

So the idea must have been based upon considerable caring thought procedures, for the benefit of all concerned. Now I believe that Religion as such is Man's attempt to satisfy his longing for something or Someone, that is for want of a better word, A Spiritual Supernatural Being that could when required perform deeds of miraculous construction! And One that you could always call upon in times of need and when things were going well, then Man could offer up prayers and homage so as to show his feelings towards the God of His Creation!

Now that I have written that I realise it can be taken in two ways.

First that God is Man's Creator, and second that God as visualised by Man is 'His Creation'!!! Two very different aspects to be sure!! And that also goes for Religion doesn't it? It's Man made and NOT GOD'S!! To my way of thinking HE doesn't need or even want all of this adulation from man!! A sincere heartfelt 'Thank You' would I'm sure be perfectly acceptable to the Deity, for all forms of 'service' that God bestows upon man, without expectations of any kind on 'His' part!!!

But I feel that that expression would not satisfy man or perhaps I should say man's ego!!! Have you not noticed when either in Church services or other less 'orthodox' as it were places where there is a congregation, when the Vicar or whoever is taking the place of an authorised teacher / preacher! That when they are talking to God from a rostrum or pulpit, such a lot of what is being said to God almost takes on the form of telling him what the speaker thinks God should be aware of. And he the speaker is humbly (?) giving his Creator the benefit of his the 'speaker's advice' on who the prayers are for, and hopefully God will be listening and will do something about it!!!

Do they not understand that God is already aware of what is needed without having to be reminded of his 'duties'!!! When I hear these people who are genuine in what they are saying, when I hear their forms of supplication to their Deity, I'm afraid I inwardly 'cringe' at what is being said. And would love to cry out 'He already knows all of that, just offer up your Silent thoughts and keep quiet!!!

For it's in the Silence that He can draw closer to you and answer your unspoken thoughts, even if the answer is not what you expect! He knows what you and others 'need', and not what you think you 'want'!!! Which is quite a different matter is it not?!!

Mankind in general it seems visualises His GOD from a human being's standpoint and GOD is NOT some form of Supernatural Human Type Being. He is the Creator of Human beings, He doesn't need to look like one!! Even when the ancient scriptures said that 'He' said, 'Let us make Man in our own image!!' Was anyone there at the time those words were voiced?!! I somehow think not! Though I must admit that the sentiments expressed are very pleasing to the ear!!!

What a lot we have to learn about everything connected to Esoteric literature of what was said and what was not said, and what was implied!!! Today is the beginning of the New Age, when to criticise is an acceptable form of understanding of what is being said and NOT what is actually being meant, either by those of the past or those now of the present! We must all use our innate intuitive powers of deduction, use your free will, it was given to you for a purpose! Use it! And Use it wisely in everything you say and do!

You are judged by your actions and those who are the judges are your own peers, not 'Someone' up there sitting on a seat of judgement looking through Your book of Life! Pen in hand, ready to exact justice! 'Karma' in fact and you all know what that word implies! Good or Bad!! The choice is yours, make sure it is the right one for 'tis you who is on trial!!!!

I had intended when I started this writing to talk about the way we visualise our God, for I think I have some rather peculiar ideas about it, but I have how gone off that idea for the present. But I will come back to it sometime, even if it's only to satisfy my own curiosity on that subject, which I feel is very vast and complex to say the least. So for now I shall bring this writing to a close, shall I bid you Farewell like my Brothers in White do? Yes, I think I will, and so I say Farewell to anyone who may have read this manuscript, perhaps long after I have left this troubled Planet of Earth.

Farewell and God bless You.

So much for me saying Farewell! I've decided to continue writing for a little while longer. And remember, these are only my personal thoughts and if they cause offence to some people I apologise before I start, but I'm still going to write what I think, so here goes!!

I cannot understand how Church Authorities, by which I mean the clergy, the ministers, the Bishops, the Archbishops, the Cardinals etc! etc! etc! I cannot understand how they stand up and talk to, and about God, in the way they do. It's as if He is some form of, how on Earth can I put it without causing offence to someone's sensibilities? Well it's as if He is some form of Super Natural Being that leaves you awe-struck to even think about what He may look like and be!!!

If they and 'they' are usually quite intelligent people, if they really stop and think and yes, look at what has and still is being created, they surely must realise that God, that is 'their God' can't possibly be anything like a likeness of a Human or Super Human being. Take for instance the smallest insect, and put it under a microscope and see the wonder of its minute creation, beauty and intricacy of construction that Man for all of his technological achievements could not replicate! And the spectrum of Created achievement is beyond our feeble comprehension! And that creation includes Us!!

The Mind simply boggles, and what about the 'Universe' and the Stars and the Planets, the Force of Nature and the elements that go to make up a viable form of habitation for Man to live upon. Oh! The mere thought of all of that Creative urge to Create and to go on creating and to keep it going and in check as it were. In spite of the turmoil that Nature seems to get herself into at times! Which is in reality Just Nature behaving Naturally!!

So how can these people of intelligence think that their God of super human like structure could possibly be the Instigator of all of this 'Ordered Chaos'. Have they ever given that real thought, because if they have then they can't possibly believe, let alone go on preaching that the God that they talk to can be explained in the way they seem to expect the laities to go on believing in!!! You may possibly think that I don't believe in God, but you would be wrong for I DO! And most sincerely I can assure you!! I talk to Him just like everyone else, I say 'Father' but… and here is where perhaps I am different.

I think of God in a sort of abstract fashion, the idea of what He may look like doesn't influence me in any way, there are times when I feel how can I put it? I feel sort of Close to Him like a friend, in fact some times I feel a bit 'cheeky' towards Him, but I know He knows I don't mean it, though I do duck my head just in case there's a hand close by to cuff me for my impudence!!! But I do Love Him in my own way, whether He feels the same about me I'm none to sure! Yes I am! I know He does!

Well at least I've no hang ups regarding how I feel about God, but then I also accept the premise that there are Other Gods, even if I don't know about them. But I'd like to, just out of curiosity on my part!! I write books, which include these other Gods, only in passing you understand. But as far as I am concerned My God, is My God, of course He's yours as well, but to me it's on a personal level and please don't think I'm being presumptuous, that is not my intention. But I think perhaps I have a better form of working relationship with Him than a lot of the Church clergy and their authorities do!!!

I accept the fact that the God I refer to in this narrative is NOT the Overall Unknown Unfathomable Essence of Life Force that has always been in existence and I have NO knowledge of that Force, but I do honestly and sincerely believe in IT! Though I have no illusions about ever understanding its existence! But I do have my own theories on that subject and I do not propose to air them here!! And this is where I think I will end all of my thoughts upon the subject in hand!

Has it got me anywhere? Well I have aired my views for what they are worth, and when I read what I've written perhaps I'll find I've got some further thoughts that I didn't know I had!!!

So I'll say Farewell and this time I mean it!! So it's Farewell, and May Your God Bless You as I know He does.

Little scribe chela, May you be blessed and in the name of Allah we bid you farewell.

Well I didn't expect that! But thank you!!

Chapter 56

November 25th, 2.30 a.m., 2008

THE LABYRINTH OF THE MIND.

Peace little Brother, we greet you in the name of the Master Jesus!! And in His Name we will continue with this night's discourse. You are wondering what it is that you are going to write about are you not? Well little friend cease your wondering, empty your mind of those intriguing thoughts and allow us to take them over, and we will see what this night's journey of the minds will reveal.

Just sit quietly and wait, there that is better, now relax and show us this privilege of the union of the Minds! Yours and Ours!!

The Mind! That intricate form of formless substance that can take you upon journeys of both the mind and the physical equivalent, the Imagination. One and the same are they not? For what may start off as a flow of the imaginative stream of unborn thoughts, can become a positive reaction resulting in a flight into the unknown into the realms of fantasy. That takes on the illusion to you but the reality lies with Us, upon the realms of the worlds of Spirit substance, that we can offer to you in the form of 'mind travel'. Where you, the physical can become as it were for just a brief spell part of the Spirit illusion of physical reality! And all because of this union of Minds!! That distance has no power over, yea and even Time itself!! For is not Time just another word for 'distance of perception'.

In other words Illusion of the senses, not just the physical but **also the Spirit, and with the input of the Spirit's insight, the** imagination of the physical can become the positive reality of the Spirit!!! Or perhaps that should read the Imagination of the Spirit becomes the reality of the physical counterpart of the Mind essence that pervades the Whole of the Spirit planes of existence!! For the Mind or Thought medium of the Spirit governs all forms of Thought Illusion and its other side, Reality of the Physical!!!

For the Internal reality of the Mind substance though not as a visible essence, is nevertheless, the very core of what can become a positive reality upon the plane of Earth!! Such is the power of Imaginative thought that from an abstract vision of an intangible as yet unborn element of substance from the Spirit, can become a positive Reality of permanent structure upon the realm of the **Earth plane!!! How do you think your 'inventions' that become** almost household necessities had their Birth? They stem from the interchange of Spirit illusion to the physical expression of **'material reality'.** And that goes equally for the expansion of the Spiritual side of Man's physical body of expression!!

The two are 'inseparable'. For one without the other is not complete, they remain as Thought expression residing in the Mind substance of both parties that need that extra impetus that bonds the two thoughts into a reality, that can be perceived as such upon the plane of the **Physical! And yet the 'Blue Print' as it** were, was originated as a form of Spirit illusion before it becomes a physical reality!!!

Such is the complexity of this union of the two essences or aspects of the Creative Mind Power that permeates the whole strata of 'Creation' from beginning to end!!

Thought is the very essence of seen or unseen Creation, nothing can be accomplished without the impetus of Thought, whether upon the planes of the Spirit or the lower dense planes of **the 'Earth's', and notice we have said Earth's and not just Earth** singular! Come to your own conclusions as to what we are implying!!!! 'As above, so Below!!' words from the distant past and yet they are equally applicable to today's society as they were then!!!

Change comes about from **the Inner perceptions and isn't** always as a physical seen reality, though paradoxically it does quite often result in a positive form of reality in both Worlds!!! It is Creation or Evolution that is an ongoing manifestation of Divine Thought, it never ceases in one form or another!!! And Creation as such is NOT just confined to one sphere of existence or even to One Creator of it!! Make of that what you will and accept or reject that statement, it is entirely up to you, but please **don't dismiss it out of ha**nd, keep an open mind and you may well be surprised at where your thoughts will take you to!!!

Creation comes from Thought and thought stimulates the art of Creation, it is a circle of never ending varieties and can never be broken, unless otherwise decreed by that Unknown Source of all created life force. And here is where we will cease this nights treatise and leave you to ponder upon its outcome!!

We bid you Farewell, which is our accredited form of departure.

And to you Brother Scribe, we bid you Farewell and yet we remain in essence, with you at all times!! Time for reflection little one. Farewell!!

Chapter 57

November 25th 2008 Continued!

MAZE! OR LABYRINTH! TAKE YOUR PICK!!!

It is now 3 o'clock p.m. and there have been a lot of thoughts milling around in my head, after reading the previous chapter about the Mind and the thoughts that it generates!!

I know that in one of my books I hinted at the thought 'waves' that circumnavigate our Earth plane, well now I'm going to elaborate on that theoretical assumption of mine and afterwards see if it makes any sense, I hope it does. So when I write I'm assuming that I know what I'm talking about so bear with me if you think differently!!

Well the 'waves' of thought that I mentioned are not 'waves' in the sense of the ocean waves! These waves or streams of invisible (to our mortal senses!) particles of light that are actually thoughts that are of a 'positive' nature, which makes them a viable force that could be classed in physical terms as a substance of matter that is not usually associated with that word! But then 'matter' as such is a variable commodity depending upon which sphere you happen to be. Upon Earth matter is considered as Heavy and Dense, upon other spheres it could be in a liquid form, and yet again it could be seen as a vapour!! All aspects of Electrical discharge in one way or another!!

Well these waves or bands that move constantly around in the Earth's atmosphere, are in varying degrees of shall I say substantial 'matter', in this case they are of a vapourish substance of fine plasticity. And can be tapped into and part removed from the continuous stream, which immediately joins up the vacant space so that there is no noticeable break in the circle!! Now the Key to this form of part removal is Your own Thought pattern! **Your positive thought creation would 'lock on' as it were to the** appropriate section that would deal with what your thoughts required.

Now all of this procedure is not only automatic it covers but a fraction of a second and the thoughts then generated come from **'Your Mind' and remain yours until they are no longer needed** and then they can reinstate themselves with your added creative positive thoughts. So forming an ever increasing volume of **'thought matter' for others to take advantage of!!!**

These thought streams are quite separate from each other for there are many of them depending upon the quality being generated by those whose thoughts are considered to be of Universal value, though not necessarily of any specific positive use!! There are Beings of High Moral standing who Monitor all of these Thought substances, that if not carefully vetted could, **left on their own get 'out of hand' so to speak!**

As you are well aware Thoughts are not always, shall we say of 'High and lofty ideals'. And these thoughts are not part of the 'Monitors' judgement!!

They come under the heading of 'rogue elements' and so are not considered in a Universal manner, but are nevertheless **administered by a special Band of almost 'outsiders' that are not** allowed access to the ordered wave bands spoken of previously!!!

Now you can appreciate that thought regulation on the part of **mankind should be seriously 'thought about'.** For Thoughts can be tools of Great Virtue and likewise the opposite can also be applied!!!

Your Mind (another invisible substance!) is a storehouse of **thought activity, which often incorporates 'memories',** memories of yesteryear, situations, experiences, good and not so good, but all part of the building of a character! These memories can be brought to the surface at almost any time when a situation of today jogs the memory of a past situation of similarity!! Sometimes the mind allows the Brain to store some of these memories, special ones that need to be looked after and treasured. And should the occasion arise, the brain will activate those memories that are pertinent to a present day situation that perhaps the Mind has forgotten about!! You have as it were, a sort of safety net should it be needed!!

So thoughts though not perhaps a visible substance can become electrically charged so that they are once again a viable agent of expectation and yes, even physically observed or perceived if that is what the Mind desires!!! We are indeed a wonderful piece of Thought generated matter are we not?!!

So take care of your own thought machine, your essence of Divine thought emanation, that makes of you the Highest form of Created life upon Planet Earth!! And by the words Planet Earth, that more or less implies that there may well be even Higher forms of Created Life substances akin to Man's likeness upon other Spheres, other Worlds, other Planets, and shall we add other 'times'!! And that can be read as past, present, or Future!! For 'time' is irrelevant when considering Creation and those who are the Creators!!!

And here I feel I have come to the end of my thoughts regarding that previous chapter called 'The Labyrinth of the Mind', which could easily have been called 'The Maze called the Mind', either version will probably leave you somewhat bewildered no doubt!! And as for me? Well I've yet to read all of what has been written, so my comments will stay with me in my Thoughts!!! I'm tempted to write AMEN! Which translated is I believe, SO BE IT!!!

Chapter 58

November 29th, 2.15 a.m., 2008

UNIVERSES WITHOUT NUMBER!!!

Welcome Brother, you are wondering what it is that you will be writing about are you not? Cease your wondering for we are about to take charge of your passive thought mechanism, relax and let your pen do the thinking for you!!!

Worlds, Planets, Stars, galaxies, the list is endless, for there is far more out there in Space than you have any knowledge of and it is ever increasing if you could but see it!! You have a saying upon earth that 'You can't see the wood for the Trees'!! Well then substitute the word Wood and replace it with 'Stars'!!! Does that make sense to you? For when you look up to the Heavenly firmament on a clear night, you might even say your view is somewhat blurred by those millions upon millions of star like objects that seem to be, almost in the way of what you hope to see!!!

Well do not be deceived, for those millions of Stars represent the basis for cosmic expansion!!! You could almost call them, Heavenly Debris!! They are the building blocks of unseen Worlds yet to be born!! You see what you see, but you see what you think you see, and not what is there in reality!!! Many of those so-called Star like objects are merely reflections of others and so it would be difficult to say which is the real and which is the substitute for the real!!

Many of those 'seen' objects of twinkling appearance are actually fronting what is behind them!! And others are merely photographic memories of past events that died a natural death many, many aeons of time ago!!

The Cosmos is one gigantic form of 'Space Illusion'! You just cannot believe everything you think you observe. What you see just gets in the way of what is still there in the background, just waiting to make an appearance upon that vast canvas called Sky!! Your Scientists talk about 'Black Holes' as if there are many of them dotted about! But take another look, your whole view of Space is one 'Big Black Hole', where stars and worlds come and go and then amalgamate to become something else!!! 'Something' unheard of by present day man!!

There are 'Worlds' out there that almost defies description. This Universe of yours is like a 'boiling pot' and do you know what for? It is for the benefit of other 'Universes' outside of your perimeter!! They receive what has been created in 'your' Cauldron of Molten Prime Ordial substance, the Chaos of Creativity and these creations 'slip through' your Black Hole of Space to emerge within the waiting Universe of expectation. The start of a brand new cycle of Life Creation, All that is needed to complete this circle are People!! And they come from Another Universe of 'Building material' if you don't mind calling Created life forms 'Building Material'.

Universes are all part of this gigantic scheme of Divine Inspiration!! They form a chain of 'linked' Life Force, a sort of Umbilical Cord that joins them all together.

Separate but still belonging to the 'Mother Universe' the size of which defies description for she is the 'Womb of Creation'. 'Resting in the Sea of Eternal Space'!!!

Do not try and fathom that out dear Earth friends for it is beyond Mans comprehension at this present time. In fact it is doubtful if He will ever be allowed to understand what the Meaning of Life Force is about! He will perhaps in time, but he will have ceased to be recognisable as a human like being!! And

The Little Scribe

here we propose to cease this part of tonight's treatise and let the Scribe go back to his bed of rest and resume at a later date.

It is now 3.45 a.m. and I feel I need some rest. Mental as well as Physical!!!

It's now 9.35 a.m. and I've just read what has been written in the early hours of this morning, which seems ages ago. But it's reminded me of something that I wrote and made a diagram of, and that was a 'string' of Universes somewhat in the shape of a 'necklace'. Oval, and in the middle was an enormous 'Magnetic core'? But I realise now that it was the 'Mother Universe' with her brood of offspring Universes, some small, some large but all having a place in this Necklace of Universal Life Force!! And all contributing in one way or another to this unified Life aspect of the Sublime Creative Force of Unknown Energy that permeates the Whole of Existence! The Original 'Alpha and Omega' yet not quite, because the 'Omega' joins up with the tail of the Alpha, so completing the Circle, the Unbroken Circle of All that there is or ever was and yea, ever will be!!

Welcome once again Scribe of the Night! We have already taken command of your thoughts, as you have rightly guessed!!! Your 'Necklace of Universes' is a very apt description of the Manifested life Force of that Unknowable Energy of Creativity. And what you have described is only just a 'part' of that 'Life Force'. For the Womb of Space is Boundless in its endless promotion of what the 'Divine Thought' decrees!!! And remember that that 'Unknown Essence' has Created not only Universes and their various appendages but also the 'Creator Gods' to administer those Creations, which includes their own ability to Create on the Sublime Creators behalf!!!

Do not be surprised at the mention of 'Creator God's' for if you truly think in terms of Eternal Eternities, you will know that the word 'God's' is the only applicable conclusion that you can come to if you wish to make sense of What Creation in its

Broadest sense really means!! It is not just confined to this One Universe wherein you dwell, for the present! Or even the Planet, your Planet that spins endlessly in its orbit of Space, its 'allotted orbit' we must add. Nothing is left to chance, believe that, for even chaos is 'ordered' even if sometimes it seems it is out of control!

Those Vast 'Beings' of Cosmic Structure that are the Monitors of Natures behaviour are constantly alert to its vagaries!! And do not hesitate to take steps to limit what might be termed or seen as Catastrophes!!! All part of the Destinies of Created Creations!! And even Man cannot escape his Destiny however much he feels he has control of it!!!

Accept your Limitations but as a paradox do not limit your expectations of what life has to offer you! Your Freedom of Will is your 'safety net' use it wisely and who knows you may even one day be able to control your own destiny instead of having it done for you!!! And by Whom!? We leave that in abeyance!! We seem to have dealt only with the physical aspect of Man haven't we? But those of you, who are on the upward path of enlightenment, know of the Spirits interaction with the physical mortal body and what that involves. And so we feel that in this discourse we can safely, shall we say, ignore that subject for the time being!!!

Take heart little scribe, we are coming to the end of this treatise, for we feel we cannot take your readers or listeners any further along the Evolutionary trail of Eternal Expectation of what the meaning of Life is all about!!! And so we will bid those travellers of the mind Farewell and hope that we have given you much food for thought!!!

And to you our faithful and patient little Scribe, you have plenty to think about and to add to your already store of wisdom and knowledge!! We greet you as one of Us dear friend and we leave you with our heartfelt thanks for this Union of Minds!!

The Little Scribe

Farewell and God bless You, and our friend from afar wishes to say,

May Allah smile kindly upon you little traveller upon life's path! May Allah be praised. May Allah be praised!!!

Praise be to Allah!!!

We now Depart!!!

Chapter 59

November 30th 2008

THOSE BEINGS OF ANTIQUITY!!!

In a previous chapter there's a mention of 'Vast Beings of Cosmic Structure' and I expect many people will wonder what is meant by that reference to 'Beings'!! Well there are Beings of Enormous Size that Monitor the four corners of this Earth!! In actual fact they are in a way, in control of the elements of Nature!! They are NOT all the same in feature or form depending upon the 'location' that they belong to! They are not visible shall we say, to those upon Earth, unless of course those people have clairvoyant and mystic persuasions and even then it's very, very rarely that those 'Beings' are actually 'seen' in Physical form, or perhaps that should read 'Physical or Spirit' comprehension!!! Their efforts can be acknowledged as seen 'effects', but not known as to there origin, they are just thought of as part of Nature's erratic behaviour patterns!!!

These Beings are from another Dimension and yet they form part of the Planet's protective strata of equilibrium and Cosmic orbital equation!!! In some of the ancient volumes of 'Esoteric Supernatural diagrams of this World', you can see a portrayal of some of these Beings, usually perhaps just a head and face of one where 'his' cheeks are puffed up.

And his lips are rounded with the force of the air being expelled, and as the air becomes gale force to billow out the sails of the ships that ply the oceans and the trade routes that circle the globe!!!! All very fanciful you may say, but many a myth has its roots in bygone folk-lore that perhaps at one time was an accepted fact, passed down through the generations and the origins lost and so becomes what is known as folk-lore!!!

Now whether you believe in these Beings or not, does not alter the fact that Natures wayward behaviour, especially of late needs **careful Monitoring by Something or even 'Someone'.** But a 'Someone' would need to be so powerful and have at 'His'? command, forces that could out manoeuvre Natures own secret **Force that can turn a Summer's day into a night time's** catastrophe in an instant!!!

Such is the awesome power that has been generated to keep this little planet called Earth on its allotted course and to protect it from Outside interference from those elements that seem to thrive on the destruction of anything that gets in their way, which must inevitably involve their own suicidal tendencies!! These **forces, both for Good or its opposite are beyond Man's physical** comprehension, and his feeble attempts at curbing them without outside help as it were, are without a doubt, doomed to failure!!

Man seems astonished when perhaps in the middle of some catastrophic event, it suddenly becomes almost passive! And it leaves Man wondering how this sudden reversal of events could come about.

And he lifts his eyes heavenwards and Thanks his God for this timely intervention!! Remember the saying that God moves in mysterious ways his mission to be fulfilled!!! And could that mission be accomplished by one of these Unknown Beings of His own Creation that are the invisible guardians of our Planet?!!!

Nothing is impossible when that Creative Genius allows his **thoughts full rein on Man's behalf!!** So do not dismiss lightly the mystic occurrence by those unknown, shall we call them 'Guardian Angels' of Ancient literature, that started out as fact, only to become folk-lore!! 'Guardian Angels' they are, even if they do not conform to Man's idealised version of a 'Guardian Angel'!!! When you view everything with an Open Mind, then

Size or the lack of it, or even the exaggerated version of it, becomes somewhat irrelevant when handing out explanations of what to some must seem to be the Unexplainable!!! It's all in the 'Perception' the mental Perception and not the 'logical one' as is so often the case when trying to deal with 'Cosmic Esoteric Illusion'. Just remember what we have said, Nothing but Nothing is Impossible to the Creator of All Creation!!!

Does that perhaps give you food for thought as to what you have always been told about 'God' and here we encompass All 'Gods' known and unknown, personal or Universal!!!

Think about it you seekers and searchers after the Truth, for Truth has many facets to it, turn it around and your view maybe different.

But it doesn't alter the basic fact, that 'Truth is Truth', whichever way you choose to look at it!!! Don't be frightened of thinking the impossible for quite often the impossible turns out to be 'quite possible' in certain circumstances!!!

And here is where we are going to take our leave of you and our dear friend the little scribe who, as so often starts out these discourses of his mind, only to find that we have taken them over before they finish!!! So we bid you the readers or listeners Farewell.

To you Brother that word does not really apply for we are always around you in Thought, never far away, and that is because we want to be near you!! God bless You little one, God bless You!!

Chapter 60

December 1st 12.05 a.m.–1.15 a.m. 2008

WHAT IS IN A NAME?!!!

Which God is your God? Do you want my God? Do I want Yours? And are all of these Gods, God's? Or are they Aspects of the One God? Why is it that when it comes to talking about God, people can become very cagey and it seems they feel that the questioner is trying to 'muscle in' on their particular one, because they feel uncertain about theirs!! Do we on the whole expect too much from our chosen God, and when I say chosen, I'm referring to the particular culture that has always insisted that the God of their choice is the only one. He was good enough for their Fathers and even their Father's Father, and you can trace the line back for generation upon generation, and so of course He Must be the right One, but is He still the right One for You? Or to try and think any differently is **just 'not on'**!!

To Question anything about the so-called Authorised version of God is just asking for trouble!! And so the easiest way out of this situation is to go meekly along with the rest of the population whose God happens to be Yours as well!! Does the same criteria apply to all those others whose conception of God differs from others upon this Planet you call Earth? But where is the verifiable proof that any one of these accepted versions of God is the right one?!!

If you say to some of those earnest adherents to their particular God that All of these various assumptions regarding these different feelings about the Word God, really means that All of those variations actually refer to the One Same God and No

Other!!! So what is all the fuss about?! If you see him differently to others and call Him by another name, it makes not the slightest difference to Him!! He is beyond a Name, for what is in a name? It's only for Mans benefit and not the accredited Deities!!!

Why not stick to the word 'Father' and leave it at that, for after all we are supposed to be a Family are we not? And 'Father' is such a comforting expression of sincere affection that should satisfy the most hardened of die-hards who insist that the Name their group culture has always associated with, the Word God is the one and only one that He deigns to accept?!!! How arrogant of Man to limit the existence of the Almighty to a particular Nom de plume!!! Of Man's choice!!!

If calling the One and Only God by various names gives those groups of Religious Culture a feeling of personal satisfaction, then go ahead and call Him what you like. But always keep in mind the change of Name does not mean the change of God. He remains the same for 'ALL PEOPLE THE WORLD OVER'. And once that fact is accepted, then these feelings of being different from your neighbour whoever he may be and wherever he may reside should be put aside once and for all!

Confrontation because of the presumed difference in Religion should be relegated to the past and forgotten, just as childish fancies are when you have grown up!!! And that is just what we say to you GROW UP!!! And then you can begin to live in Harmony, we are tempted to say Once More!! And that implies that in the beginning, so-called Religion did not mean a stumbling block to Unification of all the groups or tribes if you like, that could trace their very roots back to the one and only Creator to be called 'Father'!!! And here is where we are going to allow the little scribe to cease his writing on our behalf and return to his bed of rest, for an hour and a quarter has slipped by without him realising it.

So we bid you Goodnight little friend and thank you for your willing participation in this unexpected mind union of yours and ours!!

May God bless you and keep you safe. Fare-thee-well little scribe. Fare-the-well!!!

AMEN!!! So Be IT!!!

Chapter 61

December 2nd 2008

PLANETS! WORLDS! AND WHAT ELSE?!!

Rub the sleep out of your eyes little one, for there is work to be done this night!! Now we shall begin, heed not what your pen may write for we have command of it, as we have of you!!!

This is the time of year when you of the Christian Faith celebrate the Birth of your Saviour, known the World over as Jesus Christos!! How many times we wonder has that One had to enact this episode in His Mortal life and shall we add, Just where in this vast Universe this chasm of unknown expectations. Your world is one of many that has witnessed the rise and sometimes thought of fall, of the chosen one that was chosen by no other than Himself in his service for that Omnipresent Unknown Source of Life Force that permeates the very structure of this Universe of High expectation!!!

As long as there is a being of Humankind in its allotted Span of Evolution of the species, there will always be a need for a Saviour, a Teacher, One who is prepared. Nay, has been prepared over many incarnation periods to bring Enlightenment to those who hunger and thirst for the reason of this enforced sojourn upon a Planet of programmed life that to many seems like exile from the land of their birth!!

You may not yet be aware that Planets and Worlds are interchangeable, that is in their designated populations!! Hence this inborn desire of the enlightened ones to return to their place or plane of Origin!! And this desire is sometimes manifested in **those chosen beings of light that you call 'Saints'!! A word that** has no real meaning in various parts of this Universe! For to be a so-called Saint does not necessarily require the person to be recognised either in their lifetime upon Earth or the other Earths that abound in the space you are so fond of trying to explore!!!

These other Earths that you upon this one have no knowledge of, are the training grounds, the planes of experimentation of untold varieties of the being that you identify as the Human one!! You see, you upon the Earth are part of this Universal form of species experiment!! There dwell amongst you prototypes of some of the root races that are destined to take over this planet in due course!! Most of the **populations of this Earth are the 'misfits'** from various planets, they belong to the groups that do not conform to their original place of birth!!

That is one of the reasons for this form of hostility that you witness amongst the various races, they do not belong to the same Root Race. They seek to find that race within the confines of this Earth and those who do belong to this aforementioned Root race are those who are called the thinkers, the seekers and searchers, the ones called Idealists, the ones who do NOT belong to this Planet and they are forever aware of this.

But they understand that they are here for a purpose and that purpose is to try and enlighten those who show an interest in the World of the Spirit, the Esoteric mysteries of Why they are upon this dense planet that some feel is Alien to their nature!! Which it is, and it rests with those who can be classed as teachers (though not in the accepted sense!) as teachers of those who seriously desire to return to their plane of origin. To once more be a part of their lost civilization that is not lost but are merely half-forgotten memories that need to be returned to a form of reality. Not all of these other Planets are what you would term physical! They are of a Highly Spiritual form of an abstract creation that takes many forms of manifested existence quite unknown to Mankind upon this Earth!!!

Those seekers and searchers we spoke of were volunteers to be incarnated upon this lower Earth. For the main reason of trying to make aware to those who showed a sincere desire to understand the complexities of Creation and how they fit into this vast Enterprise of Universal Structure of God the Creator!! **We mentioned the phrase 'Saints' earlier and that is exactly what** these teachers are, though they would be the last to think of **themselves as such!!! When their shall we say, their 'job' has been** accomplished, they can if they wish return to their own Planet once again and enter once more into their previous life style. And even prepare a place for some of those earth pupils that now qualify for this Higher sphere of learning!! To some this is the Heaven that they have been told about. For this Plane is one of the many Spirit Ones.

By which you now understand that they are fully cognisant **with the idea of 'Spirit and Physical!! Evolution of the species** takes many twists and turns during its progress ever upwards!! **And not all of the Earth's populations evolve at the same time!!!** But when, and if they ever do, then you really will see your Heaven upon Earth as has been promised in ancient literature!! A **good point in which to conclude this nights foray into Earth's Planets and what they mean in the Universal Sense of Man's Evolution!!!**

We bid you Farewell. Little Scribe you may now retire once more to your bed of rest.

Farewell and sweet dreams!!!

Chapter 62

December 3rd 8.30 p.m.–10.00 p.m. 2008

SPACE! TIME! WHAT DO WE MAKE OF THEM?!!!

Little Brother, you were watching a programme on your Television last night about Time and Space!! And the conclusion that the presenter of it came to was that when this Universe, your Universe was created by what is called 'The Big Bang' some thirty and a half Million Years ago, was the start of Time as you have come to know it!! All very feasible sounding but is it true?! For the 'Big Bang' to take place there had to be the ingredients with which to create this 'Big Bang' that resulted in the Universe being born, and Time and Space must have been in existence before that Cosmic occurrence could take place!!

So Space even on its own Must have existed and not only existed, but must also have been the spawning ground for all of those molecular elements of life force to coagulate together to form what you know of as Primordial Substance or Chaos if you like! Because all aspects attributed to what the Universe houses i.e. Stars, Planets, Worlds, Galaxies, Debris, the list is endless and they don't all come about overnight, so to speak!! When the Universe was Created, formed as such, it was virtually an Empty Void, yet that actually is a miss-statement, for the Universe trapped inside of it, SPACE!! The very SPACE that exists OUTSIDE of it, then and NOW!!

And that Space that was trapped was chock-a-block with organisms of Life elements, darting here and there, swirling and turning around, forming and then coming apart, only to be engulfed by other molecular structures that are virtually invisible to the naked eye. Yet are the very 'building blocks' of all forms of Life, right through the stages of inanimate life force to the Highest form of Animate Creations.

And by that we talk not of just Mankind but of the very Worlds and Planets and Stars that one day he was destined to inhabit and maybe conquer, and bring into subjection the very Force of Life that you call Nature!! Man was not created to be 'Nature's Slave' But her 'Master' once he had come to terms with Her eccentricities, her seemingly wayward behaviour patterns, which once understood, can be, shall we say tamed and harnessed for the good of all concerned!!!

Do not think that your Universe is the only one in existence for in the Space beyond it, are many, and yea, are still in the womb of the Eternal Life Force that stems from the Thoughts of the Unknowable Essence of All Creations, seen and unseen known and unknown. For Universes of various sizes have been in existence since that Unknowable Essence as it were 'gave birth' to the very first and original Creation that burst forth from the Fiery Primordial Chaos. To become the Prototype for all subsequent Creations of which your Universe belongs as it were to the Family of the same.

And think not in Millions but in Trillions, in Zillions of so-called Years of Light. When Time Stood Still and was non existent, awaiting the call from its enforced slumber to be re-awakened as a measure of Awareness of its own abstract phenomena of calculation, of the passage from one Dimension to another, and another and another, ad infinitum through its brother in Creation namely SPACE!!

For Time is but another creation that can be halted can be catapulted; can even be dispensed with entirely. And that would come about when Creation in All of Its Aspects is put into a stillness, a form of Slumber, to re-emerge as yet another Aspect of that Thought Instigator, that Nameless Unknowable Essence of the Life Force that some call 'The Breath of God'!! Whose name can not be pronounced and yet that very silence is of 'Pure Love' and manifests itself in all that can be observed either in SPIRIT, or in PHYSICAL interpretation of that Divine essence of Thought Creation!! Most High!!

Close not your minds to what cannot as yet be understood by Mortal Man in his present stage of Evolution. There are among you 'Beings of Light', that are to bring to Man's inner consciousness the light of Reason and understanding, but for the foreseeable future they will be in the minority of those dwelling upon this planet.

But remember there are other Planets, other Worlds of habitation and their populations may well be further along the path of what is loosely called Evolution, which is only another name for Change!

Change of Thought! Change of Direction! Change even of Destination! If you can understand our meaning. Think about it and come to your own conclusion. We will say that 'Time is on Your Side!!!' Use that 'time' that is at your disposal wisely, for Time like Space is full of Illusion, make sure you know how to make the most of those two commodities! For neither of them can be considered as permanent fixtures!!

We bid you Goodnight and Farewell if you are students who study Time, Space and where they fit into the Eternal mystery of the meaning of LIFE!!!

And to you Brother, thank you for your Time. You had no idea when you sat down, pen in hand and gave to us your thoughts to be used as we wished. You are a very patient scholar dear friend and it is much appreciated by Us All!!!

Farewell and May God bless You, as we know He does. Farewell!! ALLAH BE PRAISED!!!

Post Script!

Time just as is Space varies all over the Universe! You cannot pin point it as a certainty. And so in your travels either in the physical body or as mind travel, Time and Space will take their toll upon your comprehension of it, when you pass from one time zone or **Vibration to another your body 'clock' is affected, and affected in** very peculiar ways!!

In other words, your programmed existence of your life span has been tampered with, both by Time and its mentor Space!! Your life span could be accelerated and your proverbial three score years and ten, could well end up minus several of those promised years. And then on the other hand those years of **expectancy could be 'stretched' so making your existence one of** distant speculation. And all of this form of alteration has to be taken into account, as you begin to delve ever deeper into the Cosmic wilderness you observe as Space!!

And remember that Space is not just a straight line, it jumps about, it forms mental contortions and plays tricks with the mind!! You may even find that you suddenly come to, shall we say A Brick Wall of Space, where your passage through it is halted! And you have then to find a way round it or through it and that will include the Time that it takes to re-adjust your mental and physical awareness of the phenomena presenting itself to you. For on the other side of the Blank Wall, should you be **able to overcome its 'thought of density', you could easily find yourself in the 'Past' where Time has been cocooned into a dream** like non-existence. And your ability to adjust to this state of affairs means that you may even be tampering with the Destiny of **that entrapped 'Time scale'!**

And who knows what that Pandora's Box of tricks will be **unleashed upon the unsuspecting wanderer in that Time warp's** illusion of reality!!!

Be warned, be careful when you seek to unravel the mysteries of the Universe, you may well end your days living in the past of someone else's civilization, that shouldn't really exist outside of the imagination!!! And here is where we really will end this post script, which in actual fact is not the 3rd of December but the 4th and is 2.45 a.m. on that day, we have aroused the little Scribe from his bed of rest, much to his surprise and now we are going to let him return to it!!

So this is the final Farewell to him!! Until next 'time!!' There!! That word pops up all over the place does it not?!!

Chapter 63

December 5th 12.05 a.m.–1.35 a.m. 2008

A MIND JOURNEY!!!

Dear Friend and Brother in Christ Consciousness we bid you welcome and extend our hands in true friendship in this joint enterprise of your Mind and Our Thoughts!!

So let us begin this nights treatise that involves a journey One of the Mind that does have a basis in Reality, at least for Us shall we say, for you it is of the mind only, and not the body physical!!! But the outcome will be the same!!!

We, as it were ascend into the clouds that wend their way across the Midnight Sky where the Stars illuminate our path. We are now engulfed in these clouds of coloured vapour, in fact we are part of them as they twist and turn in an endless flow of energy that is somehow soft and fluid. And we are being carried along what appears to be a corridor of cloud that in its movement give off a sound like that of distant voices in harmony. We catch snatches of the sounds of Monks chanting and then again we are aware of faint whispering sounds that seem to be telling us that all is well. And all of this is part of our feeling of being a part of these clouds of ceaseless movement.

Then all of a sudden they have left us and we are on a plateau of grass like substance that shimmers as if with the morning's dew!! Like liquid diamonds that sparkle in the Sunlight that is everywhere and yet we are not aware of the actual Sun, just its rays of golden light that covers the whole area in a mantle of gold and silver and pale, pale mauve. We now glide along this path that is strewn with petals and the smell of Jasmine pervades the

The Little Scribe

very air we breathe!! Our path leads us towards what appears to be a city of Light.

There are towers that point their fingers to the sky, huddled together in small groups, each tower pure white with pinnacles of Gold encrusted with jewels so thick the whole effect is like miniature rainbow hues of iridescent colour that sparkle in the mornings sunlight!!

These clusters of tower like buildings line a tree-lined avenue of slim Cyprus trees that look like sentinels, they almost mirror the towers with their straight-lines of form!!! The avenue is broad and of a substance that looks like crystal, so that to walk upon it is like walking upon water and is quite a peculiar sensation!!

As we travel along this avenue we are being led to an Archway, that is covered in a hanging cascade of what appears to be a form of Wisteria that obscures our view of the beyond. We move effortlessly through it and the view that meets our eyes is quite staggering. It is a golden domed Mosque that seems to be supported on pillars of turquoise coloured marble, slim so that the whole effect is if the dome is suspended upon these almost finger like columns there are no walls and so you can see straight through to the other side.

Where there appears to be a fountain surrounded by a shallow lake the bottom of which is the same turquoise coloured marble. The fountain seems to be suspended in Mid air with no support just the cascading water giving off a scent of roses. Upon the waters of the lake float swans but not the accustomed variety for these are the colour of turquoise and emerald and pinky mauve, **and their wings are like the fans of the Peacock's tails when they** are spread out. And the sound that they make as they move around is like the gentle cooing of the doves!!! By now we have moved right through the open Mosque like Building and are upon the grassy like sward that surrounds the lake.

There are many people just strolling about in earnest conversation male and female, **but they don't seem to notice us,** so obviously we cannot be seen. This place is a place of Learning, and we presume it is some form of open air university and the people we observe are in a way like pilgrims of some sort. Though what the Religion that they are studying is new to us, though we are being informed by thought that it is one of the oldest ever to have been discovered, and involves not only the physical being but also the spirit companion. And so the two of them are in joint mental communion that points to a way of Life which incorporates both at the same time!!

No wonder that the feeling we experience is one of awe and of reverence for a highly Spiritual community, we are tempted to say of Saints in the making!! Perhaps they are to be part of the New Ages that are to permeate the whole of the Universe in due course!!

We feel we have been very privileged to witness what is the beginning of a New era of understanding of the true values of what Life is all about. We are being gently informed that it is now time for us to return to our own time and place of origin, and so reluctantly we close our eyes upon this glimpse of what is to be, but for Whom? This we do not know!!!

And so dear friend of the night time's excursion into the realms of thought participation we bid you Farewell and allow you to return to your sleep state!! Farewell and God bless you little scribe. Farewell.

<u>Post Script</u>.
I wonder if I shall be permitted to go on that journey again, for I would like to know more about those people and the Religious culture that they are being taught, and if it is one of the oldest **that has been discovered and shall I say 'Resurrected'?** To become one of the foremost in the years to come that is to encompass the

'Whole Universe' and so Unifying all the various populations and diversities of created Mankind and Spiritkind so that the two are as One. That seems to have been the original intention of all of those Deities of Creation that form the Hierarchy of that Divine Circle of Celestial Beings of Light who do the bidding of that Unknown Life Force. That sublime Creator of Unknown Antiquity, that Alpha and Omega, of all that is and ever was and yea, ever will be!! And when that mission has been accomplished Then What?!!

Perhaps it is best that not to know is our own form of Salvation. So I had better cease my speculative thoughts on the subject of what Creation really means to those who have been created, and where that pathway to Eternity will take us? Perhaps to the beginning of yet another Eternity, upon another Universe in another 'Time'?!

'We Forbid You to go any further little Scribe. Put your writing implement away and think of other things!'

Farewell!!! FINISH!!!

Chapter 64

December 7th 2008
Late Evening to Early Night!

THE FREEDOM OF THE WILL!!!

These are going to start off as my thoughts, though I expect that they will be 'taken over' before I get very far with them, for which I shall be grateful. Because these thoughts are only Hypothetical conjectures on my part and probably won't be anywhere near the truth as such. So I hope that you will bear with me if what I write may seem to you either fanciful or just an over imaginative speculation!!!

Well here is where I start on this thought journey and we'll see where it takes me!!! The word 'Programmed' seems such a final word, as if whoever or whatever has been programmed has no say in the matter, and probably that is the case. I feel that it certainly applies to the animal kingdom and more, what about the birds, and the fishes, and the insects, and what else? Well I'm going to include Man in this statement, and I expect people who may read this will say 'That's rubbish! Man isn't programmed. He doesn't have to be, what about his Free Will?!!' Well that is the point that I shall be coming to. He has been endowed with that God given aspect, though I do have a feeling that we are in a way 'programmed' but not as the rest of the Creations I've already mentioned!!

And here is where I'm going to say that our 'Freedom of the Will' is for the very purpose of, how shall I put it? The very purpose of allowing us the chance to 'Opt Out' of the programmed schedule that affects all of Mankind, even if he doesn't accept that He is programmed in some way!!

The people who take advantage of this gift, when it is used in the way it was intended to be used!! Are the Thinkers of this World, and the Seekers and Searchers who make up this trinity of wanting knowledge, Esoteric knowledge, of the reasons of Why we are upon this dense planet called Earth. When sometimes it seems almost like an Alien one, to those seekers and searchers and thinkers!! And it Is!! Because we originally came from that other World, the World of the Spirit!! Though to many people that explanation wouldn't cut much ice, especially if you were to also say that the Mortal body is only a temporary dwelling place for that Spirit!!!

People often use the word spirit without ever associating it with the 'Actual One' that is their Companion for the whole of their mortal life!!! People say 'That's the Spirit' or 'That's not the right spirit!' and many more such comments, but tell them they have one that dwells within them and they will probably say, 'Oh Yes!! Well I haven't seen it, have you?!!' And in all honesty you have to answer in the negative!! At least the majority will have to answer in that way!!! So in a way they, that is most of the population that do not give much thought regarding the possibility of having a Spirit companion or guide, are sort of programmed by themselves.

Which is a pity for they are missing a lot, by not exploring the possibility that they are actually Spirit essence and are only using their physical body for a set period i.e. a life span!!!

Now going back to those Seekers and Searchers who can 'Opt Out' of the constriction of that form of 'programming'! Because they know how to use their Free Will that encompasses the 'Mind' when dealing with Esoteric knowledge and understanding! They are free from the bonds of what most people consider as

'Taboo subjects'. They can use their free will to explore and evaluate what they are learning, they use that gift with great care and combined with their attained highly developed Intuitive powers, their physical, mental, and Spiritual lives are truly enriched!!

Their free will has enabled them to bring another dimension into their Spiritual as well as their physical lives, but with that freedom they have a duty to impart to others, those who perhaps are starting out on this first rung of the Esoteric ladder. They have this duty to share their knowledge with those who thirst for it, but only if they show a real aptitude for what is expected of those who wish to become part of that ever increasing band of the **'Seekers after the Truth'**!!

You will find them from the four corners of your Globe. For in time they will bring together Nations and Nationalities all with the same purpose, to try and bring back to this Planet what was **intended as its birthright, One of God's many mansions!!** A Heaven upon Earth!!

And it is You, the Thinkers, the Searchers, and the Seekers who are the forerunners of these enlightened beings who will one day transform this sad little Planet into one of joy and happiness!! So you see that Free Will of yours is a true blessing when used in the right and proper way. And that is not just for oneself but for all those who merit your trust and fellowship those travellers **upon life's path that will, God Willing, one day become citizens** of not just this World, but of the Universe itself!!!

So cherish your 'Free Will' and encourage others to do the same so that God can see His gift is multiplied a thousand fold more! And not squandered in selfish desires of the flesh. And remember, Your Spirit also has a free will, learn to work in Harmony with it and life really will be rewarding in every way. So that Heaven upon Earth can become a reality and not just a wishful dream of the imagination!!!

The Little Scribe

We bid you Goodnight and Farewell you travellers of the Light. And let that Light shine for everyone to see!!

Farewell Brother not quite what you expected is it? And Yes, we did help you out now and then with a thought or two!!!

God Bless You little one and keep you safe is our sincere wish. Fare-thee-Well.

Chapter 65

December 10th 2008

ILLUSION AND REALITY!!?

I've been thinking about the power of Thought and how it can influence others!! Thought! A product of the Mind, that enables that thought to put into practice what it is that it wants to impress, either upon 'others' or even as a subject of discussion with 'oneself'! For let's face it we do have discussions with ourselves, sometimes verbally, sometimes mentally and sometimes through the medium of the written word!!! And just what am I getting at? Well to be frank it's about Illusion!!! That is the Illusion of Reality, that is often practised by those who we call Spirits when contacting a medium or clairvoyant, either during a Spiritualistic service in 'Church' or perhaps during a 'private sitting' with a person who has asked for one!!!

What intrigues me is the ability of the 'Spirit person' to be able to convey to the clairvoyant / medium various senses of perception, for instance, the sense of smell, the sense of an illness that the Spirit person suffered during their lifetime upon Earth, and even sometimes the actual 'pain' that they had endured!!! Now all of this 'phenomena' comes under the heading of 'Illusion'. For though the intention is to convey a sense of Reality (and it is Real to the medium!) in actual fact it is the Illusion of the Mind by both parties!!! So how is that accomplished?!!

The Medium is upon one 'vibration' while the Spirit is upon another one, albeit the Spirit or rather an 'essence' of it is temporarily a 'visitor' upon the medium's vibrationary field!!!

How is it that the Spirit essence can actually transmit this feeling of reality, for example the smell of flowers, or even the aroma of 'baking'! So that the medium is completely aware and is in perfect harmony with what is transpiring??!!

We upon the Earthplane, if we want to convey to someone else those similar examples, we have to rely upon the listener's ability to associate themselves with what they have experienced personally. So that when the speaker mentions 'baking' for instance, the listener knows exactly what is meant, but! They do not experience the reality just a remembrance of it!! So what is it that the Spirit does, that allows the Illusion of Reality to be so 'Real' that the clairvoyant person can actually feel or smell what is being mentally conveyed from one being to another, and all via the Mind apparatus!!! Now assuming that the basis of all of this Mind and Thought conveyancing is generated by 'Electrical currents', how is this done?

I'm thinking of those Illusionists that perform upon the Stage and are able to hypnotize people into thinking either that 'they' are something or someone else, or that they can 'taste' perhaps fruit or something that has been cooked. And when the Hypnotist does something that triggers a response in the subject that has been hypnotised, they 'do' what they have been 'programmed' to do, without realising the origin of their response!!!

So! Is it all a matter of suggestion? And the Mind has for a brief period been 'taken over' as it were by the one, who shall we say, is in charge on a temporary basis??!!!

Just what is 'Illusion' is it another form of 'Reality' or is 'Reality' another aspect of Illusion?!! So is this Earthplane though Real in its substance matter, a conduit for that form of Mind interpretation of Illusioned Reality of the Mortal bodies Mental powers? So is the Spirit World, one of unknown spirit essence or a form of matter, which is capable of creating the illusion of

Reality or is it the Real Reality that to some is a form of 'Illusion' because of 'its' ability to shall we say, to 'Be' and then again 'NOT to BE!!' In other words being able to create this transparency of Physical reality that can be termed a form of 'Illusion'?? And are there degrees of that 'sense' and when as Spirit we learn to differentiate between them and use them when and if the occasion requires it??!!

For we do know that upon the Realms of SPIRIT the two Aspects 'Illusion and Reality' are accepted as perfectly 'normal'. Perhaps we upon Earth ought to do the same and then we wouldn't get so disappointed when reality doesn't live up to its word!!! I guess it's all in our own perception of what we want things to be, perhaps that's one of the lessons that we have to learn, after all nothing in life seems to be of a permanent nature does it? Including our very own bodies!!! In a way I suppose we are our own 'illusionists'.

For it seems we show a different side of our character to many people, who would probably differ widely if you were to ask them to say how they 'see' so and so!! You would probably think they were speaking about someone else entirely!! So, what price 'Illusion' and what price 'Reality'??

And here I think is where I will retire from this treatise of those two illusive aspects of the same coin!!! Before I begin to wonder just who I am or am not! As the case may be!!! Now! Have I learnt anything from this foray into those realms of mind illusion or am I still in the dark?! It's the way Spirit manages to bring a sense of reality to all of this that in a way baffles me!! How on Earth (NO pun intended!!) can you create the sense of smell and taste and feeling out of shall I say 'Nothing!!' Yet even nothing must contain something of substance for it to become a vision of reality even when that reality is really an illusion of it!!!

We've got a lot of updating to do when we return to our Spiritual home haven't we? In the meantime we'll just have to accept that the Spirit friends know what they are doing and be grateful that they do!!! And here is where I really come to a closure of this treatise (if you can call it that!!!) and hope that you are not as confused as I am!!!

So I'll say Farewell for the time being, so this is it!

Farewell!!

Chapter 66

December 11th, Mid Morning! 2008

GOD! ALLAH!
A NAME IS BUT A NAME!!!
AND WHAT IS IN A NAME?!!!

As usual! I'm going to sit here with my pen in my hand and Wait! And see if Inspiration comes upon me, for quite honestly I haven't the slightest idea what to write, so here starts the pause in my writing!!!

Brother! You may take up your pen once more for we are ready to begin your mornings discourse. What is the subject that most people fight shy of actually talking about either in public, or privately amongst friends of like minds?!!

And that subject is 'GOD'!!! a very emotive and personal subject for most people, at least in the Western Hemisphere it seems to us! In other parts of your globe people seem to be more open minded or even broad minded when discussing their particular Deity or as the case may be 'Deities'.

But in the West even a hint that there maybe more than one Deity whose familiar name is GOD, causes them to as it were, close their minds on that subject and hope it will go away and leave them with their own private thoughts intact!!! A great pity for the subject of God, or Many Gods is a very fascinating and intriguing subject that just cries out for discussion on many different levels!

Now that society is becoming 'multi cultured' that subject is bound to crop up far more than it has in the past!! When certain Religious Cultures were considered as the only ones worth talking about and yes, even being thrust upon an unsuspecting Society belonging to another country!!! And usually without any consideration regarding their particular form of 'Worship'!!!

And the word 'Worship' we feel is a subject on its own, needing very careful handling for that word covers a very wide area of how that particular form of adoration is practised, and to site any one group's activities would no doubt cause bitter resentment all round, and so we pass over that aspect of Religious Culture!!! And proceed with an even more delicate one of how 'we' that is all of the humanities perceive their own particular, shall we say 'Brand' of God perception!!! And we can assure you it is very, very, varied to say the least!!! And that includes Our World of the Spirit also!!! Diverse Religious Cultures is not just confined to the Earthplane, far from it!! We too have heated arguments on that topic, but it never results in acrimonious feelings on either side!!

But upon Earth!! Well that is a different matter! You go to extreme lengths to make your point, 'War' to be exact!! And just what does a so-called 'Holy War' achieve? Bitterness and resentment on the part of those who are being invaded both mentally and physically!! And to actually call a War 'Holy' is an affront to the Deity whose name you call upon to sanction your excursion into another's domain!!

If the Powers that be truly believe in the Precepts of their particular Religious culture they could Never, Never, sanction this wanton sacrifice of Human Life in order to placate the God of their choice!! 'Hypocrites', and we repeat that word 'Hypocrites', and that word is too mild a one to actually convey our sentiments on the subject!!

It doesn't matter to what God or Gods you extend your allegiance to, Their names should never be uttered in conjunction with the words 'A Crusade', as if that sanctions all forms of atrocities too vile to even mention!

The word 'God' should be a word that conjures up all that is 'Good' and should be the precept by which all of Mankind should live by. Doesn't matter if you only believe in One, or in Many, they are all Aspects of That One on High, that we know absolutely Nothing about!! See God how you want to see 'Him'! He allows you that freedom of expression You have your Free Will, use it wisely and respect others and let them use their Free Will as they see fit.

Even if you cannot go along with their sentiments, Surely 'Your God' is Big enough to accept what you, that is Mortal Man seems unable to, that Loving your fellow Man is loving your God as well, and that is all that He asks of you! Is it so difficult? It shouldn't be, For you were created by, and in Love, 'His Love'!!

Just accept God as He is, as you 'see' Him or 'Them' as the case may be!! Diversity is a wonderful thing and should Never become a hindrance to Unity of purpose.

And that purpose is 'LIVE AND LET LIVE' GOD'S LAW IN PRACTICE.

And here is where we take our leave of you and the Little Scribe who has been a willing participant in this form of Thought Unification.

We bid you Farewell.

And to you Brother!! Well you can put away your pen, your morning's work is complete, and we Thank You. Farewell little friend and scholar, we extend our Love to you and wish you well in the coming days and months and look forward to renewing this partnership in person one day!!

Farewell and God bless You.

May Allah be Praised as indeed He is!!!

Chapter 67

December 12th, 2.20. a.m., 2008

WHO ARE WE??!!!

Let us commence with the words: Who am I?!!

A bold statement you must admit and just what does it mean or imply? 'Who am I?' And the 'I' being Not this Mortal body of clay but that illusive one that is called 'Spirit'! And just who is this Spirit? And where did it come from and how is it that I call it 'I!' 'Me!' The Unknown One!! What is Spirit and why is it called Spirit? Is that just a name for this unknown substance, this ethereal essence of the Divinity that we dimly call God? And how can we 'All' be aspects, or facets of that Holy One?!!

Are we perhaps in our own way trying to come to terms with the fact, that we really do NOT know who or what we are, or even what it is that we are 'made of' that we loosely term 'Our Immortal body'. And by using that word in an explanatory fashion we are trying to justify our very existence, and to Whom I wonder? Ourselves? Or that Unknown Source of All life that we call upon as God, Our Father in Heaven? And even that expression 'In Heaven' is perhaps an ambiguous statement for as a being of Mortal substance, we cannot have come from that place that exists - Where?! Somewhere up there in the Sky that is called Space?

As a mortal being we could not even survive for one day in that illustrious and mysterious province that we call Heaven?

Or is there yet another unknown area of Cosmic effulgence that was the spawning ground of what we term 'Our true Self'?

That essence of Spiritual growth that in its embryonic stage is but a minute particle awaiting its gestation into a life form of intrinsic beauty that encapsulates what has come to be known as the very **'breath of the** Almighty'! from which we emerge as a living breathing aspect of that Unknown Life Force that permeates the Whole of the visible and invisible arena of Cosmic activity, the womb, in fact of Creation itself!! Before its very Thought inception!!! **Of the 'One'** who must remain Nameless!! Our starting point that culminates in that Aura enveloped organ of Mind essence that is called the Immortal Spirit!! From which emerges Our Soul, our very capacity of creative possibility that transcends all other forms of known creation to become the manifested facet that we as Spirit use and what is known as the Mortal being of Human Emancipation.

That other aspect of our true Self that allows us to operate upon the dense plane known as Earth, for the life span of our chosen **representative that we call 'ME'!!** The being of identifiable mortality that is our vehicle of human mental expansion that is needed for the awakening of our Spiritual growth upon the evolutionary Spiral of Esoteric advancement that will take us back to the Source of our own creation. And the Creator who instigated our very first being of awareness that allowed us to assume our identity that could be considered as a mirrored aspect of that Divinity we call God!

The Father from whose bosom we long to return too when our series of incarnations upon the various planes of existence, have resulted in our advancement of Spiritual education that will fit us for our position if accepted, as a Co-worker for the God of our choosing, who in turn decides if we merit the accolade of being called Chosen!!!

Our journey, far from being over is only just beginning. We **can now assume our 'true identity' of 'Pure Spirit'** our Immortal self, truly a God in the Making, as was envisaged by that Creator who breathed the Breath of Life into that embryonic particle of Divine thought all those aeons of lives ago!!!

And so we come to the end of this stage in our treatise of the **Spirit, the 'ME' of realization and of emancipation.** No, not the end but the beginning, the beginning of What? And here we leave you to your own conjectures of where that will lead you to!!!

Farewell you Students of Life and its inner meanings!!!

Farewell Brother, this has been a very busy time for you has it not? We bid you Good night, or rather Good morning according to your clock!

So we say Farewell and God bless You. Peace we leave with you little one, Peace!!!

It is now 4.25 a.m. I shall go back to bed for a couple of hours I think!!

Well I did go back to bed and slept until 7.30 a.m. and Now **it's time for me** to record this treatise onto a cassette tape and see **what I make of this night's work!!! Which came as quite a surprise** when I picked up my pen and thought, what shall I do now?!!!

And the result? Well I must leave you to be the judge of that!! **Mustn't I?!!** Farewell! Farewell!

Chapter 68

December 12th, 10.10 a.m.–11.40 a.m., 2008

THE WORD IS MULTIPLE!!!

After listening to the tape of the previous chapter on 'Who are We,' it's set me thinking do we really know who we are? Or are we just part of an elaborate illusion of our own making? It would seem that to others in our circle of relatives and friends and acquaintances that we are almost a multiple sided complex creation, with innumerable facets of expression and personality and yet to ourselves none of those adjectives would seem to apply to our own perception of who we think we are!!! So what is it that makes of us such a complex person of seemingly endless forms of identification?!

Do we feel we are more than one person when we stand in front of a mirrored reflection of ourselves? Or are we quite content to accept that reflection as being who we consider as the 'ME' the 'I' of known identification that we consider is the one and only 'ME' and no other!! Yet if you were able to eavesdrop on perhaps a conversation pertaining to your character or personality that was being voiced by a group of your contemporaries, you might well be in for a shock when you discovered that the person they were discussing was no other than your very self!!! Would you recognise any of the comments that were being voiced as being a true evaluation of your character and personality?!

And would it give you cause for concern that perhaps you are 'NOT' the person who you think you are!!!? Or would you feel you would like to explore these other facets that other people see in you and that perhaps you were not aware of?!!!

Now if I tell you that you are not just one person, not even two but almost multiple, would you believe me? Well unless you are one of the seekers and searchers and thinkers that we hear about, your answer would probably be,

'Well No quite frankly I can't believe what you are saying, it doesn't apply to me I'm sure!!!'

And no one could blame you for thinking that way, for after all most people are completely unaware of their other selves and **unless you could parade them in front of you there's very little** possibility of being able to convince you of the argument in **favour of accepting the fact that these other 'YOU' really do exist!** And exist outside of yourself!! Another conundrum for you to come to terms with!!!

And yet further, if we tell you that they (that is aspects of the YOU) dwell upon various planes of existence and also lead not exactly a parallel life as yours but one of Higher Spiritual Quality, that can and does at times influence your physical mind via your **Spirit companion's ability of communication with your sense** perception, of shall we say your own intuitive powers of deduction!!

Do you think you could take all of that in, without actually wondering if **perhaps the speaker wasn't a good candidate for** 'certification'!!!?

When dealing with anything to do with Esoteric or Occult persuasion you have to approach the subject with a completely **'OPEN MIND'. For if you don't then you will lose the true value** of what is being given to you!!! Creation as such is a very complex form of Creativity. In actual fact it is very simple in its abstract form, but in reality of judgement it is all the colours of the **Rainbow and more!! And here we are speaking in a 'metaphorical'** form of explanation!!

We beg of you do not dismiss out of hand what you perhaps do not quite understand at this present time of your mental evolution, come back to it after perhaps reading what others have to say upon the subject. And then perhaps a clearer picture will emerge upon your inner 'screen of perception'. And then the whole idea of actually being more than one aspect of the Divinity would be more feasible and would explain why at times we all feel that we are more than just one person. And sometimes we may even catch more than a glimpse of one of those other selves that go to make up the complete Whole of who we are and not who we Think we are!!! And here is where 'I' or perhaps 'WE' and I'm not thinking of 'me' when I say 'We' I am referring to my Brother guides who influence so much if not all of my inspirational writings!!

So, to continue, here is where this unexpected treatise of the 'You', the 'Me', and the 'I' of identification comes to an end with the accustomed departure words of Farewell Brethren of the Earth. Farewell.

And to you Brother! What a busy little person you have been this morning and no mistake!

Farewell dear friend until next time your pen accosts the pages of this journal. May the blessings of Allah the God of all Mercies by upon you, now and forever.

Farewell Scribe Farewell. Farewell!

Chapter 69

December 16th, 1.30 a.m., 2008

A DIP INTO THE PAST AND MAYBE EVEN THE FUTURE!!!

It is now 2 a.m. and as I haven't received any inspirational thoughts I shall go back to bed!!

It's now 1.45 p.m.! Shall I wait and see if I am prompted to put my pen to paper with a discourse of some sort?? I'm not going to pretend, and if I don't get the inclination to write I'll postpone it till I do!!! Well it's now 8.45 p.m.! Still no form of inspired thoughts, though I did see a programme this afternoon called 'Catastrophe'. All about an Asteroid that struck this planet Earth some 65 Million Years ago! Which 'may' have accelerated the process of Evolution, which includes the creation I take it, of Man!

That made me think about what must have come 'before', and that I presume would be 'umpteen millions' of years, going back, and back, and back!! To What? To What was in existence, before this Universe or should I qualify that statement by saying 'Universes' came into existence! And the thought that came into my mind was The Unknowable Indestructible Essence of Life Propulsion that Was and Is and Forever will Be! And We, that is Mortal Man will never be able to Comprehend its Existence, and so we fall back onto what we feel comfortable (if that is the right word!!!?) feel comfortable with, and the name that comes to mind is 'GOD'!!!

And I will add in 'HIS MANY DISGUISES', by which you may also add All the various Religious cultures that shall I say, boast their own version of the 'God' of their choice!!! So that 'Unknowable Essence' has many, many aspects or facets of its existence!!! And where do I go from here?!!! Well, by admitting at least to myself, that I have no quarrel with what might turn out as a fact that This Universe of Ours could quite easily be the home of 'Many Creator Gods' of diverse persuasions of what to create, or what not to entertain as created, living species of, what shall I say? Experimental organisms of as yet unheard of species that have no previous category to which they belong to!!!

Now that does pose a question, a question of How far should Creation go? or even be allowed to go, when taking into consideration that whatever is Created must be of Universal Value to the 'Whole' and not just to the 'few', metaphorically speaking!! And here I am thinking of Man's, that is Mortal Man's exploration into the art of what is His interpretation of a created species, Human or otherwise and I leave you to interpret that statement for what it is worth!!!!

For remember, This Physical World that is the original creation for the population of all 'living' species, can only cater for the dense body or bodies of all species that come under that heading, 'The Spirit', that is an essential part of the Human body cannot be created in any shape or form by any known or unknown scientific enterprise!!

The Creation of the SPIRIT, is in God's domain and cannot be replicated by any other form of Creativity!!!

So, whatever Man or any of His distant cousins upon other Planets or Worlds yet to be discovered, may create, they can 'never, never, duplicate' a 'complete' facsimile of their own species!!! 'The Gods would NOT allow it!!!'

So Mankind in his various forms had better not venture down that avenue of Creation however altruistic his motives may be!!

Remember what happened those millions of years ago that I mentioned, was shown in picture form on the Television. Not only did the Dinosaurs become extinct but all Hell was let loose upon this planet creating devastation of the very earth itself!!! So what would happen if the Unthinkable did happen, because of **Man's stupidity in attempting to emulate 'God'** That aspect of the Indestructible Essence of Life Propulsion!!! That is Forever!!! Unlike Man's life span of programmed expectancy!!!

And all of this stemmed from just my unexpected thought **excursion Though I'm sure they are not all my own original** thoughts. You're right there young man!!! **And here is where we** are told to bring this treatise to a close. Do you agree? Yes, we see you do, and so we will bid you Farewell and we also say Congratulations!! Farewell and Goodnight little friend!!

God bless You.

As a form of Appendage to the above treatise Personally **speaking I'm quite happy in the way I see God.** That is the God of I suppose of the Western Hemisphere!!

But what puzzles me is this desire by most people (regardless of which God they pay lip service to) this desire on their part for **a form of 'Religion' whereby they can show to their Deity how** much they Worship and Adore Him!! Why all this adulation? And for whose benefit I wonder? Themselves or their chosen God figure? Who to my mind must surely be above all of this degree of pious intention? I expect I won't get agreement on that, by those of 'orthodox' Religious Persuasion! And I certainly don't blame them for feeling that perhaps I'm somewhat akin to being a Heretic!!! It's just that I don't see God (Whoever He is) needs all of that continual ritualistic idolization!!!

Well that's all I'm going to say on the subject, and I expect you'll say 'Thank God!!!'

So I leave you on that note! Farewell and just remember it's all my personal feelings and no one else's!! But I am sincere even if you may think otherwise!!!

Chapter 70

December 17th, 7.30. p.m.–8.45 p.m., 2008

THE UNIVERSE AND ITS SECRETS!!!

I've been thinking about the Night Sky when all of the Stars and constellations come alive and beckon the weary traveller to once more let his imagination have full reign, as to where perhaps one day he may be permitted to venture even further than what is now visible. It is almost like a fine gauze curtain studded with diamonds that in actual fact hides from view what is really there waiting to be discovered. And I say by Earth man, because I do believe that Others out there in the gloomy depths of Space have most likely 'beaten us to it'.

For one thing they are nearer to their intended goal, than we can ever be, and for another Their modes of 'transport' are so far advanced that they would make our Space Craft seem like children's toys if you were able to compare them. Which by the look of it that won't happen for a very, very, very long time if you are calculating in Earth Years, which in actual fact are not even relevant when discussing the vastness of Space within the confines of this Universe!! And believe me we do not even know how 'Our' Universe behaves when it comes to trying to ascertain the complexity of its inner structure! For the Universe is a living breathing, pulsating creation that spreads itself and then withdraws once again, it never stays the same.

It is like a gigantic heart, beating, beating, beating, and in its efforts it does not take into account those millions of Planets and Worlds and Stars, and it is they who are the ones who suffer with all of this untamed energy. **And by 'suffer' I refer to their demise!** Their death if you prefer!! They disappear in a cloud of dust particles to make way for even more creations!!

You cannot take for granted what your probes and telescopes tell you, for what is visible today is gone tomorrow, leaving just a photographic imprint upon the Cosmic curtain of Illusion!!! And by 'today' and 'tomorrow' you must read as millions of light years. Theirs! Not Ours!! So remember do not trust what you think you see, for you may well arrive at your chosen destination, only to find either an empty space or even another Stella creation in the making!!!

In the deepest areas of Space where blackness is the norm, you may find that nothing is actually existing there, just vast, vast, emptiness, yet cross that chasm and you will discover Worlds without number, Life in abundance. Civilizations that are beyond your wildest imaginings!! You could be forgiven for thinking that you had stumbled upon yet another Universe within your Own!!! And who knows perhaps you have!! Nothing is impossible when creation is on the agenda!!! And think in the broadest of terms. **For the word 'Civilizations' can mean Past, Present, or Future.** For Time in Space is Flexible and not the immutable commodity you may think it is!!!

Could it be that those Worlds and Civilizations are the lost ones of your Universe that were once chronicled in those Akashic records of Antiquity that disappeared oh! so long ago that people believed that they never really existed only as speculative folk-lore??!!! **So much of the Earth's history lies hidden that if it ever** does come to light then our whole understanding of it will have to be completely re evaluated as to what Our (that is our Earth's) what is our true position in this Universe that we call 'Ours' when in truth we might not even belong to it!!! And that explanation regarding the Planet Earth and its various Births and Deaths and

Resurrections of its molecular structure would need another book to clarify it satisfactorily, but not this one I'm afraid!!

We have so much to understand about 'Life' and that word encompasses not only Human life but Planetary life as well, and also the prime aspect of the 'Spirit life' that is the true driving force of all Creation. For Spirit is the essence and aspect of the Unknown Source of All Life Force before it is manifested in all that we see around and within us!!!

And here is where we, the Brothers in White of that Brotherhood are to bring this, our Brothers discourse to an end. You have done well Brother, and we salute you, and bid you a fond Farewell. May Allah be Praised! May Allah be praised!

All praise be to Allah the God of All Mercies!!

Chapter 71

December 18th 2008

PROGRAMMING!!
WHAT'S IT ALL ABOUT??!!

About a week ago in the circle that I belong to, one of the sitters read an extract from a book, which stated that animals have NO Spirit and I presume by that remark no Soul either!! And I was asked what I thought about the subject!! First thing was that I did not agree with what the writer had said, and this seemed the universal reaction by the other sitters. Still it made me think, and we got onto the subject of 'Group Soul', we all thought that that was the only answer regarding when birds (especially Starlings) when birds at dusk congregate in vast numbers and whirl about the Sky in complete unison. Sweeping up and down from side to side and in their hundreds making a huge dark cloud in the sky, before eventually going off all in the same direction to their 'resting' place for the night!!!

A spectacular phenomena but how is it achieved?! Then there's all of the other bird species that do this joint flights display! And what about the Shoals of fish in the ocean's depth? Another aspect of joint endeavour!!! So is this the 'Group Soul' in action or What? They must in someway be 'programmed' so that when a certain 'something' triggers something in their 'genes'? I can't say 'brains' or 'minds', so 'genes' will have to suffice!!

And I presume it's by an electric current so that 'they' (the birds in this instance) so that they behave with one accord and nothing seems to stop them, and that must apply to those other creatures as well. For the formula seems to be the same! One way, then the other and back again!! As if there's no tomorrow!!! One might even say it's a 'mindless exercise' and yet of course it isn't, it's a form of survival isn't it? Especially regarding the fishes!!!

So that must mean that each individual right from birth, is programmed not only for that exercise but also it seems for their very 'lifestyle'. A lot of what animals and other created species do is a form of automatic reaction, not requiring shall I say, thought on their part!!! And yet some animals do display a certain degree of 'thought procedure'! Especially with the Primates you can see it in their expressions, and the resulting actions that come from their thought expansion!!!

Other creatures are clever at mimicking what they are being shown. Now is that individual thought or a programmed response? And now this 'Group Soul aspect'. Where does it come from? Outside of the flock of birds or from 'One of them'? Almost shall we say, the 'Leader'!!

No, I don't think so, that is regarding 'the leader'. That one if they were the leader, would I'm sure have to be 'programmed' in some way. But that still needs a lot of explaining doesn't it? Personally speaking I feel that even we as human beings are up to a point, sort of programmed in some way!! It's only our Free Will that probably takes us beyond that boundary line of being programmed.

Without it, I'm sure we would join the ranks of other Creations that need that outside/inside impetus, that somehow almost, but not quite makes them a form of automation, but a very sophisticated one I must admit!

Is that what all this cloning amounts to? A perfect replica of the original, but would that clone be able to think for itself and come to the right and proper decisions, or would it have to be programmed in some way. Because I can't see scientists being able to create a brain that does a lot of our work, though thinking about it, do we programme our Brain with things that can be considered as automatic responses to certain situations, without us having to give those situations much thought regarding the outcome?!!

Quite a thought there!!!

And as we (that is the thinkers etc. etc!) as we understand about our Spirit companion and the influence it can exert upon its mortal counterpart, there must be a lot of ('behind the scenes sort of') that we have as yet not properly comprehended regarding this liaison of Body and Spirit!!

Perhaps there's far more to this programme business than we will ever know, at least I'm tempted to say while we are in this Mortal human being stage!!!! We do accept this 'life span' part of our two way relationship, so that is one aspect of programming isn't it? And what about this Planet that we are on? Has that a 'life span' programmed into it? And why stop there? How about the Universe itself? I feel that I'm getting into very deep water here and so perhaps I'd better call a halt to all of this hypothetical conjecturing on my part before I sink without a trace!!!

Quite so! Brother, we've been watching your thoughts with interest and if you hadn't called a halt we feel we would have had to, done so!!! Lesson learned little One! Lesson learned!!! So say Farewell and we will join you in that departing gesture!!!

Farewell and God bless You as we know He does!!! Farewell!